Andrew Linn
Cambridge 1991

CAMBRIDGE STUDIES IN LINGUISTICS

General Editors: W.SIDNEY ALLEN, B. COMRIE, C.J.FILLMORE
E.J.A.HENDERSON, F.W.HOUSEHOLDER, R.LASS, J.LYONS
R.B.LE PAGE, F.R.PALMER, R.POSNER, J.L.M.TRIM

*The phonetic description of
voice quality*

In this series

Issued in hard covers and as a paperback

THE PHONETIC DESCRIPTION OF VOICE QUALITY

JOHN LAVER

Reader in the Department of Linguistics,
University of Edinburgh

CAMBRIDGE UNIVERSITY PRESS

CAMBRIDGE

LONDON · NEW YORK · NEW ROCHELLE

MELBOURNE · SYDNEY

Published by the Press Syndicate of the University of Cambridge
The Pitt Building, Trumpington Street, Cambridge CB2 1RP
32 East 57th Street, New York, NY 10022, USA
296 Beaconsfield Parade, Middle Park, Melbourne 3206, Australia

First published 1980

Printed in Great Britain at the
University Press, Cambridge

British Library Catalogue in Publication Data
Laver, John
The phonetic description of voice quality. –
(Cambridge studies in linguistics; 31
ISSN 0068–676x).
1. Phonetics
2. Voice
I. Title   II. Series
414   P221   79–41643

ISBN 0 521 23176 0

Contents

Figures

Acknowledgements

My major debt in writing this book is to David Abercrombie. The book owes its genesis directly to his suggestions about the analysis of voice quality in the postgraduate course in phonetics taught by him in 1962 at the University of Edinburgh. But my indebtedness to him is much wider. His humanity and lucidity, his insistence on speech as a social phenomenon, and on the necessary linguistic base to rigorous phonetic theory, have been a model to a whole generation of phoneticians. On the occasion of his retirement in September 1980, this book is dedicated to him.

An early version of the middle three chapters of the book formed part of my Ph.D. dissertation for the University of Edinburgh in 1975. I have had the great benefit of editorial guidance in writing the book from John Trim, and I deeply appreciate his incisive suggestions. I am very grateful also to the staff of Cambridge University Press, who have made the production of the book a very pleasant process. For help with the experimental analysis of voice quality data, I owe much to Francis Nolan of the University of Cambridge, Peter Roach of the University of Reading, Robert Hanson of the University of California at Santa Barbara, and to Roger Brown of the University of Edinburgh. I am indebted to Mrs T. L. Harris of the Edinburgh Dental Hospital for radiographic help. I am particularly grateful to G. J. Romanes, Professor of Anatomy in the University of Edinburgh and editor of *Cunningham's textbook of anatomy* and *Cunningham's manual of practical anatomy*, for his generous guidance on many details of muscular anatomy.

I am also very grateful to the group of postgraduate and postdoctoral researchers who formed the first panel to learn the use of the descriptive system, at the University of Edinburgh in 1976: Roger Brown, Luiz Cagliari, Fatiha Dechicha, John Esling, Jimmy Harris, Cynthia Shuken and Wilfried Wieden. Frances Macnamara, Frances Taylor and Margaret Strachan typed the manuscript, and Norman Dryden wrote the

viii

computer program for constructing the Index. The preparation of the book was also partly supported by a grant from the Medical Research Council.

I would especially like to express my appreciation to Istvan Anhalt, of Queen's University, Kingston, who first convinced me of the usefulness of the descriptive scheme for paralinguistic purposes, and who has been very supportive over a number of years.

I have reserved until the end the expression of my gratitude to those who always pay the highest price for any book – one's family. Above all, to my wife and colleague Sandy Hutcheson, in personal and professional terms, I owe a very great deal.

John Laver
Edinburgh, October 1979

Introduction

In his *Institutes of Oratory*, Quintilian wrote that 'The voice of a person is as easily distinguished by the ear as the face by the eye' (c.III, Book XI). The importance of an individual speaker's voice in everyday social interaction, as an audible index of his identity, personality and mood, could hardly be overstated. Yet we know now only a little more about the factors that give rise to different qualities of the voice than Quintilian did. Abercrombie was recently still able to write, with justification, that 'voice quality is the least investigated' of the different strands in the production of speech (Abercrombie 1967:91). This book is an attempt to apply the principles of phonetic analysis to the description of voice quality.

Voice quality is conceived here in a broad sense, as the characteristic auditory colouring of an individual speaker's voice, and not in the more narrow sense of the quality deriving solely from laryngeal activity. Both laryngeal and supralaryngeal features will be seen as contributing to voice quality. Perceptually, voice quality in this broad interpretation is a cumulative abstraction over a period of time of a speaker-characterizing quality, which is gathered from the momentary and spasmodic fluctuations of short-term articulations used by the speaker for linguistic and paralinguistic communication. Following Abercrombie, the term 'voice quality' will be taken to refer to 'those characteristics which are present more or less all the time that a person is talking: it is a quasi-permanent quality running through all the sound that issues from his mouth' (Abercrombie 1967:91).

It has sometimes been maintained that the analysis of voice quality is quite external to the proper study of language (Sapir 1921:47). One might then ask, given that phonetics shares with linguistics the responsibility for describing how spoken language works, why phonetics should take any professional interest in an apparently extralinguistic area such as voice quality. One obvious justification lies in the attitude that the semiotic function of linguistic communication can be better understood

1

when seen in a wider semiotic context. Voice quality, as a major vehicle of information about physical, psychological and social characteristics of the speaker, has a vital semiotic role to play in spoken interaction (Laver 1968; Laver and Trudgill 1979).

There is, however, a further justification for a linguistic interest in voice quality. It springs from the essential nature of phonetic data, and involves a distinction between phonetic segments and phonetic 'settings'. Considering phonetic segments first, it is striking that despite the alternative approaches that are possible, most general phonetic theories that have been put forward have given major prominence to one particular way of dissecting the continuum of speech. They nearly all segment the continuum into short stretches approximately correspond-ing to the basic linguistic units of consonants and vowels. It is not difficult to understand why phonetic theory should organize its descriptive taxonomy in such a way as to facilitate the correlation of phonetic segments with phonological units. Phonetic theory is properly pre-occupied with linguistic uses of the vocal apparatus. In addition, the intellectual roots of modern phonetics are embedded in an orthographic culture whose alphabetic influence is very pervasive.

The time-domain of phonetic segments of this sort is typically short, and there is considerable variety in the articulatory activities involved. Because phonetic description finally has a linguistic motivation, it is the differences between the segments that tend to be emphasized, rather than the similarities. There is an alternative approach to the task of articulatory description, however, that concerns itself with both differences and similarities in vocal performance in speech. In such an approach, individual segments are seen as being articulatorily related to other segments in that a particular articulatory feature could be abstracted from the chain of segments as a shared property of all or most of the segments. A recurrent feature of this sort constitutes in effect a tendency for the vocal apparatus to be subjected to a particular long-term muscular adjustment (Abercrombie 1967:93) or 'articulatory setting' (Honikman 1964:73). One example of such a setting would be a quasi-permanent tendency to keep the lips in a rounded position throughout speech. Another would be a habitual tendency to keep the body of the tongue slightly retracted into the pharynx while speaking. Another would be the persistent choice of a characteristically 'whispery' mode of phonation. Settings give a background, auditory 'colouring' running through sequences of shorter-term segmental articulations.

It is important that the analytic relationship between settings and segments should be stated as clearly as possible from the very beginning. It is not proposed that settings and segments are complementary divisions of phonetic quality. The standard attitude that phonetic quality should be fully exhausted by a comprehensive segmental analysis is maintained. The analysis of phonetic quality into settings is a second-order analysis, abstracting data from a prior segmental analysis. It is true that it will often be analytically convenient to discuss the relation between settings and segments as if a given setting had a perturbing effect on the articulation of some particular segment, and therefore had some notionally independent existence. It would be extremely tedious to have to spell out the analytic priority of segmental analysis at every mention of the relationship between segments and settings. Let this discussion stand, then, as a general caveat. Having said that, it is also true that a phonetic theory which incorporates an account of settings as well as segments is demonstrably a richer theory, with a wider application, than one which focuses merely on the first-order description of segmental performance.

Settings can have different time-domains. Being by definition poly-segmental, a setting must be a property of a stretch greater than a single segment. But there is no upper bound to its extent in time. A setting can thus be used for phonological purposes, usually as a relatively short-term activity. The phonological use of settings has been described by many writers in the prosodic school of phonology, and also by Zellig Harris, in his article on simultaneous components in phonology (Harris 1944). As Lyons points out, Harris, like the prosodists, showed that 'in many languages the "simultaneous components" recognized in the analysis extended over more than one segmental phoneme and could frequently be associated with the whole of a higher-level structure: e.g. tongue-retraction in Moroccan Arabic, nasality in Swahili, etc.' (Lyons 1962).

Settings can also be used for paralinguistic purposes, usually on a somewhat longer-term basis, in signalling affective information through tone of voice, and regulating the progress of conversational interactions. On a quasi-permanent basis, it can also be used for extralinguistic purposes, as a phonetic component of voice quality identifying the individual speaker.

A useful example is offered by the different signalling functions of nasality. Nasality can be exploited phonologically both as a segment and as a setting. As a segmental quality in vowels, for example, it is used for contrastive lexical identification in many languages, including French, Portuguese and Yoruba. As a setting, nasality is used phonologically in Sundanese, a language of Java, as a marker of verb forms. Once initiated by a nasal consonant in any position in the syllable, nasality in Sundanese runs forward through all syllable boundaries until checked by a word boundary or a supraglottal consonant (Robins 1953, 1957). Nasality as a setting is also manipulated for paralinguistic purposes. Crystal cites Key (1967) as reporting that in Cayuvava, a language of Bolivia, nasality is used stylistically with an honorific function: 'an individual of lower social or economic status addresses one of higher rank with a prominence of nasalization for all vowels of the utterance; and similarly with a woman being polite to her husband, or a man asking a favour' (Crystal 1970: 191). Finally, nasality is a very common setting component of voice quality, either idiosyncratically or as an indicator of membership of particular sociolinguistic groups. It characterizes most speakers of Received Pronunciation in England, and many accents of the United States and Australia.

One fundamental principle emerges from these illustrations: if we leave aside matters of time-domain as such, then it is impossible to establish from considerations of auditory quality alone what the communicative function of some given vocal setting might be, on any *a priori* basis. Classification of a particular setting as having a linguistic function, or a paralinguistic function, or merely an extralinguistic function, has to await later knowledge, not available to the analyst solely on a phenomenal basis. If the phonetic settings which can be exploited in voice quality all have potential use for phonological and paralinguistic purposes also, then a descriptive phonetic model of settings in voice quality is directly available for application to each of these two other areas. In fact, the settings which will be discussed have almost all been discovered to be used in the phonological repertoire of different languages, or in conventional paralinguistic communication of different cultures. Although discussion will be directed chiefly to the occurrence of the settings as components of voice quality, comment will therefore also frequently be made about their use in individual languages, or in paralinguistic communication.

The study of voice quality has a further relevance to linguistics, springing from perceptual considerations. In order to decide which aspects of vocal performance count as linguistically pertinent in a particular language, the linguistic phonetician must be able to isolate these aspects as figures against the perceptual ground of the other aspects of vocal performance. The perceptual relationship between figure and ground is reciprocal: the figure gains its clarity by virtue of the relative definition of the ground against which it is set. The question of what counts as linguistic data is thus the obverse of the question of what counts as voice quality data. Neither question can be answered independently of the other. Paralinguistic data completes the triad of complementary relations with linguistic and voice quality data. A phonetic theory which proposes an adequate account of the data of spoken language therefore cannot avoid taking voice quality into account.

The above argument stands even on a narrow definition of the concept of 'language', as might be used by those linguists whose interest in phonetic data is limited to the phonologically distinctive aspects of spoken language. A broader view of language will be adopted in this book, however, in which the phonetic material of spoken language and the phonetic component of voice quality overlap to some degree. In this broader approach, the view that is taken of the linguistic accountability of phonetic theory is that phonetic theory should be responsible for describing all recurrent, patterned, phonetic activity that characterizes the spoken language of the speech community concerned. In a famous passage in his article on 'Modes of meaning', Firth wrote that

Phonology states the phonematic and prosodic processes within the word and sentence, regarding them as a mode of meaning. The phonetician links ... this with the processes and features of utterance. Such processes are characteristic of persons, of social groups, even of nations. Moreover, the general feature of voice quality is part of the phonetic mode of meaning of an English boy, a Frenchman, or a lady from New York. Surely it is part of the meaning of an American to sound like one. (Firth 1951)

If the speech patterns of a community such as Liverpool, say, are characterized by persistent velarization and denasality, then this is a most important phonetic index of sociolinguistic and regional group membership, and should not be omitted from a phonetic account of the phonology of English as spoken in Liverpool. A formal linguist might of course object that these settings play no part in signalling distinctive linguistic contrasts in Liverpool English, and are therefore of no interest to his version of linguistics. To oppose that view would be merely to set one value judgement against another about preferable motives for constructing a linguistic theory. It is perhaps sufficient simply to say that in the perspective of this book language is seen partly as a social instrument, and that a rich analysis of all the material of spoken language, including distinctive and non-distinctive aspects, allows a closer approach to the social texture of language.

A particularly good example of this approach, showing how an interest in settings can enrich a phonological analysis in a sociologically relevant way, is offered by Trudgill (1974). He showed, in an investigation of the speech of Norwich, that the articulatory patterns of working-class speakers, compared with those of middle-class speakers, are marked by the habitual use of a number of settings. These include: creaky phonation, a high pitch range, a loud loudness range, a fronted and lowered tongue position, a raised larynx position, a particular type of nasality and a relatively high degree of muscular tension throughout the vocal apparatus (Trudgill 1974: 186–7; Laver and Trudgill 1979). The relevance to phonological description here is that Trudgill found that by incorporating a setting rule very early in his sequence of phonological rules, he could use it to generate multiple surface phonetic data which in a more conventional segment-focused approach could not easily have been seen as related. Perhaps the chief benefit of this approach is its success in relating linguistic to sociological factors. As Trudgill comments:

Different social types of Norwich English may be characterized by the presence or absence of, say, rule 100 [a setting rule – J.L.], rather than by a whole series of rules. This is an important point, since it is clear that perhaps the single socially most significant feature of linguistic differentiation in Norwich is the type of voice quality produced by the particular type of setting employed by the speaker. It is in any case this feature which most clearly distinguishes WC from MC speakers. This point, of course, did not emerge at all from our atomistic analysis of the co-variation of linguistic and sociological phenomena. (Trudgill 1974: 190–1)

The advantage of setting rules in the phonology of Trudgill's comparative sociolinguistic description is thus that 'they can relate different types of Norwich English to each other in the diasystem in a much more generalized and significant way than a whole series of individual rules' (Trudgill 1974: 190).

In a similar vein, Esling (1978) has shown that in Edinburgh social class correlates with laryngeal settings, in that higher social status corresponds to a greater incidence of creaky phonation, and lower status to a greater incidence of whisperiness and harshness.

As a general point, then, to the extent that settings characterize social and regional groupings of speakers, a descriptive model of such settings should be of value to comparative sociolinguistic investigation of those groups. By extension, the analysis of code-switching within the speech of a single socio-linguistic group should also be facilitated.

A basic attitude in this book is thus that the study of phonetic components of voice quality is not irrelevant to the study of spoken language. But of course the study of voice quality also has a great deal to offer to the many other disciplines that take a professional interest in speech. For all these disciplines, speech is a partial interest. For phonetics, the entirety of its subject is defined by speech, in all its aspects. Before beginning to discuss the descriptive model in more detail, it may therefore be appropriate to comment briefly on the characteristics that it should possess in order to qualify as a *phonetic* model.

Firstly, the model should rest on a scientific base, and not rely on impressionistic description which is idiosyncratic to the individual analyst. The advantages of standardization are self-evident. Secondly, the descriptive analysis of a given voice must be communicable in writing, without requiring an audible demonstration of the qualities to which reference is being made each time particular labels are used (Laver 1974). Part of this requirement is a useable transcription system. Thirdly, the analysis the model provides must be replicable. Judges must be able to be trained in the use of the system, and be able to make judgements which are consistent both with those of other judges and with their own judgements of the same material on different occasions. Lastly, as an optimal requirement, the model should be integrative, drawing on work from the same areas as segmental phonetic analysis – namely, auditory and articulatory analysis, acoustics and physiology.

On these criteria, the descriptive system for voice quality offered in this book is a general phonetic model, applicable to the vocal performance of all human beings of normal anatomy and physiology.

The descriptive system that is proposed stands on an auditory foundation. But the auditorily-identified components all have correlates specified at each of the three other levels of analysis, all capable of instrumental verification – the articulatory, physiological and acoustic levels. These specifications are offered on my own responsibility, but I have tried wherever possible to draw upon the authority of specialists in the relevant disciplines, particularly in physiology and acoustics. Attribution to individual sources is made throughout.

A comment on level is necessary at this point: although the book was written as a monograph, it is hoped that it might also be of interest to students. With their needs partly in mind, a deliberately schematic account of the muscular anatomy and physiology is given, and physiological detail is kept to the minimum necessary to understand the hypothesized working of the muscular apparatus as a mechanical system. No claim is made to be advancing the state of knowledge in physiology as such, and the criterion for judging the degree of detail in the physiological presentation was one of phonetic relevance, at a level capable of being assimilated by senior undergraduate and beginning postgraduate students. The same is true of the acoustic presentation.

The prescription of acoustic correlates of supralaryngeal and laryngeal settings that is offered is based on two types of sources. The first is the available literature on acoustic phonetics. The second is instrumental investigations of my own performance of the settings. The analysis of the acoustic correlates of supralaryngeal settings was carried out by Francis Nolan, of the University of Cambridge Department of Linguistics, on recordings made by myself of the first paragraph of the Rainbow Passage (Fairbanks 1960) in the Phonetics Laboratory of the University of Edinburgh. The analytic method involved a computer program using a linear prediction pole-finding routine, developed in the Engineering Department of the University of Cambridge by Stephen Terepin, supplemented by visual examination of spectrograms. Some of the computer-based results are presented in Chapter 2, in Table 1, and some of the spectrograms in Figure 19.

The analysis of acoustic correlates of laryngeal settings was carried out in the Speech Science Laboratory of the University of California at Santa Barbara, by Robert Hanson, using the Sondhi-tube method of analysing glottal volume–velocity waveforms (Sondhi 1975; Monsen and Engebretson 1977), with myself as subject. Data on the spectral slope of glottal waveforms from this experiment is included in Chapter 3.

Illustrative recordings of glottal adjustments in laryngeal settings were made by Peter Roach, with both himself and myself as subjects, using a Fourcin laryngograph in conjunction with a PDP-8 computer, in the Phonetics Laboratory of the University of Reading. Some of these are included in Chapter 3.

The account of each type of setting will follow a standard pattern. First, a schematic account is given of the muscular physiology of the setting; then the acoustic characteristics are discussed; and finally, phonological and paralinguistic uses of the setting in question are briefly mentioned.

The point of departure for the descriptive system was Abercrombie's account of voice quality (Abercrombie 1967: 89–95). More sporadic comments on voice quality are to be found scattered through a wide range of phonetic literature. I have tried to incorporate these insights wherever relevant, because I believe that a subject should be thoroughly conscious of its historical roots. There was not enough space, however, for more detailed comment on historical aspects, and a further commentary on this topic can be found in Laver (1975, 1977, 1978). A classified bibliography of research into voice quality is available in Laver (1979).

The analytic approach used in this book is one of componential analysis rather than holistic identification. Each given voice is analysed into the independently controllable settings whose composite auditory effect characterizes the overall voice. In this way, with some forty basic settings available in the descriptive repertoire, a very large number of different composite voice qualities can be described. Attaching a scalar label to the effect of a given setting makes the system yet more delicate: these scalar labels are discussed in Chapter 5. In a holistic approach one would have to have a single label identifying each of this very large number of different voices, giving an impossibly cumbersome system. Holistic labels of an impressionistic sort, such as 'heavy voice', 'light voice', 'tinny voice', or 'thick voice', are therefore avoided.

The learnability of the system depends on the possibility of the user being able to discriminate and identify the different auditory elements. Demonstrations of the settings can be heard on the tape-recording accompanying this book, and a suggested transcription system, based on International Phonetic Association conventions, is given in Chapter 5. The descriptive system was initially taught to a group of postgraduate and postdoctoral researchers in 1976 (see Esling 1978). The preparation of a full set of self-instructional materials is the subject of a current project funded by the Medical Research Council in the Phonetics Laboratory at the University of Edinburgh. These are primarily intended to be used by medical personnel, but should be capable of wider usefulness.

The possibility of learning to use the descriptive system is enhanced by the fact that the vocal qualities concerned are all capable of being imitated by all anatomically and physiologically normal speakers. This is because voice quality derives from two distinct factors in vocal performance. The first of these is to do with the nature of the individual speaker's own vocal apparatus. The particular anatomy of the speaker constrains his voice quality by the effect of such physical features as the dimensions, mass and geometry of his vocal organs. Thus, *organic* features such as the length of his vocal tract, the size of his tongue, velum, pharynx and jaw, the shape of his laryngeal structures and the volume of his nasal cavity, will all contribute their effect to the overall quality of the speaker's voice.

The second factor is to do not with the nature of the vocal apparatus at a speaker's disposal, but the use to which he puts it. Each speaker, as part of his habitual style of speaking, tends to use particular settings of his vocal apparatus. The descriptive system offered here largely excludes consideration of the first, organic type of influence on voice quality, except as a ground against which the figures of individual settings are perceptible. The concern of the descriptive system is primarily the second, *phonetic* type of feature.

Since these phonetic setting features are all by definition a matter of a mode of control of the muscular apparatus for speech, then all normal speakers should be able to learn to imitate the articulatory basis of the settings, and to recognize their auditory correlates. The descriptive model therefore refers to settings of an idealized vocal apparatus, and ignores inter-speaker differences of anatomy. The generality that this assumption permits is one of the essential attributes of a *general* phonetic theory.

Phonetics is inherently a synthesizing subject, drawing its methodology and its descriptive concepts from a wide range of different disciplines. It would be pleasant to think that this book might hold some appeal for a correspondingly wide range of readers. Linguists, phoneticians and speech scientists are amongst the primary groups of readers envisaged, as are speech therapists and speech pathologists. It may be worth emphasizing that the book concerns itself only with the 'normal' voice; but it is assumed that an indication of the enormous variety of potential qualities that the normal voice can achieve will be of interest to those concerned with speech and voice disorders.

Given the wealth of speaker-characterizing information conveyed by the voice, it is hoped that the descriptive model outlined here will also be useful to those researchers interested in the complexities of nonverbal interaction in face-to-face communication, including psychologists, psychiatrists and ethologists. In addition, since voice quality can signal membership of many types of social and regional groupings, sociologists, social anthropologists, social psychologists and sociolinguists may find the descriptive system of interest.

Spoken communication between men and computers is almost certain to be a widespread social reality in the not-too-distant future. There are very many intelligible speech synthesizers. Speech-recognition systems are becoming increasingly sophisticated and successful. Many speaker-recognition systems already exist, in voice security applications, for example. In all these areas, voice quality is an important consideration. Communications engineers are therefore part of the envisaged readership.

Finally, I am very conscious that this book represents only a beginning to the study of an area as rich and subtle as voice quality.

1 *Basic analytic concepts*

The originator of the term 'articulatory setting' was Honikman (1964: 73). But while the term was new, the general concept was not (Laver 1978). Early writers on phonetics such as Wallis (1653), Wilkins (1668), Holder (1669), Cooper (1685) and Herries (1773) all made comments on the settings that characterized the pronunciation of particular languages or particular individuals. While the general concept of a setting was clearly established over three hundred years ago, the concept had to wait for a specific name until the second half of the nineteenth century, when phoneticians such as Sweet, Sievers, Storm, Jespersen and Viëtor became interested in the topic. Kelz (1971) gives an excellent account of the widespread adoption of Felix Franke's term 'Artikulationsbasis', coined earlier but published posthumously in an article in 1889 edited by Jespersen. Franke's term replaced slightly earlier terms such as Siever's 'Operationsbasis', Storm's 'Mundlage', and Sweet's 'Organic basis'. The term in most general use nowadays is the English translation of Franke's original term, 'basis of articulation'.

The term 'articulatory setting' is preferred here to 'basis of articulation', because it encourages consideration of the articulatory relationship between the setting and the segmental articulations through which it runs. Honikman had a clear view of relationship, when she characterized the notion of a setting in the following way:

Broadly, it is the fundamental groundwork which pervades and, to an extent, determines the phonetic character and specific timbre of a language. It is immanent in all that the organs do. Articulatory setting does not imply simply the particular articulations of the individual speech sounds of a language, but is rather the nexus of these isolated facts and their assemblage, based on their common, rather than their distinguishing, components. The isolated articulations are mutually related parts of the whole utterance; they are clues, as it were, to the articulatory plan of the whole; the conception of articulatory setting seeks to incorporate the clues or to see them as incorporated in the whole. Thus an articulatory setting is the gross oral posture and mechanics, both external and

12

internal, requisite as a framework for the comfortable, economic, and fluent merging and integrating of the isolated sounds into that harmonious, cognizable whole which constitutes the established pronunciation of a language. (Honikman 1964: 73)

This is a complex characterization. A simpler view of the notion of a setting will be used in this book, based on the aspect of Honikman's definition that isolates 'the common, rather than [the] distinguishing, components' of sequences of individual segments. A useful preliminary way of envisaging an articulatory setting is to imagine a cineradiographic film being taken of the vocal apparatus in action over, say, 30 seconds. If the individual frames of the film were superimposed on top of each other, a composite picture might emerge which would represent the long-term average configuration of the vocal organs. This configuration constitutes the setting underlying the more momentary segmental articulations, and settings will often be conveniently described as configurations of this sort. In fact, a less static view is closer to the truth, where a setting is a constraining influence on segmental action. This notion of a constraint on dynamic segmental articulation is perhaps best expressed in terms of an articulatory 'bias' (John Holmes, personal communication). However, the 'configurational' image is a convenient initial characterization.

The minimal example of a setting constraint on the dynamics of segmental articulation is any assimilatory interaction between two adjacent segments. There has been a good deal of research in this area, which since Öhman's influential articles (1966, 1967) has come to be called 'coarticulation'. Fujimura discusses this in a recent article on articulatory constraints:

In the domain of articulatory dynamics, interaction between consecutive articulatory events using the same (or physically interacting) articulators may be described as what we may call hard coarticulation (Fujimura and Lovins 1978). Much has been discussed about the effective temporal domain of such interaction (see Kent and Minifie 1977 for a review). Hard coarticulation, defined as a direct mechanical smoothing effect, which may contain for example language-dependent and speaker-dependent time constants, would account for only part of the so-called coarticulation phenomena. The Henke type look-ahead mechanism (Henke 1966), for example, goes beyond this notion, and should be described as a feature-copying (or agreement) process, i.e. soft coarticulation. (Fujimura 1980)

Feature-copying is one example of the phonetic operation of a setting, over a short temporal domain. Mechanical smoothing, in Fujimura's definition, would be another example, to the extent that phonetic control of articulation is involved.

The purpose of this chapter is to explain some basic analytic relations before embarking on the detailed discussion of the settings themselves. Relations between different settings will be discussed first, and then relations between a setting and the segments superimposed on it.

1.1 Relations between settings

The settings will be described in terms of their relation to a standard reference setting, which will be called the 'neutral' setting. This neutral setting should in no way be confused with any idea of some putative 'normal' setting, nor with any concept of the 'rest' position of the vocal organs. It may be that the neutral setting coincides, in some given individual, with either the setting he habitually adopts in normal, unemotional speech, or it may coincide with the habitual position of his vocal organs at rest: whether it does or not is irrelevent to the definition of the neutral setting, which only has the status of a descriptive datum-point, as it were, by reference to which other settings can be conveniently described.

The neutral setting of the vocal organs is more properly to be thought of as a constellation of co-occurring settings at different locations in the vocal apparatus, each of which constitutes the neutral reference for the description of other settings at that location. This constellation of neutral settings has the following specifications:
- the lips are not protruded
- the larynx is neither raised nor lowered
- the supralaryngeal vocal tract is most nearly in equal cross-section along its full length
- front oral articulations are performed by the blade of the tongue
- the root of the tongue is neither advanced nor retracted
- the faucal pillars do not constrict the vocal tract
- the pharyngeal constrictor muscles do not constrict the vocal tract
- the jaw is neither closed nor unduly open
- the use of the velopharyngeal system causes audible nasality only where necessary for linguistic purposes
- the vibration of the true vocal folds is regularly periodic, efficient in air use, without audible friction, with the folds in full glottal vibration under moderate longitudinal tension, moderate adductive tension and moderate medial compression (van den Berg 1968)

– overall muscular tension throughout the vocal apparatus is neither
high nor low

Each setting to be described can then be contrasted with at least one of
these requirements.

The acoustic characteristics of the neutral setting are well established.
If we take an adult male speaker with a vocal tract of 17 cm in length and a
larynx of corresponding normal dimensions, then a number of statements
can be made about typical acoustic values. When the vocal tract is most
nearly in equal cross-section along its full length, and assuming that there
is no acoustic coupling to the nasal tract, then the frequency of the first
formant will be 500 Hz, and those of the higher formants will be odd
multiples of this value (Stevens and House 1961: 308) – 1500 Hz for the
second formant, 2500 Hz for the third, and so on. The bandwidths of the
first three formants are normally 100 Hz (Fant 1956: 111; Stevens and
House 1961: 311). The frequency ranges for the first four formants in an
average male speaker have been suggested by Fant (1956: 111) to be F_1
150–850 Hz, F_2 500–2500 Hz, F_3 1700–3500 Hz and F_4 2500–4500 Hz.
Fant (1960) suggests 60–240 Hz as the typical range for average male
fundamental frequency, and comments that 'females have on average one
octave higher fundamental pitch but only 17% higher formant
frequencies ... children about 10 years of age have still higher formants,
on the average 25% higher than adult males, and their fundamental pitch
averages 300 cs' (Fant 1960: 242). Average values for fundamental
frequency in adult males and females are 120 Hz for males and 220 Hz for
females (Fant 1956: 111).

In a later article, Fant slightly amends his comments about the
relationship between the formant frequencies of adult males, adult
females and children. He writes that:

The common concept of physiologically induced differences in formant patterns
comparing males and females is that the average female F-frequencies are related
to those of the male by a simple scale factor inversely proportional to the overall
vocal tract length (i.e. female F-pattern about 20% higher than male) ... this ...
simple scale factor rule has important limitations. (Fant 1966: 22)

Fant points out that deviations from the rule are obscured if an average is
taken over all vowels, and says that female–male relations are
characteristically different in rounded back vowels, very open unrounded
vowels and close front vowels. The reason for this is that 'The main
physiological determinant of the specific deviations from the average
rule is that the ratio of pharynx length to mouth cavity is greater

for males than for females' (Fant 1966: 22). 'The scaling of children's data from female data comes closer to a simple factor independent of vowel class' (Fant 1966: 29).

From this point on, in general discussion the average adult male vocal tract of 17 cm will be taken as representative, and the acoustic consequence of supralaryngeal settings will be discussed in terms of changes, relative to those of the neutral setting, in average values of formant frequencies and bandwidths, as would be found in a long-term average spectrum of the voice concerned. In Table 1, which is a compilation of results found by Nolan in his computer-based analysis, verified by spectrography, of my own performance of a number of settings on the first paragraph of the Rainbow Passage (Fairbanks 1960), the average values of the first three formants do not quite conform to the 'odd-multiples-of-the-first-formant' ratio required for a strictly neutral setting. The second formant is somewhat low, as is the third, suggesting a slightly lowered larynx. In addition, the absolute frequency values indicate that my own vocal tract length is longer than 17 cm. However, it is relative values that are relevant, and it will be seen that, with the exception of raised larynx, nearly all the results are in fair agreement with the theoretical predictions cited in the discussion of each of the settings, in terms of the directions of relative difference from the neutral values. Spectrograms of a number of supralaryngeal settings, including the neutral setting, are shown in Figure 19.

The average value and range of the fundamental frequency has already been stated. It will be further assumed that the laryngeal excitation of the resonatory system consists of a train of larynx pulses of approximately triangular waveform, regular in frequency and amplitude, where the maximum excitation occurs during the closing phase of the glottal cycle (Miller 1959), with the closing phase lasting approximately 33% of the glottal cycle (Monsen and Engebretson 1977). The spectral slope of the glottal waveform will be between -10dB and -12dB per octave (Flanagan 1958). Phonation at moderate effort is assumed; and Stevens and House (1961: 305) calculate that in this condition the spectral slope of the glottal waveform is -12dB per octave above 250 Hz, and less steep at frequencies below that value.

The regularity of the glottal waveform means that frequency jitter and amplitude shimmer will be absent. It is also assumed that in the neutral mode, there is no aperiodic noise produced by the laryngeal vibration.

Acoustic specifications of laryngeal settings will be given in terms of

Table 1. *Average formant frequencies for the first three formants in the author's performances of different settings on the first paragraph of the Rainbow Passage (Fairbanks 1960). The results are from a linear prediction computer program, supplemented by visual analysis of spectrograms (data from Francis Nolan, personal communication). The data points in the three vowel classes were from the following vowels: High front – /i, ɪ, ɛ, eɪ/; Low – /ɑ, ʌ, ɒ, aɪ, aʊ/; High back – /u, ʊ, ɔ, oʊ/.*

		Neutral setting	Lowered larynx	Raised larynx	Close rounding	Retro-flex	Dental-ized	Palat-alized	Velar-ized	Pharyng-alized
Overall mean (67 data points)	F3	2414	2401	2297	2265	2226	2465	2536	2565	2254
	F2	1348	1285	1277	1277	1317	1416	1524	1439	1263
	F1	495	452	511	475	540	479	475	474	539
High front vowels (21 data points)	F3	2512	2513	2375	2328	2344	2599	2666	2640	2313
	F2	1707	1606	1614	1616	1628	1775	1945	1860	1587
	F1	378	396	410	375	437	376	350	362	448
Low vowels (17 data points)	F3	2351	2397	2271	2272	2215	2443	2433	2447	2202
	F2	1206	1139	1160	1115	1207	1253	1326	1297	1152
	F1	760	578	744	680	774	724	763	729	756
High back vowels (10 data points)	F3	2211	2116	2072	2061	2067	2239	2378	2553	2060
	F2	1103	1069	1038	1036	1080	1145	1195	1099	1043
	F1	446	462	465	437	517	435	417	417	526

the shape, relative to that for the neutral setting, of the glottal waveform, its spectral slope, the presence or absence of spectral noise, average values for fundamental frequency and amplitude and their ranges, and the presence and degree of jitter and shimmer.

The acoustic specifications of overall muscular tension settings will be given in terms of changes, relative to the neutral setting, of the overall spectral slope, and in the slope of the spectrum of the glottal waveform, and in formant bandwidths. Associated changes of fundamental frequency and amplitude values will also be mentioned.

The relationship between the neutral setting and the other settings is a descriptive relationship. Because voices are to be described as the product of potentially composite settings, we turn now to the acoustic, auditory and physiological relationships between settings in terms of their possible co-occurrence.

Each of the settings will be described in analytic isolation. In reality, however, the different settings interact in various ways. One aspect of such an interaction is that the supralaryngeal vocal tract and the larynx are to a certain degree acoustically interdependent (Flanagan 1965: 154). Coupling factors between the resonatory system and the vibratory source result in each different supralaryngeal setting being associated with a slightly different pattern of laryngeal vibration. The effect is usually very small, with writers such as van den Berg (1954b), House (1959) and Stevens and House (1961) preferring to maintain that laryngeal activity is 'relatively unaffected' by supralaryngeal configurations; but in some cases the effect is more evident, as when the nasal tract is coupled to the resonatory system and has a more substantial impact on the fine detail of the mode of laryngeal vibration.

Acoustic interdependence is of more major importance when two settings co-occur which exploit different parts of the supralaryngeal vocal tract. For example, the effect of rounding the lips will be different, in absolute terms, when the back of the tongue is simultaneously raised in velarization than when the front is raised in palatalization.

The general principle of interdependence is an important factor at the physiological level. The muscle systems that make up the vocal apparatus are all anatomically interlinked, to varying degrees. Because of the mechanical linkages that exist between the different parts of the vocal apparatus, the use of any particular setting has effects on the possible actions of other settings. In some cases, the anatomical relationship between particular parts of the vocal apparatus is such that settings of one part can only be achieved if 'enabled' by the other part. For example, the jaw has an enabling role vis-à-vis the tip of the tongue in allowing the latter to be set in a retroflex position. There are many other examples of a facilitatory relationship of this sort between different types of settings.

Another type of relationship between settings is one where different settings compete for the use of the same part of the vocal apparatus. This is often the case in laryngeal settings, where the physiological action for one type of setting is sometimes incompatible with the action that would be required for a different setting of the same part of the larynx. Falsetto and the neutral mode of voicing are mutually incompatible in this way. Where two laryngeal settings use the same part of the larynx for their implementation, but are mutually compatible, then the action of the one setting modifies that of the other, as in whispery voice, where whisper and the neutral mode of voicing are combined.

Compatibility is a principle which extends beyond physiological requirements alone, however. Auditory and acoustic compatibility are factors which have to be taken into account in discussing the relationship between settings. One facet of this is that some settings have auditory aspects which are mutually overlapping. Thus both whisper and harshness have as part of their acoustic specification a necessary aperiodicity. In this particular respect, adding harshness to whisper would have no consequence for auditory quality.

A further facet of auditory compatibility is that the auditory effect of some settings is masked by the effect of other settings. Nasality is a vulnerable setting from this point of view, being perceptually less prominent when overlaid by any of a variety of other settings. Presumably, most settings could be arranged in a hierarchy of vulnerability to auditory masking by other settings.

The final aspect of the relationship between settings that needs to be considered is the interaction of settings with individual anatomy. Although the descriptive model refers explicitly to an idealized vocal apparatus, it is important to point out that, because of idiosyncratic anatomy, not all speakers will be able to achieve all possible settings with equal ease. A speaker with an anatomically markedly protruded lower jaw, with a corresponding dental overbite, will not be able to achieve a retroflex tongue setting as readily as a speaker with a more standard anatomy.

1.2 Relations between settings and segments

Interdependence and compatibility are thus basic concepts in the consideration of the relationship between different settings. They can also be seen to be relevant to the relationship between individual segments and the particular setting underlying them. In this context, appeal can be made to a principle of segmental *susceptibility* to the articulatory, auditory and acoustic effect of a setting. No setting normally applies to every single segment a speaker utters. The performance of a given segment may over-ride the parametric values of a setting, as in the case of a velar stop in the speech of someone generally characterized by velarization, or a nasal stop in the speech of a speaker with a nasal voice quality. In these examples, the influence of a setting on segmental performance is redundant. Alternatively, the performance of a given segment may momentarily reverse the value of an articulatory parameter normally exploited by a setting, as in the case of oral stops performed by a speaker with a nasal voice quality. It is therefore useful to propose a distinction between segments which are susceptible to the influence of a given setting, and those which are non-susceptible, because of their pre-emptive articulatory, auditory and acoustic requirements (Laver 1978). Using the notion of segmental susceptibility to the effect of a setting, we can now define a setting a little more precisely, as that aspect of the performance of a segment that it shares with other susceptible segments. By extension, settings can be abstracted from the chain of segmental performance as the shared properties of segments with a common susceptibility.

Susceptibility is a scalar concept, rather than a binary one. If we explore the potential perturbatory effect of a setting on different types of segments, then a hierarchy of influence is evident. As a hypothesis, in the case of the relationship between a setting and potential vowel segments at least, the effect of a setting on a segment will be proportional to the distance between the articulatory locations of the setting and the segment. Taking velarization as an example, the nearer the location of a potential vowel segment to the velar sector, the less susceptible that vowel will be to a shift in articulatory location caused by the velarizing setting. Close back vowels will be (redundantly) non-susceptible to velarization, while open front vowels will be maximally susceptible; intermediate vowels will be affected by the setting in a hierarchy of susceptibility.

The potential susceptibility of consonantal segments to a setting is more complex. Taking velarization as an example again, the effect of the setting can be either to shift the articulatory location of the segment closer to that of the setting, or to add a secondary articulation to the production of the otherwise unperturbed segment. In both cases, it seems not unreasonable to propose that the scale of the effect of the setting on an individual consonantal segment will be proportional to the distance between the articulatory locations of the setting and the segment. Thus, analogously to the vowel situation, velar stops would be (redundantly) non-susceptible to the effect of velarization, and dental stops would be maximally susceptible, with stop articulations between these two locations being affected by the setting in a hierarchy of susceptibility.

If the scalar nature of segmental susceptibility is a valid suggestion, and if acoustic and auditory susceptibility is organized in a similar way, then parallels with such notions as phonological strength immediately suggest themselves, and applications of the concept of scalar susceptibility to problems in comparative and historical linguistics and in sociolinguistics, can be readily conceived.

One rider needs to be added to the suggestions about segmental susceptibility to the effect of settings. Stevens (1972) has offered a persuasive account of the quantal nature of the relationship between articulatory and acoustic parameters, arguing that there are zones in the articulatory–acoustic graph where articulatory changes have a negligible acoustic effect, and are thus auditorily insignificant. In these plateau-like zones of the articulatory–acoustic graph, the scalar nature of suscept-ibility is necessarily suspended.

Because the successive segments in the stream of continuous speech vary in their susceptibility to the effect of settings, a setting is audible only on an intermittent basis, and even when audible, varies in its prominence, depending on the susceptibility of the segment currently being uttered. It was presumably intermittency on this basis that led Abercrombie, as quoted in the Introduction above, to describe voice quality as referring to 'those characteristics which are present more or less all the time that a person is talking: it is a quasi-permanent quality running through all the sound that issues from his mouth' (Abercrombie 1967: 91).

Another basis for intermittency of settings is that speakers sometimes adopt settings which are either incompatible with each other, or of a low degree of mutual compatibility, and use them on complementary sets of segments. This typifies the articulation of languages which exploit vowel harmony or consonant harmony as phonological devices. It can also be postulated as a possible explanation for historical sound change in a language, accent change in foreign language acquisition and stereotyping in accent imitation.

Intermittency of settings is sometimes due to a different type of partial distribution within the speech of a single speaker. Although dynamic features are largely left out of account in this book, there is a strong tendency for some settings to be associated with particular ranges of fundamental frequency, for instance. (Indeed, the notion of a 'setting' is just as applicable to the dynamic parameters of fundamental frequency and intensity as to parameters of phonetic quality (Laver and Trudgill 1979).) The neutral mode of voicing, for example, is usually associated with a medium range of fundamental frequency. Many speakers often change their phonatory setting when their fundamental frequency level drops below this, falling into a 'creaky' phonatory setting.

Lastly, voice quality settings can be intermittent for a different reason. That is, the communication of affect by paralinguistic manipulation of tone of voice depends partly on the momentary deviation of the speaker's voice from his habitual quality. The conventions of paralinguistic communication in English allow the speaker to signal confidentiality, for example, by switching his phonatory setting momentarily to whispery voice. To the extent that a speaker's utterances are paralinguistically coloured in this way, his 'base-line' voice quality will be less in evidence.

2 Supralaryngeal settings

The neutral configuration of the supralaryngeal vocal tract was characterized in the first chapter in the following way:

the lips are not protruded

the larynx is neither raised nor lowered

the supralaryngeal vocal tract is most nearly in equal cross-section along its full length

front oral articulations are performed by the blade of the tongue

the root of the tongue is neither advanced nor retracted

the faucal pillars do not constrict the vocal tract

the pharyngeal constrictor muscles do not constrict the vocal tract

the jaw is neither closed nor unduly open

It was also specified that, in the neutral configuration, the velopharyngeal system causes audible nasality only where necessary for linguistic purposes. It will be assumed for the moment that this is equivalent to maintaining velopharyngeal closure throughout speech, except for phonologically nasal or contextually-nasalized segments.

A radiographic diagram of the vocal tract in a neutral setting, based on an X-ray photograph of the author made in the Edinburgh Dental Hospital, is shown in Figure 1. (It may deserve comment that the hyoid bone, though accurately represented, is unusually oblique.)

This neutral configuration can be modified by three different groups of settings, which will each be considered in turn. Firstly, modifications of the longitudinal axis of the tract; secondly, modifications of the latitudinal, cross-sectional axis; and thirdly, velopharyngeal modifications.

2.1 Longitudinal settings

Modifications of the longitudinal axis of the vocal tract can result from at

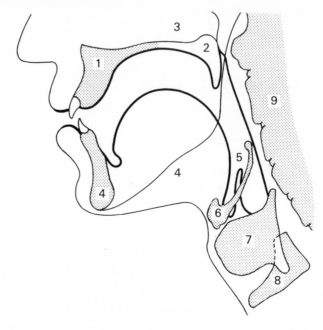

Figure 1. Radiographic diagram of the vocal tract in a neutral setting

1. Hard palate	6. Hyoid bone
2. Soft palate	7. Thyroid cartilage
3. Nasal cavity	8. Cricoid cartilage
4. Lower jaw	9. Vertebrae
5. Epiglottis	

least four different types of displacement of vocal organs from their neutral position.

The first two involve vertical displacements of the larynx, and its associated supporting framework, upwards or downwards from its neutral location, giving *raised larynx voice* and *lowered larynx voice* respectively. The third type of modification concerns the protrusion of the lips, and the fourth involves a raising and retraction of the lower lip, in *labiodentalized voice*.

2.1.1 *Raised larynx voice*

The key to vertical movements of the larynx is the hyoid bone, from which the larynx is suspended. The hyoid is a 'U'-shaped bone with the open end pointing backwards, itself nearly horizontally suspended above the larynx by a triple sling system of muscles. The first sling pulls the hyoid upwards and backwards towards the skull and middle pharynx; the second sling pulls the hyoid forwards and towards the jaw and the tongue; and the third sling pulls the hyoid downwards towards the larynx (Heffner 1950: 25; Kaplan 1960: 147; Van Riper and Irwin 1958: 363–9). The hyoid bone is unique in being the only bone in the body which is not articulated with any other bone, and its muscular suspension from the larynx, pharynx, tongue and jaw, with the muscular tensions of

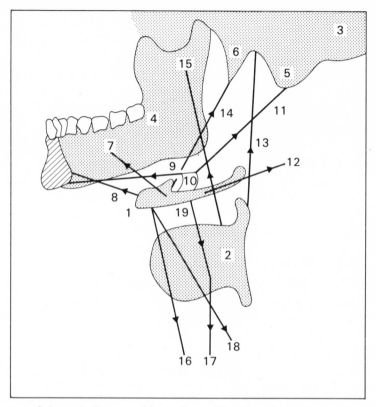

Figure 2. Schematic diagram of the action and location of the muscles of the hyoid complex

1. Hyoid bone	11. Posterior belly of the
2. Thyroid cartilage	digastricus muscle
3. Skull	12. Middle pharyngeal
4. Internal surface of lower jaw	constrictor muscle
5. Mastoid process	13. Stylopharyngeus muscle
6. Styloid process	14. Stylohyoid muscle
7. Mylohyoid muscle	15. Palatopharyngeus muscle
8. Geniohyoid muscle	16. Sternohyoid muscle
9. Anterior belly of the	17. Sternothyroid muscle
digastricus muscle	18. Omohyoid muscle
10. Fascial sling	19. Thyrohyoid muscle

the different sling systems having to be appropriately balanced for the accurate production of almost every single act of the vocal apparatus, makes the hyoid complex the prime example of mutually-influencing interaction of different muscular systems in speech.

Figure 2 is a schematic diagram of the three muscular hyoid slings. There are two chief possibilities of using these slings to raise the larynx from its neutral position. The first is to immobilize the hyoid and pull the larynx up towards it. This is done by using mainly the *hyoglossus, geniohyoid, mylohyoid* and *middle pharyngeal constrictor* muscles to fix the hyoid in position, and pulling the larynx upwards using the laryngeal muscle connecting the larynx to the hyoid, the *thyrohyoid* (Kaplan 1960: 147).

The second possibility is to raise both the hyoid and the larynx together. The hyoid can be raised by contracting the *geniohyoid, genioglossus, mylohyoid* and anterior belly of the *digastricus*, which act to pull the hyoid upwards and forwards, while simultaneously contracting the *stylohyoid, posterior belly of the digastricus, palatopharyngeus*, and the *middle pharyngeal constrictor*, which pull the hyoid upwards and backwards (Van Riper and Irwin 1958: 366). The forwards and backwards components of these mechanisms are made to balance each other, giving the overall result of raising the hyoid. The larynx can then be raised in two ways: either by actively contracting the thyrohyoid and shortening the distance between the hyoid and the larynx; or passively, by allowing the rising hyoid to carry the larynx up with it by means of the *thyrohyoid membrane*, whose median section thickens into the median *thyrohyoid ligament* (Kaplan 1960: 121), which acts as a mechanical link between the *thyroid* and the hyoid. The thyrohyoid membrane and ligament have been described in this passive action as 'a checkrein to limit the distance separating these structures' (Saunders 1964: 76).

Any of these possibilities allows the larynx to be kept in a raised position throughout continuous speech, with momentary positional fluctuations caused by the movements of the muscles directly involved in, or passively affected by, the production of segmental articulation.

There is also the possibility of pharyngeal muscles such as the *stylopharyngeus* being directly involved in the physiology of raising the larynx (Greene 1964: 48).

Kaplan (1960: 147) comments that the 'elevation of the larynx tends to decrease the length and caliber of the laryngopharynx'. One might also speculate that, because of the muscular interconnections between the larynx and the other components of the vocal tract, the articulatory activities of the tongue and the jaw might also be affected. Sundberg and Nordström (1976) have shown, however, that in vertical shifts of larynx position of up to 1.5 cm, the main resonatory consequence can be explained by the resulting change in the length of the pharynx. Associated local changes of cross-sectional area apparently contribute little to the overall effect on formant frequencies.

The conclusions in the study by Sundberg and Nordström are based on a comparison of spectrographic analyses of two subjects (a phoniatrician and a singer) who were able to control vertical larynx position during speech, with the predictions of a computer model of vowel-formant correlations with vocal-tract length. The computer predictions for raised larynx voice were as follows: all formant frequencies tend to rise. The third and fourth formants rise as the larynx rises; there is a substantial rise of the second formant for close front vowels, without a comparable rise of the first formant; and both the first and second formants rise in open vowels (Sundberg and Nordström 1976: 38–9; see also Fant 1960: 170).

The results from the live subjects agreed closely with these predictions for the first two formants. 'The major trend ... is that the first formant frequency of close front vowels is almost unaffected, whereas the second formant rises considerably when the larynx is raised. Vowels with lower second formant frequency exhibit substantial increases in both the first and the second formants' (Sundberg and Nordström 1976: 37). For the higher formants, the trend (with some complicating counter-tendencies because of the difficulty for subjects of altering larynx height without changing other articulatory factors) was for the third and fourth formant frequencies to tend to rise with larynx height (Sundberg and Nordström 1976: 38).

In the compilation in Table 1 of Nolan's computer-based analysis of my own performance of the settings, the average values for the first three formants in raised larynx voice match the predicted values only in the case of the first formant, and even there not very satisfactorily. The values for the second and third formants show a drop compared with the values for the neutral setting, where a rise was predicted. The analysed pattern is strongly like that for pharyngalized voice, and in fact the recording was of an extreme version of a raised larynx position, where the sustained muscular effort to keep the larynx high may very well have unwittingly resulted in a severely constricted pharynx. In this case credence should be given rather to the Sundberg and Nordström figures.

There is a tendency for laryngeal elevation to be accompanied by a rise in the fundamental frequency, and most voices produced with a raised larynx seem comparatively higher-pitched. This, however, is not mechanically inevitable, and can be compensated by adjustments of the pitch-control mechanism of the larynx. Since the laryngeal mechanism for achieving higher pitch has as one of its contributors a raising of the larynx (presumably 'because the larynx is braced up to the hyoid bone to withstand the strong pull of the cricothyroid muscle acting to stretch the vocal folds' (Catford 1964: 34)), then to raise the larynx and leave the pitch undisturbed necessarily requires a compensatory adjustment of some sort.

Conversely, it is possible to compensate for a naturally low pitch range, in singing, for example, by raising the larynx as a continuously-held setting. In this way, many would-be tenor singers, whose organic vocal equipment endows them with an optimum natural pitch range slightly lower than that appropriate for a tenor voice, manage nevertheless to achieve a (slightly strained) tenor-like pitch range.

Raised larynx voice often sounds to have a particular mode of phonation associated with it. This can be attributed to two factors. Firstly, the interaction of anatomically-linked muscle systems in the vocal tract and the larynx allows the supralaryngeal adjustment to perturb the muscular setting of the larynx. Secondly, the acoustic coupling of the resonatory system of the vocal tract and the phonatory mechanism of the larynx source may slightly affect the fine detail of the vibratory pattern of the vocal folds. At the present stage of research, not enough is known about the details of very small phonatory adjustments of this sort. Only impressionistic auditory labels are available for their description, and comments offered here are speculative.

Auditorily, and with an implication of an empathetically-sensed physiological state, raised larynx voice often sounds rather strained. Van Riper and Irwin (1958: 310) offer this physiological explanation:

When, in phonation, [the larynx] is raised, and the thyroid is tilted in the direction of the position used in swallowing, many abnormal patterns of muscular contraction take place. Certain muscles, which in normal phonation need only make movements of fixation, anchoring with their antagonists any of the laryngeal structures, must now make strong contractions. Other muscles, normally not employed, must be brought into play to operate the displaced larynx. The whole activity is productive of localized tension.

There is a discussion in Chapter 4, on settings of overall muscular tension, of the effect of this sort of tension on the auditory and acoustic characteristics of voice quality.

2.1.2 *Lowered larynx voice*

The larynx can be depressed by the action of the infrahyoid group of muscles, schematically represented in Figure 2. Together with the *sternothyroid*, which runs from the thyroid, the cartilage shielding the front of the larynx, to the breastbone, the infrahyoid muscles form a third muscular sling system connecting the hyoid to the breastbone (*sternohyoid*), and to the shoulder blades (*omohyoid*, which comes horizontally forward from the shoulder blades before travelling upwards to insert on the lower border of the hyoid bone (Kaplan 1960: 150)). Kaplan (p. 149) also suggests that the sternothyroid is 'perhaps the most significant in such activity' as depressing the larynx.

Depression of the larynx increases the length of the laryngopharynx, and one acoustic result of this is to lower the frequency ranges of the lower formants (Fant 1960: 64). Lindblom and Sundberg (1971) give some detailed calculations for a vertical drop of larynx position of 1 cm:

> [larynx lowering] lowers all formant frequencies, especially those that can be regarded as a back-cavity resonance . . .
>
> For most vowels, the effect on F_1 keeps close to $5\%–6\%$. For [u] and [ɑ], the effect is stronger and for [a] weaker. The effect on F_2 in the vowels articulated with a tongue shape similar to that of [i] is quite large (around 8%). This appears to be a consequence of the fact that F_2 tends to be a half-wave resonance of the back cavity for those vowels. F_2 for the back vowels [u], [o], and [ɑ] is much less affected, but is large for [a]. For all vowels except [u], F_3 is rather insensitive, which might be explained by the front-cavity affiliation of this formant. On the average, F_4 drops by about 5% – somewhat less for [o] and [i], somewhat more for [ɑ] and [a].
>
> Summarizing, we may say that F_3 is least sensitive to an expansion of the pharynx cavity in the epiglottal region and, in terms of percent, F_2 is the most sensitive formant. The absolute formant frequency change is largest for F_4. The net effect of the larynx lowering on F_3 and F_4 is to decrease the frequency distance between them. (Lindblom and Sundberg 1971: 1176)

As an indication of the absolute frequency values that may be involved, we can note that Sundberg and Nordström made long-term-average-spectra of a singer singing the same song twice, once with raised, once with lowered larynx. The values for the first formant fell from 650 Hz to 400 Hz, for the second formant from 1500 Hz to 900 Hz, and for the third from approximately 3500 Hz to 3000 Hz (Sundberg and Nordström 1976: 38).

In Nolan's computer measurements in Table 1, the values for the three formants are fairly closely in accord with the Lindblom and Sundberg calculations, both in terms of overall averages, and in the three subclasses of vowel types. A spectrogram of a phrase pronounced with a lowered larynx setting is shown in Figure 19.

Together with the lowering of formant ranges, there is a concomitant tendency (again, not inevitably, and which, as in the case of raised larynx voice, can be compensated for), to lower the fundamental frequency. Fundamental frequency compensation in lowered larynx voice seems uncommon, however, and a lowered fundamental seems to be an almost ubiquitous accompaniment to lowered larynx voice. One explanation for this lowered fundamental lies in the relaxing effect on the pitch mechanism of the larynx by the mechanical downwards pull of the infrahyoids.

A lowering of the larynx was said by Passy (1914: 20–1) to be a component of what he called 'sepulchral voice'. Sweet, on the other hand, thought that 'sepulchral tone' was merely the combination of low pitch and an exaggeration of what he assumed to be a typical English tendency towards a 'muffled', 'dull' quality, due to habitual 'slight separation of the jaws and neutral lip position' (Sweet 1890: 72). Sweet had earlier attributed the 'exaggerated dulling' in 'sepulchral tone' to the effect of what he called 'cheek and lip rounding' (1877: 97–8), rather than to the neutral lip position referred to in his later work.

If Sweet and Passy were using 'sepulchral' as an impressionistic term to refer to the same sort of quality, and if we concede that a lowered larynx setting is genuinely a component of such a quality, which Sweet's comment (1890: 72) on its characteristic low pitch might support, then perhaps Sweet's earlier comments (1877: 97) on the lip-rounding component are not so unlikely as they may seem at first sight. Passy might have agreed that lip-rounding is also a possible feature of the holistically-labelled 'sepulchral voice', but in any case it is striking that lip-rounding, and especially lip protrusion, as a component of many sorts of lip-rounding, have much in common with lowering of the larynx, acoustically, and hence auditorily. In all three cases, lowered larynx, lip-rounding and lip protrusion, the acoustic effect (Fant 1960: 64) is to lower the frequencies of the lower formants (though the effects are not identical, in that in lowered larynx voice it is the lower formants which are most affected, and in labial protrusion and lip-rounding it is the higher formants which are most changed). The configurational similarity of lowered larynx voice and lip protrusion is particularly interesting, in that they both effectively lengthen the longitudinal axis of the vocal tract.

It may be, then, that the concept of a 'sepulchral voice', for Sweet and Passy, was basically an auditory concept. In seeking an articulatory correlate for the auditory quality, they individually arrived at very different conclusions, but ones which gave acoustically and auditorily somewhat similar results.

As in the case of raised larynx voice, lowered larynx voice seems to have a special phonatory quality associated with it, by virtue of the same principles of interdependence of the muscle systems involved and of possible acoustic interactions in the vocal system.

Auditorily, the effect is of a somewhat breathy voice. Breathy voice is discussed separately in Chapter 3, as an independent phonatory setting, but one feature which may be relevant here is that breathy voice is produced with a marked relaxation of muscular effort, laryngeally. Speculatively, it may be that to enable the infrahyoid muscles to pull the larynx down effectively, the antagonistic suprahyoid muscles are allowed to relax, and that this relaxing mechanism is similarly involved in the production of breathy voice.

Speakers who use lowered larynx voice often seem to adopt a posture with their chin 'tucked in', as it were, together with a slight rotation downwards of the head. One consequence of this is to reduce the angle between the neck and the under surface of the chin, thus facilitating the process of lowering the larynx by minimizing any potentially-antagonistic mechanical stretch on the suprahyoid musculature. Another consequence is to facilitate the lower range of fundamental frequency noted earlier, by not opposing the pitch-lowering effect of infrahyoid contraction on the cricothyroid pitch-control system.

2.1.3 *Labial protrusion*
In this third type of longitudinal setting, voices with labial protrusion increase the longitudinal axis of the vocal tract.

The physiology of protruding the lips forwards from their neutral position touching the central incisors is chiefly a function of the *orbicularis oris* muscle, which acts as an oral sphincter, and is 'composed, primarily, of the fibers of other muscles – particularly the incisive, buccinator, caninus, and triangularis – that attach into the lips. The orbicularis oris fibers blend rather freely at the corners of the mouth and thus form an almost continuous sphincter' (Van Riper and Irwin 1958: 374). As well as serving to close the lips and to pull the upper lip down and the lower lip up, it protrudes the lips, in conjunction particularly with the *mentalis* muscle, which runs from the upper part of the front of the lower jaw down to the skin at the central point of the chin, and which in contraction can evert the lower lip, a usual component of lip protrusion (Hardcastle 1976: 116; Kaplan 1960: 274–5; Van Riper and Irwin 1958: 375). See Figure 3 for a schematic diagram of the muscles involved in labial protrusion.

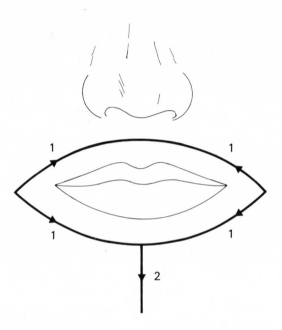

Figure 3. Schematic diagram of the action and location of the muscles involved in labial protrusion
    1. Orbicularis oris muscle   2. Mentalis muscle

The action of protruding the lips, which in effect adds a short section of variable length to the vocal tract, has the acoustic effect of lowering the frequencies of all formants, with the higher formants more affected, as mentioned above (Fant 1960: 64; Lindblom and Sundberg 1971: 1176).

There is usually an interaction between the longitudinal protruded setting and a latitudinal factor if more than the most moderate degree of labial protrusion takes place. Anything more than slight protrusion usually involves a certain amount of horizontal constriction of the space between the lips (Sweet's 'inner rounding' (1890: 17)). This latitudinal action tied to protrusion is not a mechanical inevitability, since it is physiologically possible to have substantial protrusion without any such horizontal compression, but protrusion without lip-rounding of this sort seems rare.

Protrusion of the lips is occasionally asymmetrical, in either the vertical or horizontal plane or both, but discussion of such idiosyncratic factors is beyond the scope of this book.

2.1.4 *Labiodentalized voice*

Habitual labiodentalization has the effect of slightly shortening the length of the vocal tract, by retracting and raising the lower lip while leaving the upper lip more or less in its neutral setting. Given that the labiodental setting is usually insufficiently constricted to cause local friction, the auditory effect of this type of setting tends to be minimal except on certain segments. The effect is most obvious on the segments articulated nearest to the lips: oral and nasal stops normally made bilabially are made labiodentally, and dental and alveolar fricatives are subject to a very prominent auditory modification.

Phonetic labiodentalization of this sort must be distinguished from the auditorily similar effect arising from organic causes such as protruding upper front teeth or a short lower jaw.

A labiodental setting is often combined with various types of lip-rounding, both with and without protrusion. When protruded lip-rounding is added to labiodentalization, the lower lip is frequently slightly everted, presenting part of the oral surface of the lip towards the upper front teeth.

The physiology of labiodentalization is particularly complex. The action of retracting the lower lip while raising it is left undiscussed by all the standard sources in the literature. The explanation offered here must be regarded merely as a possibility, therefore.

Three muscles at least seem to be involved, all shown in Figure 6. Kaplan (1960: 272) suggests that the orbicularis oris, in conjunction with other muscles, can act to draw the lower lip upwards. This is also stated by Van Riper and Irwin (1958: 373). When protrusion is involved, the mentalis muscle can co-operate with the orbicularis oris to evert the lower lip, as described earlier. The third muscle involved is the paired *levator anguli oris* muscle (also sometimes called the *caninus* muscle). According to Zemlin, the levator anguli oris is 'a flat triangular muscle, located above the mouth angle, but deep to the quadratus labii superior ... Its fibers converge as they course towards the angle of the mouth, where some fibers insert. Other fibers cross over to insert into the lower lip. Upon contraction [it] draws the corner of the mouth upwards and also helps to close the mouth by drawing the lower lip upwards' (Zemlin 1964: 239). The acoustic effect of labiodentalization is broadly the same as that of any tendency to constrict the labial aperture – a lowering of the formant frequencies, with the higher formants more affected. The acoustic effect of a secondary labiodental constriction on front fricatives is very audible: the lower limit of frequency distribution of the fricative noise is lowered for alveolar fricatives and is raised for dental fricatives.

As a secondary articulation modifying linguistic segments, labiodentalization has been reported in a number of languages. Catford summarizes some of these findings as follows:

Labiodentalized alveolar or postalveolar fricatives occur in several African and Caucasian languages, and perhaps elsewhere. In West Africa, Kom and Kutep are reported to have labiodentalized sounds (Ladefoged 1964, 1971) and in the Caucasus, the Fij dialect of Lezgin (Meilanova 1964), Tabasaran, some Eastern varieties of Aghul, and Abkhaz all have labiodentalized fricatives and affricates. In Sechuana there is a special type of labiodentalization described in Jones and Plaatje (1916). The Abkhaz and Tabasaran labiodentalization is of a somewhat similar type. (Catford 1977: 191)

A labiodentalized setting is often a consequence of the paralinguistic action of smiling.

2.2 Latitudinal settings

Latitudinal settings of the supralaryngeal vocal tract involve quasi-permanent tendencies to maintain a particular constrictive (or expansive) effect on the cross-sectional area at some given location along the length of the tract, relative to the cross-sectional area appropriate to the neutral vocal tract.

These latitudinal constrictive and expansive tendencies can be brought about by the action of a number of the vocal organs, and the different settings will be discussed in five groups, according to the organ principally responsible. The five groups relate to the activities of the lips, the tongue, the faucal pillars, the pharynx and the jaw.

2.2.1 *Labial settings*

A description of the habitual muscular settings of the lips in voice quality entails a discussion of the well-established but somewhat under-differentiated phonetic concept of *labialization*. However, a consideration of the concept of labialization does not exhaust the field of potential settings of the lips, and it may lead to a clearer exposition, therefore, if we initially approach the area of labial settings without reference to labialization as such.

The latitudinal muscular adjustments involved in labial settings consist of tendencies to constrict or to expand the space between the lips (the 'rima labiorum'), which will be called here the *interlabial space*, in two dimensions of the coronal (vertical, side-to-side) plane of the lips, compared with the neutral setting defined earlier. The interlabial space is delimited not by the vermilion border of the outer anatomical edge of the lips, but by the maximum horizontal and vertical dimensions of the aperture through which the airstream can pass. The assumption is made that these horizontal and the vertical dimensions lie on exactly the same coronal plane. This is in fact not quite true – for example, both in protrusion of the lips, and in lip spreading with the angles of the mouth pulled laterally and backwards, the coronal plane of the maximum vertical dimension of the interlabial space is further forward than the coronal plane of the maximum horizontal dimension (see Lindblom and Sundberg 1971: 1171). Nevertheless, for descriptive convenience the assumption will normally be held to apply.

All possible states of the horizontal and vertical parameters, leaving aside scalar variations within a parameter, give a total of eight latitudinal settings which deviate from the neutral: *horizontal expansion* of the (*vertically neutral*) interlabial space; *vertical expansion* of the (*horizontally neutral*) interlabial space; *horizontal constriction* of the (*vertically neutral*) interlabial space; *vertical constriction* of the (*horizontally neutral*) interlabial space; *horizontal expansion* with *vertical expansion*; *horizontal constriction* with *vertical constriction*; *horizontal expansion* with *vertical constriction*; and *horizontal constriction* with *vertical expansion*.

We have already discussed labial protrusion as a longitudinal setting: combining protrusion and the neutral non-protrusion settings with the eight conditions listed above for the non-neutral latitudinal settings of the lips, we have sixteen different types of labial settings. Together with the neutral latitudinal labial setting, with protrusion and non-protrusion, this gives a total of eighteen categories of labial settings available for

Parametric description	Non-protruded	Protruded
neutral	very common	rare
horizontal expansion	fairly common	rare
vertical expansion	rare	fairly common
horizontal constriction	common	fairly common
vertical constriction	fairly rare	rare
horizontal expansion & vertical expansion	fairly rare	rare
horizontal constriction & vertical constriction	fairly rare	fairly common
horizontal expansion & vertical constriction	fairly rare	fairly rare
horizontal constriction & vertical expansion	rare	very common

Figure 4. Tabulation of the relative frequency of labial settings

potential use in voice quality. All are physiologically possible settings, but some of the eighteen seem to be used very much more frequently than others (which is itself an interesting observation). Figure 4 is a tabulation of the eighteen settings, with an indication of the settings which, as a tentative impression at least, seem most and least common in their occurrence among speakers of English.

Figure 5 is a schematic diagram of the front view of the nine possible latitudinal settings.

A common labial setting deviating from the neutral is the one involving (moderate) horizontal expansion of the interlabial space with a neutral vertical component and non-protrusion, which resembles a fixed, slight grin. If the amount of horizontal expansion is increased, and/or vertical

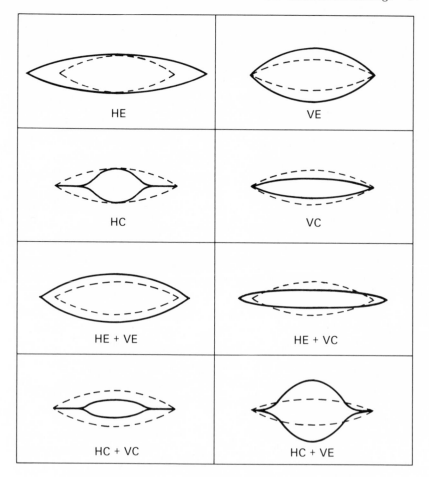

Figure 5. Schematized front view of labial settings
H – horizontal, V – vertical, E – expansion, C – constriction
The outline of the neutral setting is indicated by a dashed line

expansion is added to this setting, the 'fixed grin' is changed to a quasi-permanent 'smile'.

Another common labial setting is horizontal constriction with vertical expansion and protrusion.

A fairly common setting is horizontal and vertical constriction, a neutral horizontal component and non-protrusion; another is one with horizontal expansion and vertical constriction, with non-protrusion. Another interesting setting is the one with vertical expansion, with a neutral horizontal component; it is rare to find protruded lips with such a setting.

Perhaps the most easily identifiable setting, from auditory clues alone, is the 'lip-rounded' type of setting of horizontal constriction and vertical expansion with protrusion.

It is now possible to give some indications of the equivalence between this approach to the three-dimensional description of labial settings and the traditional phonetic terminology developed for the description of lip positions in segmental articulation. The use of terms referring to 'secondary' segmental articulations for the purpose of describing features of voice quality is discussed below in the section on lingual settings, but some translations of orthodox phonetic labels, including 'labialization', can be attempted here. 'Labialization' as a term has been used in such a variety of ways that it is probably safe to suggest that the only articulatory action to which the various usages usually have any reference in common is horizontal constriction of the interlabial space. The same applies to the general term 'lip-rounding'. It is only when the phonetic labels become more specific in their reference that detailed translation is feasible. Thus the terms 'close rounding' and 'open rounding' can be translated as follows: 'close rounding' is used usually to correspond to horizontal and vertical constriction of the interlabial space, with the degree of protrusion very marked for an articulation such as Cardinal Vowel No. 8, for example (see Jones 1962: 33, Fig. 22), but less marked for Cardinal Vowel No. 7 (*ibid*. Fig. 21).

'Open rounding' would correspond to horizontal constriction and vertical expansion of the interlabial space, with marked protrusion. The vertical expansion gives way to vertical constriction in a progression to 'close rounding'.

The term 'lip spreading' seems to refer uniquely to horizontal expansion of the interlabial space, with no protrusion, although there is a tacit convention that a spread lip position is limited to postures without much if any vertical expansion of the interlabial space.

Sweet was one of the first phoneticians to begin to distinguish between the three dimensions of labial articulation suggested here. In his *Handbook of phonetics* (1877: 13–14) he distinguishes the different parameters in this way: firstly, 'Projecting [pouting] the lips ... of course practically lengthens the mouth channel by adding a resonance-chamber beyond the teeth'; secondly, 'inner rounding' is his label for 'lateral compression of the cheek passage'; and thirdly, he sees 'lip-narrowing' as being the result of constrictive effort in the vertical dimension, whose degree of aperture normally varies with the height of the tongue, 'high vowels having the narrowest, low the widest lip-aperture'.

In his *Primer of phonetics* (taking quotations from the third edition, in 1906), Sweet makes this classification rather clearer. He continues to speak of 'pouting' (1906: 18); he implies that vertical constriction is the most important component of what he now calls 'outer rounding' – i.e. his previous 'lip-narrowing', in saying 'In outer rounding – with which front vowels are rounded – the lips are brought together vertically' (1906: 17); he then suggests in effect that horizontal constriction is the most important component of his 'inner rounding' – 'Back vowels, on the other hand, are rounded by lateral compression of the corners of the mouth, and, apparently of the cheeks as well' (1906: 17).

Another phonetician who explicitly distinguishes between the three labial dimensions is Heffner (1950). He put forward a descriptive scheme for labial articulation in terms not dissimilar to the ones used in this book. He said that, apart from the 'spread lip position', there are

two types of lip rounding. (a) A long narrow slit is produced between the two lips by bringing the lips vertically nearer each other. This is called vertical lip rounding. (b) A horizontally short, more or less oval opening is produced by closing the lips from the corners towards the center until only a small aperture remains. This is called horizontal lip rounding. (Heffner 1950: 98)

He also noted that 'protrusion of the lips is often a concomitant of horizontal lip rounding. It is much less frequently found with vertical lip rounding' (*ibid.*). Like most other writers on phonetics, Heffner pays no attention to the possibility of vertical expansion of the interlabial space, as opposed to its constriction. In fact he quite explicitly excludes factors to do with expansion from the consideration of lip rounding, in saying 'Rounded vowels are produced when the area of the aperture of the mouth cavity is reduced by contraction of the muscles of the lips' (1950: 98). But if one examines the photographs of Daniel Jones's lip posture in pronouncing the Cardinal Vowels and looks at the overall area of the 'aperture of the mouth cavity' as related to rounded versus spread vowels, then it is precisely the expanded vertical component which gives Cardinal Vowel No. 6, with open rounding, an aperture area scarcely less than that for the unrounded Cardinal Vowel No. 3 (Jones 1962: 33, Fig. 20 and Fig. 17).

No account is taken here of idiosyncratic asymmetries of latitudinal labial settings.

The physiology of manipulation of the interlabial space has been described by a number of writers, and the following comments rely chiefly on the accounts of Fromkin (1965: 93–109), Hardcastle (1976: 111–20), Kaplan (1960: 272–4), and Van Riper and Irwin (1958: 374–5). Figure 6 is a schematic diagram of the action of the labial muscles discussed below.

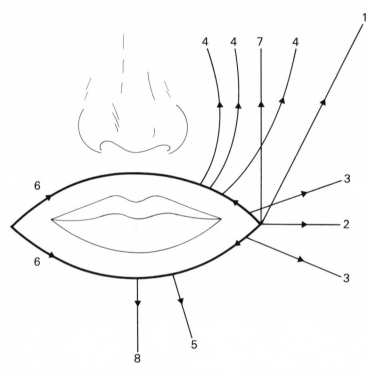

Figure 6. Schematic diagram of labial muscles involved in latitudinal control of the interlabial space (after Hardcastle 1976)

1. Zygomaticus muscle
2. Risorius muscle
3. Buccinator muscle
4. Quadratus labii superioris muscle
5. Quadratus labii inferioris muscle
6. Orbicularis oris muscle
7. Levator anguli oris muscle
8. Mentalis muscle

Horizontal expansion of the interlabial space is achieved principally by contraction of the *zygomaticus, risorius* and *buccinator* muscles. The zygomaticus runs from the temporal bone diagonally forward and down to the angle of the mouth, and acts to lift the corners of the mouth upward and outward; the risorius runs from near the ear across the cheek to the corner of the mouth as well, and widens the mouth laterally; and the buccinator is the large, strong muscle which makes up most of the cheek wall, coming from the jaw near the ear to the corner of the mouth once again, pulling the corner laterally and to some degree backwards.

Vertical expansion of the interlabial space, where this is done with no contribution from lowering the jaw, is almost entirely brought about by two muscles: the *levator labii superioris*, which runs from three points of origin (the side of the nose near the bridge, the lower edge of the eye-socket, and the edge of the temporal bone) down to the upper lip, pulls the upper lip upwards and slightly laterally; and the *depressor labii inferioris*, which has its point of origin on the chin just to the side of the point of the chin, and runs up to the skin of the lower lip, contracts to pull the lower lip downwards. (The levator and the depressor muscles are sometimes called the *quadratus* muscles.)

Horizontal constriction makes use of the *orbicularis oris* muscle, whose sphincteric effect was described in the earlier section on labial protrusion.

Vertical constriction also employs sphincteric action of the orbicularis oris, with appropriate antagonistic tension from the muscles specified above for horizontal expansion, and from the levator labii superioris helping to position the upper lip, and the depressor labii inferioris the lower lip.

The acoustic effect of horizontal expansion of the interlabial space, 'lip-spreading', is chiefly to raise the frequencies of the formants (Fant 1957: 19); the broad effect of the settings discussed above as contributing to the various sorts of 'lip-rounding' (depending on the closeness of the rounding) is similar to that of protruding the lips, and to the effect of labiodentalization – a lowering of the formant frequencies, with the higher formants more affected (Fant 1960: 64; Lindblom and Sundberg 1971: 1176). In Nolan's computer-based results in Table 1, the findings for close rounding are as predicted by Fant, and by Lindblom and Sundberg.

The descriptive scheme has been discussed so far as if it were largely one for accounting for static, postural configurations. The factors suggested as relevant for contributing to the acoustic effect of the settings have been stated only as comparative categories of dimensions relative to the neutral setting without scalar values attached to the dimensions. In particular, the cross-sectional latitudinal specification of the interlabial space has been discussed only as a shape and not as a quantified area. But cross-sectional measurements are relevant to acoustic quality only in terms of cross-sectional area, and not cross-sectional shape. Difficulties immediately arise from this position, since it seems to follow that if two settings have exactly the same degree of protrusion, and different latitudinal shapes, but exactly the same cross-sectional areas, then the descriptive model would assert that the settings, being of different categorial values, are therefore also auditorily different, while acoustic theory would require that the settings should produce exactly the same acoustic effect. Clearly, in such a situation, an acoustically acceptable explanation has to be found, if the descriptive system is not to be undercut.

Two possible explanations come to mind. First, as briefly mentioned earlier, although the descriptive scheme treats the interlabial space, for analytic convenience, as being two-dimensional, it is in fact three-dimensional, even in the case of non-protrusion, with a depth corresponding at least to the front-to-back thickness of the lips. This thickness varies with the different conditions of tension and contraction in the many interdigitating facial muscles involved in both longer-term labial settings (which can also be affected by different mandibular settings), and in momentary segmental articulations. This will result in variations in the fine detail of the rapidly-changing cross-sectional area function along the short, variable length of lip-cavity. So two settings of different shapes of the interlabial space in two dimensions, but of equal cross-sectional area at that plane of maximum constriction, may, perhaps, almost never have identical cross-sectional area functions along the whole length of the labial section. There is also the related point, explored more fully in Chapter 4 on settings of overall muscular tension, that since different shapes of the lip-apertures are created essentially by the action of different muscles or by different degrees of tension in the same muscles, then the acoustic properties of the cheek and lip section of the vocal tract may well be different for the different settings (in terms of radiation and absorption of sound through the cavity-walls, acoustically reflected as changes in the bandwidths of the formants most affected), and therefore give slightly different auditory impressions.

Secondly, and perhaps more importantly, if, instead of looking at the problem as if it concerned a steady-state, long-held posture, we consider the situation of normal, continuous speech, it is clear that the muscular adjustments of different labial settings impose differing amounts and types of constraint on the ability of the lips to execute their segmental articulations – and of course it is precisely this constraining factor that is abstracted as the setting underlying speech. This constraint operates both in the relatively steady-state aspects of articulations and in the dynamic transitions to and from such states. It is assumed that as listeners we receive our auditory clues to labial settings from both these aspects.

In considerations of the acoustic effect of lip settings in any particular individual, account may have to be taken, depending on individual anatomy, of organic aspects of the acoustic influence of the spatial relation between the lips and the front teeth. Such speaker-specific details do not, of course, enter the descriptive scheme offered here, which is speaker-neutral.

Lip spreading and lip rounding as components of both vowel and consonant segments are taken to be so familiar as phonological devices that exemplification is unnecessary.

2.2.2 *Lingual settings*

There are five different groups of lingual settings. Four major ones involve constraints on articulation in the sagittal plane of the vocal tract (that is, in the vertical, central, front-to-back plane). Three groups of sagittal settings concern the body of the tongue, the tip and blade of the tongue, and the tongue-root. The fourth sagittal setting is to do with limitations on the movements of the tongue radially away from its neutral position. The fifth setting involves a more minor aspect: it is concerned with the degree of lateral curvature of the tongue-surface in the coronal, side-to-side plane. These last two settings are among the many aspects that have to be considered in an account of overall muscular tension, and will therefore be discussed later, in the chapter on tension settings.

If we consider here only the sagittal settings of the body, tip and blade, and root of the tongue, they all involve the adoption of a setting which tends to maintain the relevant part of the tongue displaced from its neutral position in the vocal tract, either towards or away from the upper surface or the back surface of the tract. The result is thus to constrict or expand the oral cavity or the pharynx. Pike describes the effect of lingual adjustments of this sort on vowels, in terms of 'moving the vowel triangle AS A WHOLE frontwards, backwards, upwards, and downwards in the mouth during connected speech. The auditory effects are startling, and easy to achieve' (Pike 1967: 224). The conceptualization of the articulatory correlates of these overall lingual adjustments is not quite the same in this book as Pike's suggestion. In the view presented here, it is less a matter of a displacement of the whole vowel area than of a setting imposing a bias on vowel articulations such that they are constrained to fall only in a restricted zone within the vowel area. It may be that extreme examples of lingual settings push the realizations of certain vowels beyond the periphery of the vowel area – as in the 'strangulated' effect of extreme pharyngalization. But the effect of settings on vowels in less extreme instances is to push the individual vowel realizations, depending on susceptibility, into favoured parts of the vowel area, leaving some (usually peripheral) part empty.

It may be helpful at this point to reiterate a basic aspect of the relationship between a setting and a segment. It was said earlier that a setting is that part of the performance of a segment that it shares with other susceptible segments. It is not some extraneous addition to the 'basic' segmental performance, but integral to the phonetic make-up of the segment. It was also suggested earlier that settings can be abstracted from a chain of segments as the shared properties of those segments. The analytic separability of settings from segments should not be taken to imply (as the quotation from Pike seems rather to suggest) that settings are in some sense phonetically extraordinary, and of minimal concern to segmental analysis.

In the case of the effect of gross lingual displacements on consonantal segments, the segmental articulation will either be displaced towards the articulatory location of the setting, or will have a secondary articulation added to its primary stricture, as indicated in Chapter 1. We can use the traditional labels of secondary articulation, such as 'velarization', 'pharyngalization' etc., for both these effects, to cover equally the cases of vowel and consonant segments. The ambiguity that results is not important, and explicitness is easy to achieve whenever necessary. Abercrombie (1967: 93) discusses this application of the concept of secondary articulation to the description of voice quality: it is necessary here only to note that, while an analysis of the segmental make-up of a voice quality such as velarized voice may show consonantal segments with velarization as a secondary articulation, the notion of 'secondariness' applies only to that segmental level of analysis, and not to the level of voice quality analysis as such, where quasi-permanent velarization is in no sense analytically 'secondary'.

The use of labels of secondary articulation to classify voice qualities whose constituent, susceptible segments show the effect of the particular setting can be extended to apply not only to lingual settings, but also to labial, faucal, pharyngeal and velopharyngeal settings.

Returning to the analysis of lingual settings, both in the mouth and in the pharynx, it is customary, in the phonetic description of segmental articulation, to think chiefly about the location and degree of the maximum constriction of the vocal tract. This point of maximum constriction is then taken to characterize the configuration of the rest of the tongue surface, which is assumed to be regularly curved, and convex, in the sagittal plane. Using this point as the descriptive datum, either in the traditional analysis of place of articulation or in the more recent method of specifying its distance from the glottis, is valid and economical for describing segmental articulation. In describing settings, however, it is less a matter of specifying relatively fine distinctions of place of articulation than of stating general tendencies for the positioning of the bulk of the tongue. We can therefore profitably take as our reference point the long-term average speech position of the approximate centre of mass of the tongue (Laver 1968).

Figure 7 shows the centre of mass of the tongue lying nearly vertically

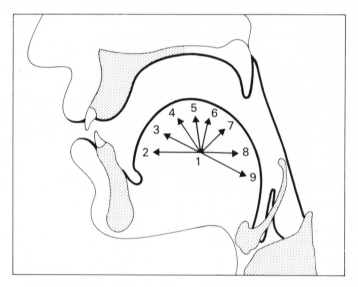

Figure 7. Sagittal section of the vocal tract in the neutral setting, showing radial directions of movement of the centre of mass of the body of the tongue in lingual settings

1. Centre of mass of the tongue	6. Velarization
2. Dentalization	7. Uvularization
3. Alveolarization	8. Pharyngalization
4. Palato-alveolarization	9. Laryngo-pharyngalization
5. Palatalization	

beneath the junction of the hard and soft palates, in the neutral configuration. The vocal tract, in a stylized version, can be seen as an arc, of about 270 degrees, curving at relatively constant distance round the centre of mass of the tongue, from the larynx to the lips. Settings of the body of the tongue can now be visualized as resulting from the shift of the centre of mass along any radius of the circle of which, in the neutral configuration, it is the centre.

The customary phonetic labels for place of articulation can be appropriately used. Various constrictive settings result from the following radial movements of the location of the centre of mass of the tongue: upwards towards the hard palate, and slightly forwards, to give a voice 'with palatalization', or *palatalized voice*; forwards and upwards for 'palato-alveolarization' or *palato-alveolarized voice*: forwards and slightly upwards for 'alveolarization' or *alveolarized voice*; forwards for 'dentalization' or *dentalized voice*; backwards and upwards for *velarized voice*; backwards and slightly upwards for 'uvularization' or *uvularized voice*; backwards for 'pharyngalization' or *pharyngalized voice* (where the constriction of the pharyngeal part of the vocal tract is achieved by retraction of the body of the tongue into the pharynx, rather than by the spincteric action of the muscles of the pharynx bringing the back wall of the pharynx forward as well, which is discussed in 2.2.4, 'Pharyngeal settings').

It is probably unrealistic to hope to be able to distinguish auditorily between finer subdivisions than these, such as 'prevelarized voice', 'alveolo-palatalized voice', and 'post-alveolarized voice', when one is gathering the necessary diagnostic information over quite a long stretch of speech. Indeed, it may be more practical for most purposes to subdivide less finely, and distinguish only between settings with a fronting component, in *tongue-fronted voice*, and those with a retracting component, in *tongue-retracted voice*.

On the other hand, it may be helpful to subdivide the lingual settings that achieve pharyngalization into *pharyngalized voice* versus *laryngo-pharyngalized* voice, where the former might be reserved for constriction chiefly of the middle pharynx, and the latter for constriction of the lower pharynx and upper larynx, with the centre of mass of the tongue moving backwards and slightly downwards. One difficulty in drawing an auditory distinction between these last two is that constriction of the pharynx almost always involves other physiologically and acoustically linked phenomena, such as a vertical shift of larynx position downwards, giving a lowered larynx component (and a somewhat breathy phonatory setting), a tendency to pull the velum downwards (because the velum and tongue are attached to each other by the palatoglossus muscle), giving some nasalization. All of which makes pharyngalized voice into a perceptual complex in which the specific contribution of the pharyngalization is particularly hard to isolate and subdivide.

Examples of a constrictive lingual setting are found in the voices of adult women adopting 'little girl' voices. In the terms just discussed, their voices are the result of a raising and perhaps a slight fronting of the centre of mass of the tongue, to give palatalization or palato-alveolarization (sometimes also raising the larynx and using whispery phonation). Something of the same effect, without the whispery voice, can be heard in the voice quality that people in our culture use (more usually older women) when talking affectionately to babies (this also often involves protrusion of the open-rounded lips). Pike discusses the palatalized voice of this kind of speech:

I have heard ... sharp changes of vowel quality in a woman using a kind of 'baby talk' which had a 'caressing' quality without mutilating the language structure or suppressing phonemic contrasts. In the instance referred to, the vowels seemed to be raised and fronted so that the net result gave a partial paralleling of the smaller vocal cavity of a child. (Pike 1947: 66)

Palatalized voice was very probably also a component in the voice adopted by a ventriloquist described by Abercrombie:

The ventriloquist ... has to have command of several voice qualities. The extreme of virtuosity, probably, was reached by a certain music-hall performer, a large middle-aged man, who had learnt to produce, completely convincingly, the voice-quality of a seven-year-old girl, showing that it is possible to compensate, by muscular adjustment, for extreme anatomical differences. (Abercrombie 1967: 94)

There is also an example of palatalized voice in the nationally-representative articulatory setting said to characterize French. The overall tendency of French speakers to raise and front the centre of mass of the tongue is reflected in comments from Wallis (1653):

The French articulate all their sounds nearer the palate, and the mouth cavity is not so wide ... (Kemp trans., 1972: 211)

Sweet (1906: 74):

In French ... the tongue is arched and raised and advanced as much as possible, and the lips articulate with energy. French therefore favours narrowness both in vowels and in consonants, its point-consonants tend to dentality, and compared with the English ones, have a front-modified character . . .

Heffner (1950: 99):

French is a language which is usually spoken with a high and tense forward basis of articulation

and Honikman (1964: 78–9), where she writes that the tongue

is anchored medially, albeit lightly, to the floor of the mouth by the tip tethering to the lower front teeth . . . Of the free, untethered part of the tongue, the *blade* (or tip and blade) and the *front* are the dominant articulators

and

In French, there is no lateral tension of the lingual muscles but strong thrust is given to the convexed dorsum, especially in articulating the front vowels. French people with whom this has been discussed say it feels as if they were 'pushing the words forward out of the mouth'.

Velarized voice (with denasality) is a characteristic of speakers from certain parts of Lancashire (Abercrombie 1967: 95). The complex of settings which typify the voice quality of the Liverpool accent has been well documented by Knowles:

In Scouse, the centre of gravity of the tongue is brought backwards and upwards, the pillars of the fauces are narrowed, the pharynx is tightened, and the larynx is displaced upwards. The lower jaw is typically held close to the upper jaw, and this position is maintained even for 'open' vowels. The main auditory effect of this setting is the 'adenoidal' quality of Scouse, which is produced even if the speaker's nasal passages are unobstructed. (Knowles 1978: 89)

Phonological uses of tongue-body settings as secondary articulations added to a primary constriction elsewhere in the vocal tract are familiar from many languages. Catford (1977: 192–3) gives numerous examples of palatalization, velarization, uvularization and pharyngalization in a wide variety of languages.

Settings where the centre of mass of the tongue moves downward, or downward and forward, as a continual tendency, seem rare.

Because the tongue is of relatively fixed volume (Paget 1930: 36), it follows that, unless there are strong, compensating, antagonistic tensions, any lingual constrictive setting will tend to have a corresponding and co-acting expansive tendency in one or more other parts of the vocal tract. Pharyngalization, for example, enlarges the front part of the oral cavity, as does velarization, to a smaller extent. Account also has to be taken, however, of factors of elasticity. Lindblom and Sundberg (1972) in comparing the tongue contour lengths in the production of spoken and sung vowels, conclude that

Our investigation seems to suggest that the tongue contour between the tongue tip and the glosso-epiglottic fold exhibits some elasticity. The tongue is somewhat stretched when the tongue tissue is raised and/or when the larynx is depressed. The site of this spring-like property cannot be determined from our measurements but anatomical considerations make it seem likely that at least some of it should be attributed to the posterior portions. Also the tissues joining the glosso-epiglottic fold with the larynx can be compared to a spring. However, it appears to be stiffer than that of the tongue tissues. (Lindblom and Sundberg 1972:4)

They establish that the line along the surface of the tongue in the mid-sagittal plane from the tip to the glosso-epiglottic fold can vary by up to 20% (11.4 cm for a spoken open back vowel to 13.7 cm for a sung close front vowel, with spoken vowels having shorter lengths than their sung counterparts).

There is one type of setting of the body of the tongue which is of a different kind from the ones just discussed. This is a setting in which the centre of mass of the tongue remains more or less in its neutral position, and the segmental articulations tend not to depart radially very far from the centre of the articulatory space. This centring setting is one usually found in so-called 'muffled voice', and it will be discussed under *lax voice* in the section of Ch. 4 on settings of overall muscular tension. Similarly, *tense voice*, the other setting in the section on overall tension, usually involves a lingual setting where the centre of mass of the tongue remains more or less in the neutral position, but with the segmental articulations being characterized by movements of greater radial distance than in lax voice. (Tense voice is often impressionistically labelled 'metallic voice'.)

After the group of lingual settings which can be seen as involving primarily a shift in position of the centre of mass, there is a small group of settings where the centre of mass is displaced from the neutral position merely as an 'enabling' factor. This is the group of settings of the tip and blade of the tongue.

One example would be the consistent use of the tip of the tongue as the principal active articulator in the front of the mouth instead of the blade. The neutral setting exploits the reverse situation, of the use of the blade instead of the tip. Honikman (1964) gives many suggestions about differences of shape and posture characteristically distinguishing the settings of the tip and blade of the tongue in English, French, Iranian, Russian and Turkish.

One further example is the tendency to maintain a hollowed, slightly retroflex setting. Both Sweet (1906: 74) and Honikman (1964: 77) suggest that this setting characterizes English speech (Received Pronunciation, rather, explicitly in Honikman, and, one assumes, in Sweet).

At least two different types of retroflex articulations need to be distinguished here. The most extreme degree of curling of the tongue tip results in the underside of the tip and blade being presented to the front of the hard palate. Catford (1977: 153) calls these 'sublamino-prepalatal' articulations, and says that Tamil and other Dravidian languages are often of this type. Ladefoged (1971: 40) suggests that while this is true in some South Asian languages, other languages from South Asia use retroflex articulations of a less extreme degree, involving the tip of the tongue articulating against or near the back of the alveolar ridge: Ladefoged calls these articulations 'apical postalveolars' (1971: 39), and Catford (1977: 152), discussing their use in Hindi and other North Indian languages, calls them 'apicopostalveolar'. Retroflex vowels, such as in accents of South West England and very many North American accents, in words spelt with a post-vocalic 'r' such as 'bird', 'earth', involve apical retroflexion much more commonly than the sublaminal type. The same seems to be true of retroflexion used as a voice quality.

For all these tongue tip and blade settings, the body of the tongue has to conform to a setting which enables the tip/blade to execute the appropriate movements. This would be particularly necessary in the case of the retroflex setting, especially of the sublaminal type, where to allow the tongue-tip to curl up at relevant moments throughout the speaker's utterances, the body of the tongue seems likely to be set in a slightly lowered and possibly slightly backed position, compared with its neutral configuration. The tongue-body is assisted in this 'enabling' function by the jaw. Honikman, for example, comments that

the frequent retroflex consonants in the languages of India and Pakistan are produced with the tongue curled back in such a way that the edge of the rim of the tip approximates or touches the hind-part of the alveolar ridge or fore-part of the palate; the open setting of the jaw enables this tongue-setting to be made comfortably. (Honikman 1964: 78–9)

In 'tip' settings, the body of the tongue is slightly retracted, and in the 'blade' setting, it is in the neutral position. It therefore seems reasonable to maintain that the tip/blade system, though capable of affecting the quality of speech to an audible degree, is only relatively and not entirely an independent system, depending to some extent on the major tongue-body system (which is in turn partly dependent on the jaw).

The limited independence of the tip/blade system is reflected to some degree in the perceptual nature of the effects of such settings. While the tongue-body settings can usually be heard underlying nearly every segment in continuous speech, the tip/blade settings (except in the case of retroflexion) exercise their auditory influence only when the tip or the blade is the active articulator and even then they are in competition, as it were, with the auditory colouring of the ever-present tongue-body setting on which any given tip/blade setting is superimposed.

The same can probably be said of a third lingual system, that of the root of the tongue. Pike (1947: 21b–22b; 1967) suggests that the root of the tongue can be adjusted in long-term muscular settings which expand or constrict the pharynx sufficiently to produce different qualities in a speaker's voice. Settings of the root of the tongue would have to be included in a comprehensive descriptive model of voice quality, with the same semi-independent status as the tongue tip/blade system, with its actions needing to be facilitated by corresponding adjustments of the tongue-body system. A descriptive statement of the physiology and acoustics of tongue-root adjustments would be somewhat speculative at this time, however, and will therefore be omitted. A brief discussion of the phonological role of tongue-root adjustment can be found in Stewart (1967) for Twi, Ladefoged (1964) for Igbo, Lindau (1979) for Akan, and Gregerson (1973) for the Mon-Khmer group.

The muscular physiology of tongue control is complicated and, in some details, controversial. The identity of the prime movers, or protagonist muscles, is reasonably well agreed, however, for the major parameters of movement of the body of the tongue (although the situation is made more complex by the fact that moving the tongue in any given direction can be achieved in a variety of ways by the synergistic action of different co-acting muscles).

The following brief outline is distilled from Hardcastle (1976), Heffner (1950), Kaplan (1960), Luchsinger and Arnold (1965), Van Riper and Irwin (1958), and Zemlin (1964).

The body of the tongue can be lifted upwards primarily by the contraction of the *styloglossus* and *palatoglossus* muscles, sometimes with some assistance of the *superior* and *inferior longitudinal* muscles and *digastric* muscles. Figure 8 shows the location and direction of pull exerted by some of these and other lingual muscles involved in settings of the tongue.

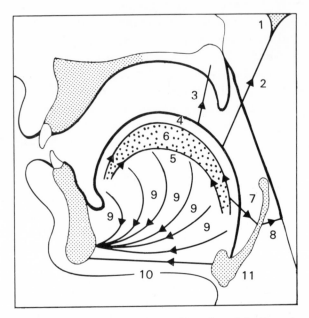

Figure 8. Schematic diagram of the action and location of the lingual muscles

1. Styloid process
2. Styloglossus muscle
3. Palatoglossus muscle
4. Superior longitudinal muscle
5. Inferior longitudinal muscle
6. Transverse lingual muscle
7. Hyoglossus muscle
8. Middle pharyngeal constrictor muscle
9. Genioglossus muscle
10. Geniohyoid muscle
11. Hyoid bone

The styloglossus runs downwards and slightly forwards from the styloid process of the temporal bone to insert into the sides of the tongue; its upper fibres travel along the tongue, near the margins, almost to the tip of the tongue. The effect of contracting the styloglossus is to pull the tongue up and back. It can be assisted in this by the palatoglossus, which makes up the forward faucal arch, and which starts in the forward part of the soft palate, curving laterally forward and down, to insert into the sides and upper part of the back of the tongue, with its fibres blending with those of the styloglossus (Van Riper and Irwin 1958: 379), and with those of the *transverse lingual* muscle and the *hyoglossus* (Zemlin 1964: 219). The action of the palatoglossus normally is to act as one of the depressors of the soft palate, but when the velum is fixed in position by the palatal levators, contraction of the palatoglossus pulls the body of the tongue upwards. (The palatoglossus will be discussed more fully in the section on velopharyngeal settings.) The lifting action of the styloglossus and the palatoglossus may be helped by the superior and inferior longitudinal muscles, which, located entirely within the tongue and not attached to any part of the skeleton, serve to bunch the tongue from front to back. The lifting action may also be aided by the digastricus muscle, whose posterior belly runs forwards, inwards and downwards from the mastoid process on the skull, through a fascial sling, which is a tendinous hoop, on the hyoid bone, to join with the anterior belly of the digastricus, which inserts on the inside surface of the jaw at the chin, as shown on Figure 2. When the digastricus muscle contracts, its effect is to lift the hyoid, if not resisted by the infrahyoid muscles. The tongue is then free to move upwards in the mouth, through the action of the muscles mentioned above, such as the styloglossus, palatoglossus and the longitudinal muscles.

The muscles which are antagonistic to the upwards and backwards tendency of the styloglossus and palatoglossus are the hyoglossus, which attaches the hyoid bone to the sides of the tongue, and the *genioglossus*. The hyoglossus exerts a pull on the body of the tongue in a downwards and backwards direction, if the hyoid bone is immobilized by the infrahyoid muscles. It is chiefly responsible, with the styloglossus, for adjusting the vertical positioning of the tongue-body in the production of vowels (and hence for the vertical component of the radial displacement of the centre of mass of the tongue in lingual settings). With appropriate vertical co-operation between the styloglossus and palatoglossus pulling the tongue up and back and the hyoglossus pulling it down and back, another antagonistic element is needed to counter the combined tendency to pull the body backwards, and this can be supplied by the genioglossus. The genioglossus is the big, fan-shaped, vertical muscle that makes up the bulk of the body of the tongue, running from the inner surface of the jaw, at the chin, backwards to the hyoid bone and upwards to the dorsum of the tongue. Its action pulls the body of the tongue forward, when the jaw is in a fixed position.

The body of the tongue is pulled downwards chiefly by the hyoglossus, with the hyoid braced against its upward pull by the synergistically acting infrahyoids.

The settings with an element of retraction from the neutral position are achieved by the contraction of all the muscles mentioned so far in this section, together with a contribution from the *middle pharyngeal constrictor* pulling the body and root of the tongue towards the back wall of the pharynx. The styloglossus, with the palatoglossus acting from a fixed velum, and the hyoglossus from a fixed hyoid, equalizing their vertical mutual counteraction, allow their common retracting tendency to help pull the tongue body backwards. The backwards tendency is checked and held to the necessary degree by the forwards pull of the genioglossus from a fixed jaw position.

The overall fronting component of settings of the body of the tongue is produced by the genioglossus as the prime mover, with antagonistic counteracting tension from the styloglossus, and hyoglossus from a fixed hyoid.

It is more difficult to be confident about the physiology of settings of the tongue tip/blade, because of the multiple possibilities of different synergistic muscle systems producing the same articulatory result. The following comments should be regarded as plausible hypotheses, rather than statements of established fact.

The setting of the tongue tip/blade where the tip is the principal articulator in segmental sounds with primary articulation in the front of the mouth, relies mostly on the contraction of the superior longitudinal muscle. This runs from the root of the tongue to the tip, immediately underneath the mucous membrane, and in protagonist contraction pulls the tip of the tongue upwards. In the retroflex setting, the superior longitudinal muscle contracts to a greater degree, and the tip is pulled both up and back. To be able to curl back in this way, the tongue tip has to be lengthened, and this is done by the transverse muscle. This is a horizontal muscle whose fibres cross the tongue from side to side, separating the superior longitudinal muscle from the inferior longitudinal. The transverse muscle does not reach the tip of the tongue, nor the surface, and its contraction narrows the tongue, thus protruding the tip.

The setting where the blade is the primary articulator in the front of the mouth has to have the tongue tip lowered, and this is brought about by the joint action of the inferior longitudinal muscle, which runs the length of the tongue from root to tip low down in the body of the tongue, and the upper fibres of the genioglossus.

We come now to the acoustic correlates of the different lingual settings. The commentary which follows incorporates data from publications on acoustic phonetics by Arnold, Denes, Gimson, O'Connor and Trim

(1958), Fant (1957, 1960, 1962, 1964, 1968, 1975), Peterson and Barney (1952) and Stevens and House (1963).

In *palatalized voice*, where the body of the tongue is raised nearly vertically towards the hard palate and slightly fronted, the second formant is 'maximally high and close to F_3' (Fant 1962: 14).

In settings of the body of the tongue which involve a fronting component, as in *palatalized, palato-alveolarized, alveolarized* and *dentalized voices*, there is a larger distance between the first and second formants than in the neutral setting. The second formant is high, but drops in frequency progressively as the setting moves from palatalization through palato-alveolarization and alveolarization to dentalization. The third formant is kept relatively high.

In settings of the body of the tongue which involve a backing component, as in *velarized, uvularized, pharyngalized* and *laryngopharyngalized* voices, the first formant is higher and the second formant lower than in the neutral setting. In velarized and uvularized voice, in back vowels, the third formant is raised, by the contraction in the uvular region (Fant 1975: 13). In pharyngalized voice, with the body of the tongue retracted towards the back wall of the pharynx, the first formant rises and second formant drops to cause a first formant–second formant proximity. Fant comments on the first formant that 'In all vowels F_1 is raised by a contraction of the pharynx. The expansion of the mouth cavity is more effective in rising F_1 of front vowels than back vowels' (Fant 1975: 13). Because back vowels have a necessarily retracted tongue position, they are minimally susceptible to the effects of pharyngalization.

The acoustic characteristics of the settings of the tip and blade of the tongue are difficult to specify, because they are coloured by the effects of the 'enabling' settings of the body of the tongue. The one setting that can be specified more easily is the *retroflex* setting. When the degree of retroflexion is slight, the fourth formant is lowered and close in frequency to the third formant. When retroflexion is more severe, the third formant is lowered to values close to those of the second formant (Fant 1962: 14).

In Table 1, Nolan's computer-based measurements are broadly in agreement with all these predictions, with the exception of velarized voice. In the Nolan results, velarization shows a closer affinity with palatalized voice than with pharyngalized voice, in that it has a high second formant and a low first formant, compared with the neutral setting. It may be that the performance of the setting in the recording analysed by Nolan was too fronted to be able strictly to be called 'velarized'. But it may also be that there is a difference in conceptualization about the articulatory configuration that counts as velar.

Spectrograms of a phrase pronounced with a palatalized and a pharyngalized setting are shown in Figure 19.

2.2.3 *Faucal settings*
Another group of configurational settings of the supralaryngeal vocal tract are settings of the faucal arches, or pillars, which can constrict the vocal tract in an approximately coronal cross-section at the back of the mouth.

The faucal pillars are the two sets of muscular arches, one behind the other, formed by the *palatoglossus* and the *palatopharyngeus* muscles, located at the junction of the mouth and the pharynx, connecting the soft palate to the tongue, the side walls of the pharynx, and the larynx.

The front set of faucal pillars, which are visible at the back of the mouth supporting the pendent uvula centrally between them, are called the glossopalatal arches. They are made up of the paired palatoglossus muscle, described earlier in the section on lingual settings. The rear set of pillars are made up of the paired palatopharyngeal muscle, which runs from the velum downwards in the walls of the pharynx to be inserted in the posterior border of the thyroid cartilage of the larynx. There is a triangular space between the two sets of arches, which contains the palatine tonsils.

The major function of the faucal muscles in speech is to pull the velum downwards. The palatoglossus, as we have seen immediately above in the section on lingual settings, can also function as a lingual elevator, when the soft palate is braced by the palatal elevators (which will be discussed below in the section on velopharyngeal settings). The palatopharyngeus, similarly, when the soft palate is fixed in position, can help to raise the larynx and shorten the pharynx.

When the palatoglossus and the palatopharyngeus contract against the resistance of a fixed velum and larynx, the effect is to approximate the sides of the arches, constricting the vocal tract at the mouth–pharynx junction. Figure 9 is a schematic diagram of the location and action of the faucal muscles, as seen from behind.

Latitudinal approximation of the faucal pillars has been said by a number of writers to affect the quality of the voice. Alexander Graham Bell (1908: 19–21) traced a type of voice quality that he heard in a school for the deaf (a quality he described as being 'decidedly unpleasant, the

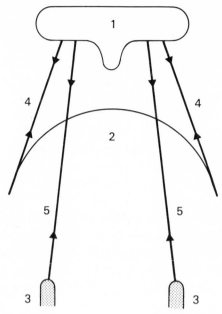

Figure 9. Schematic diagram of the action and location of the faucal muscles, seen from behind

1. Soft palate
2. Tongue
3. Thyroid cartilage
4. Palatoglossus muscle
5. Palatopharyngeus muscle

voice resembling somewhat the cry of a peacock', and as having 'a peculiar metallic ring, somewhat like the tone of a brass musical instrument') to the effect of approximating the faucal pillars. He was able to train these deaf speakers to relax the muscles of the pillars, 'and at once the voice became natural and pleasant in quality'. He also suggested, in an appendix to the same book (p. 123), that 'When the posterior pillars of the soft palate approximate so closely as almost to touch, a very disagreeable reedy quality of voice results, which can be best described as a sort of "Punch and Judy" effect.'

Pike (1943: 123–4) tentatively associates the act of approximation of the faucal pillars with a possible 'lower pharyngeal constriction, glottal tension, and usually a raising of the larynx', and calls the result 'faucalization'.

Greene (1964: 48–9) says that

The palatoglossus and palatopharyngeus may be considered in relation to the pharyngeal resonator. Their muscular arches form a flexible and variable arch of communication between the oropharynx and oral cavity, and if overtensed are capable of materially decreasing the dimensions of the oropharyngeal outlet and creating a 'cul-de-sac' resonator as West calls it.

She is referring to West, Ansberry and Carr (1957), and the 'cul-de-sac' concept is one which has been put forward to explain the acoustic–articulatory basis of nasality. This 'cul-de-sac' theory was originally suggested by Russell (1931) and West (1936), and will be discussed in detail in the section on velopharyngeal settings.

The metallic quality referred to above by Bell may be partially explained by Pike's hint that a degree of lower pharyngeal constriction and glottal tension is present in faucalized voice, suggesting a general state of marked muscular tension. Given that the palatopharyngeus is connected to the thyroid cartilage, it is not surprising that its contraction should be associated with a disturbance of the fine mode of vibration of the vocal folds, and with constriction of the lower pharynx and upper larynx. Chapter 4 on tension-dependent settings of the whole vocal apparatus suggests some acoustic correlates for the tensed condition of the walls of the vocal tract which may be relevant to Bell's and Pike's comments, and for the component of nasality implied by Greene's statement. The acoustic effect of constricting the vocal tract at the junction of the pharynx and the oral cavity is to raise the value for the frequency of the first formant, compared with that for the neutral configuration, and to lower the value for the second formant (Fant 1960: 210). The most frequent involvement of the faucal muscles in voice quality is of course in *nasal voice*, discussed in 2.3, where they contribute to the complex acoustic characteristics of nasality.

Faucal constriction plays a phonological role in Arabic, according to Catford. He describes 'faucal or transverse pharyngeal' articulation as follows:

In faucal or transverse pharyngeal articulation the part of the pharynx immediately behind the mouth is laterally compressed, so that the faucal pillars move towards each other. At the same time the larynx may be somewhat raised. This appears to be the most common articulation of the pharyngeal approximants ... The most common type of Arabic *'ain* seems to be an *upper pharyngeal* or *faucal* approximant. (Catford 1977: 163)

2.2.4 *Pharyngeal settings*

We have seen that constriction and expansion of the pharynx can be due to the effects of lingual settings involving either the body of the tongue or the root of the tongue. Firstly, the body of the tongue may be retracted

into the pharynx, constricting it, or it may be fronted, expanding it.
Secondly, the root of the tongue, acting semi-independently of the body,
may constrict or expand the lower part of the middle pharynx.

There still remains, however, the possibility of constriction and
expansion of the pharynx by means of the muscles of the pharynx walls
themselves. Apart from their function in speech, these muscles play a
large part in the physiology of swallowing, together with the muscles of
the tongue, and the details of the physiology of the pharyngeal muscles as
part of the overall swallow mechanism have been commented on at length
by Bosma (1953, 1957a, 1957b, 1961), Bosma and Fletcher (1961, 1962)
Greene (1964) Kaplan (1960), and Merritt, Nielsen, Bosma, Goates,
Haskins, Ramsell and Lamb (1957).

Zemlin (1964: 225) describes the pharynx as follows:

The pharynx is a cone-shaped tube about 12 cm. in length, and wider at the top
than at the bottom. It is about 4 cm. wide at its extreme width superiorly and
about 2 cm. from front to back. It narrows considerably until, at the level of the
larynx in front and the sixth cervical vertebra behind, it is about 2.3 cm. wide. At
its lowest extreme the pharynx is continuous with the esophagus, and at this level
the front and back walls of the pharynx are in direct contact with one another and
separate only to permit the passage of food into the esophagus.

Settings of the upper part of the pharynx (the nasopharynx) will be
commented on below, in the section on velopharyngeal settings, and
some remarks have already been made on settings of the laryngopharynx
in raised and lowered larynx voices. Discussion here will concentrate on
settings of the middle pharynx, or oropharynx, which extends from the
soft palate to the hyoid bone (Zemlin 1964: 226).

Emphasis has been placed, throughout, on the complex mutual
interdependence of the muscle systems used to achieve particular
settings, which have been analysed, for convenience, as if they were
independent of each other. Together with the hyoid complex (with which
the oropharyngeal complex itself interacts), the settings of the
oropharynx furnish one of the best examples of the intricate interlocking
of muscle systems which affect, and are affected by, settings in various
parts of the vocal tract and larynx. Laryngeal, velopharyngeal, tongue-
body, tongue-root and hyoid-positioning settings all potentially interact
with oropharyngeal settings.

The oropharynx is affected by all the pharyngeal muscles, which fall into
two major groups, an 'outer and inner layer which are not readily
separable throughout. The outer layer is arranged circularly and is

comprised of three constrictor muscles' (i.e. the superior, middle and inferior pharyngeal constrictor (Kaplan 1960: 203)).

These muscles change the diameter of the tube. The inner layer is roughly longitudinal, and it includes the palatopharyngeus, salpingopharyngeus, stylopharyngeus muscles, and other irregular muscle bundles. The inner muscles function in elevation, depression, expansion and contraction of the pharynx. (Kaplan 1960: 204)

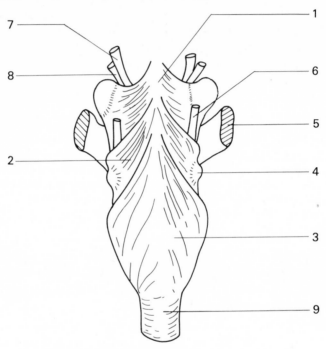

Figure 10. Diagram of the pharyngeal constrictor muscles, seen from behind
(after Kaplan 1960)

1. Superior constrictor muscle	5. Mandible
2. Middle constrictor muscle	6. Stylopharyngeus muscle
3. Inferior constrictor muscle	7. Palatal levator muscle
4. Greater horn of the hyoid bone	8. Palatal tensor muscle
	9. Esophagus

Figure 10 is a schematic diagram of the pharyngeal muscles. The *superior pharyngeal constrictor*, the weakest of the pharyngeal constrictors, acts in a sphincteric role in helping to lift the velum to a closed position, and will be discussed in the section on velopharyngeal settings. But it should be noted here that some of the fibres of this muscle have their origin fairly low down on the sides of the tongue, and in contraction tend to lift the tongue-root upwards and backwards, constricting the oropharynx to some degree.

The *middle pharyngeal constrictor* is the principal muscle involved in constricting the oropharynx. It has its point of origin on the horns of the hyoid bone, and from there it runs upward and backward round the sides of the pharynx, forming a U-shaped sling with the arms pointing forwards and down. The fibres of this muscle spread out in a fan-like shape, with only the middle fibres running horizontally, from the area of the root of the tongue round to the back of the oropharynx meeting in the midline pharyngeal raphe (Zemlin 1964: 229); the lower fibres run downwards and backwards beneath the inferior constrictor, and the upper fibres rise to cover the lower fibres of the superior constrictor. In contraction, the effect is mainly to narrow the oropharynx; the hyoid tends to be lifted, but only slightly because of the nearly horizontal plane of the fibres in that area (Hardcastle 1976: 73; Kaplan 1960: 204).

The *inferior pharyngeal constrictor* rises in a backwards and upwards fan of fibres from its origin, which is on the cricoid and thyroid cartilages. These fibres also meet at the back of the pharynx in the midline pharyngeal raphe (Zemlin 1964: 228). The lowest fibres run horizontally and the others rise upwards to cover most of the middle constrictor. In contraction it can pull the larynx upwards, but when the larynx is fixed by the infrahyoids, the inferior constrictor narrows the upper larynx and lower pharynx in a sphincter fashion. It is the broadest, thickest, and strongest of the pharyngeal constrictors (Hardcastle 1976: 126; Kaplan 1960: 204; Zemlin 1964: 229).

The *stylopharyngeus* muscle, also paired, runs down each side of the pharynx from its origin on the temporal bone to its triple insertion in the constrictor musculature, the palatopharyngeus and the back edge of the thyroid cartilage. Its contraction either pulls the larynx and the walls of the pharynx upwards, or, if the larynx is fixed by the infrahyoid muscles, widens the pharynx laterally (Kaplan 1960: 205). This is opposed to Greene's view, quoted above, that 'The stylopharyngeus and salpingo-pharyngeus muscles reinforce the lateral pharyngeal walls and upon contraction raise and shorten them, decreasing the transverse and longitudinal measurements of the pharynx.' Greene does not change her position in the latest (1972) edition of her book and cites no source. The question hinges on the exact anatomy of the course of the stylopharyn-geus muscle vertically, and Zemlin (1964: 229) supports Kaplan's description.

The small, paired *salpingopharyngeus* runs vertically from the cartilage of the Eustachian tube to the back and side of the pharynx, blending with the upper fibres of the palatopharyngeus. The muscle is not present in some individuals, and the fibres when they are present tend to be sparse (Dickson and Dickson 1972: 377). The salpingopharyngeus may contribute to lateral narrowing of the upper part of the pharynx, as claimed by Greene (1964: 46), Luchsinger and Arnold (1965: 450) and Harrington (1944), but the details of its sparse morphology make it reasonable to believe, with Dickson and Dickson (1972: 379), that the muscle 'probably has little, if any, functional significance'.

The acoustic effect of constricting the pharynx by means of either the pharyngeal muscles or by retraction of the body or the root of the tongue is likely to be similar, as far as formant frequencies are concerned. The effect, varying in degree with different pharyngeal configurations, would be a rise in the first formant and a lowering of the second, tending to cause a first formant–second formant proximity (Fant 1957: 19). A spectrogram of a phrase pronounced with pharyngalization can be seen in Figure 19.

The acoustic effect on formant frequencies of expanding the pharynx would depend partly on what correlated constrictive tendencies were simultaneously exerted elsewhere in the vocal tract, but one component would normally be a lowering of the frequency of the first formant.

Another acoustic factor than formant frequencies would be the feature of formant bandwidths, deriving from the tension, and therefore acoustic characteristics of absorption, reflection and radiation of sound energy, of the muscular walls of the pharynx. Hardcastle (1976) suggests that isotonic contraction of the pharyngeal muscles narrows the pharynx, but that isometric contraction of the pharyngeal muscles (where the configuration of the pharynx remains unchanged because the mutually-antagonistic tensions of all the local muscle systems exactly balance each other), would 'have considerable effect on the resonance quality of the laryngeal tone giving it a metallic, strident quality'. This would be because the tensed walls of the pharynx would damp the sound wave less than relaxed walls, and the resultant decrease in damping is reflected in narrower formant bandwidths.

This contribution of formant bandwidth factors to overall auditory qualities of the voice will be discussed more fully in the section on tension-dependent settings.

Adjustments of the size of the pharynx have been suggested as part of the phonetic realizations of phonological vowel harmony in a number of languages, as mentioned in the section on tongue-root settings. Akan, for example, has been described as having a phonological distinction between expanded and constricted pharyngeal configurations in non-low vowels (Lindau 1979: 176). It is not clear whether such configurations are achieved by action of the pharyngeal constrictors or not. But Lindau makes a sensible point in her radiographic study of Akan, when she warns against discussing changes in pharynx shape in single dimensions. She writes that

> the common factor underlying vowel harmony is the variation in pharyngeal size, not just pharyngeal width ... [There is] a very important contribution of the vertical position of the larynx, working in synchrony with the horizontal position of the tongue root to accomplish the desired goal: the variation in pharyngeal size which produces the important changes in the first formant. (Lindau 1979: 174–5)

2.2.5 *Mandibular settings*

In continuous speech, most speakers visibly move their lower jaw vertically upwards and downwards, moving slightly for almost every segment. This perhaps is to be anticipated, given the intimate anatomical linkage that we have been discussing above between the jaw and the tongue and hyoid bone. This linkage is reflected in the way that the jaw can be seen to move in sympathy with the articulations of the body of the tongue. Underlying these moment-to-moment variations of jaw position, a general tendency can usually be discerned towards keeping the jaw in a particular setting.

The jaw has four dimensions of movement, all of which can potentially be involved in phonetic settings in voice quality. These dimensions are: *vertical* (close and open); *horizontal* (protruded and retracted); *lateral* (left and right); and *rotational*, in the coronal plane, with one side higher than the other. All these dimensions of movement are biologically important in biting and chewing, but speech does not usually exploit all four. The principal speech-related dimension is the vertical, and most mandibular settings in voice quality are of this sort. This is the dimension which differentiates British English from Indian pronunciation, partly. Honikman points out that

> the greater part of English articulation takes place behind (loosely) closed jaws. It is this feature of English, no doubt, which helps to give foreigners the impression that we do not move or open our mouths when we speak ...

The jaw-setting for the languages of India and Pakistan is distinctive: the jaws are held rather inert and loosely apart, so that the aperture between upper and lower teeth is relatively wide and the oral cavity enlarged; this position is appropriate to the frequently occurring retroflex consonants, enabling them to be produced more comfortably than if the jaws were held closer; this setting accounts, too, for the lack of pressure in bilabial stops, and for the characteristic timbre of Indian languages. This distinctive timbre is very noticeable in the English spoken by Indians. (Honikman 1964: 80)

There are two chief exceptions to the tendency to exploit only the vertical dimension in settings of the jaw, although neither case is particularly common. The first is the use of a slightly protruded setting, usually coupled with a slightly open vertical setting. This can often be heard in idiosyncratic segmental pronunciations of the voiceless alveolar fricative [s] in English; as an audible segmental quality, it is very distinctive, and even when the posture is generalized to an overall mandibular setting, the fricative remains auditorily very prominent.

The other case is one typified by the late Robert Newton in his film role of Long John Silver in *Treasure Island*, and much imitated for humorous effect. It consists of a laterally offset position of the jaw, with a slight coronal rotation, lowering the same side as the lateral shift. The visual effect of the setting is often exaggerated, in such imitations, by the lip opening being similarly laterally distorted.

A third, minor, case which might be mentioned here, though it will be discussed below in a moment, is the open retracted jaw setting that is sometimes seen accompanying a lowered larynx setting.

Given that it is very much more common to see variations of vertical adjustments of the jaw, it will be these that will continue to be discussed here, mostly leaving the other possibilities aside.

The muscles that serve to close the jaw are very strong, and can contract very fast: Zemlin (1964: 240) states that 'although the jaw is a rather massive structure, it is . . . surpassed . . . in mobility only by the tip of the tongue'. Van Riper and Irwin (1958: 360) also point out that 'all the muscles that act strongly on the jaw act to close it. The jaw can be opened or dropped with much less strength that it can be closed. We must work to keep our mouth shut. It opens quite easily.' This last quotation has implications for the muscular setting that has been adopted here as the neutral, datum configuration of the vocal tract. Acknowledging that the tongue is to some degree independent of the mandibular setting, nevertheless it is necessary to emphasize that the position of the jaw envisaged in the specification of the neutral configuration is not one where the muscles which serve to close the jaw are completely relaxed, allowing the jaw to fall open under the force of gravity. Rather, the neutral mandibular setting is seen as the one which interferes least with the tongue and lips achieving a configuration of the vocal tract which most nearly approximates to an equal cross-sectional area along the full length of the vocal tract. This means that the neutral setting of the jaw has to be achieved by a positive degree of contraction of the muscles that lift the jaw, and that this setting lies between the two extreme possible settings, maximally open, and completely closed with clenched teeth. Many intermediate possibilities exist between these two extremes.

There are three main paired muscles which serve to raise the jaw, the *internal pterygoid*, the *masseter* and the *temporalis* muscles. Figure 11 shows the location and direction of action of these muscles.

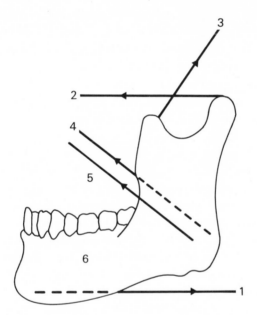

Figure 11. Schematic diagram of the action and location of the mandibular muscles

1. Anterior belly of the digastricus muscle
2. External pterygoid muscle
3. Temporalis muscle
4. Internal pterygoid muscle
5. Masseter muscle
6. External surface of the lower jaw

The internal pterygoid muscle has its origin on the skull (on the perpendicular plate of the palatine bone and on the lateral pterygoid plate

(Zemlin 1964: 243)). It runs backwards, downwards and laterally, to insert on the upper middle surface of the jaw bone at its angle and on its vertical section. Its chief function is to raise the jaw, assisting the masseter muscle, but it can also be used to protrude the jaw, and used unilaterally, to pull the jaw to one side (Kaplan 1960: 265).

The masseter muscle is the most powerful jaw muscle (Hardcastle 1976: 109), and runs from the lower edge of the cheekbone more or less vertically downwards to the angle of the lower jaw (Van Riper and Irwin 1958: 358). The more superficial part of the muscle lifts the jaw (and is used also in grinding the teeth together), and the deeper fibres can be used to protrude the jaw (Kaplan 1960: 265).

The last of the muscles which act to close the jaw is the temporalis muscle. This is a wide, thin, fan-shaped muscle which starts on the skull, at the wide end of the fan, attached to a wide arc stretching from the temple to a point on the skull above and behind the ear. From this origin, the fibres converge rapidly as they run forward and down under the cheekbone to insert on the forward surface of the whole of the vertical part of the jaw bone, down as far as the angle of the jaw (Zemlin 1964: 243). Because the fibres of the temporalis run forwards as well as downwards, it can be used to help to retract the jaw as well as to close it (Kaplan 1960:265).

Lowering of the jaw usually involves the co-operation of the three powerful muscles just described, even when the jaw is being allowed to fall open mostly under the force of gravity. The muscles which actively open the jaw are: the *external pterygoid*, the *geniohyoid*, the *anterior belly of the digastricus*, and the *mylohyoid*. Figure 11 shows the location of three of these muscles. The positions and directions of action of all the muscles have been discussed in earlier sections, except for the external pterygoid. This is a paired muscle with its origins on the skull in front of the hinge of the jaw – specifically, it has two origins; one on 'the lateral portion of the greater wing of the sphenoid bone, and the other ... [on] ... the lateral surface of the lateral pterygoid plate' (Zemlin 1964: 241). The fibres of the muscle run horizontally backwards to the temperomandibular joint of the jaw, just in front of the ear, and exercising a forward pull on the topmost extension of the jawbone just above the joint and on the capsule of the joint, both rotate the jaw downwards and pull the jaw forwards. As with many of the muscles associated with the jaw, the direction of the main pull is thus not just unidimensional. Also, being a paired muscle, it can contract unilaterally. When this is done, the effect is to rotate the jaw slightly to the non-contracting side (Van Riper and Irwin 1958: 360).

Heffner (1950) gives a concise description of the actions of the muscles which lower the jaw, although he relegates the external pterygoid to the role merely of assisting the internal pterygoid to protrude the jaw and to move it laterally. He writes:

The downward movement of the jaw can be assisted by the contraction of a number of muscles connecting it with the hyoid bone, provided the latter is not allowed to rise. The digastric muscles, from the chin to the side of the hyoid, the mylohyoid muscles, which are broad sheets of fibers from the sides of the mandible to the body of the hyoid bone, and the geniohyoids from chin to hyoid, when contracted, tend to bring the jaw to the hyoid bone. If at the same time the latter is pulled upon by the sternohyoid and omohyoid muscles, the jaw will be drawn down vigorously. Whether or not the whole head comes with it depends in part upon the action of the muscles which close the jaws. (Heffner 1950: 35)

In referring to different vertical mandibular settings, we can use the conventional phonetic terms *close* and *open*, when there is a deviation from the neutral setting. We could say of a speaker who habitually keeps his teeth clenched during speech, or nearly clenched, that he had (say) a 'velarized voice with raised larynx and a close jaw setting'. If it is needed to give labels to jaw settings which involve other dimensions of movement than the vertical, terms such as *protruded*, *retracted*, and *offset* could be used.

The acoustic effect of mandibular settings is similar to that of the longitudinal and latitudinal labial settings. Stevens and House (1955: 485) point out that in the region of the vocal tract about 15 cm from the glottis, the cross-sectional area and the length of the front 3 cm or so of the tract are controlled primarily by the mandible and the lips. The major acoustic effect of changes in jaw position is seen in the first formant, with the frequency rising as the jaw opening becomes larger. Lindblom and Sundberg (1971: 1174) have shown that 'with all other parameters constant, mandible movement alone causes considerable shifts in $F1$'. Higher formants are proportionally less affected, but also rise with the degree of jaw opening. In an earlier article, Lindblom and Sundberg (1969) showed that, for a close jaw setting, not only does the frequency of the first formant drop, but also that its range is markedly reduced.

In specifying the acoustic effect of any particular mandibular setting, the speaker's labial setting also has to be taken into account, since the relationship between mandibular and labial settings is such that each can magnify or diminish the other's effect.

2.3 Velopharyngeal settings

Apart from the neutral velopharyngeal setting, which will be defined in a moment, there are two settings, giving *nasal voice* and *denasal voice*. More has been written on the subject of nasality than about any other aspect of voice quality. It nevertheless remains an area characterized in phonetic writings by misconceptions and vagueness. Part of the vagueness is due to the lack of explicit distinction between some of the terms used to refer to the phenomena of nasality. One quite common term that might suggest itself as referring to a single phenomenon is 'nasal twang'. It is probably fair to say that it is normally restricted to the description of a voice quality setting (Heffner 1950:31), as opposed, for instance, to nasality which occurs on an individual segment. But 'nasal twang' is not consistently used for any given type of nasality in voice quality. We shall explore some of the different types of nasality in a moment, but given that different types do exist, it is not possible to be sure that 'nasal twang' is not being used for different phenomena by the various writers who use the term, such as Abercrombie (1967), Appaix, Sprecher, Hénin and Favot (1963), Berry and Eisenson (1942, 1956), Bullen (1942), Davis (1941), Heffner (1950), Greene (1972), Luchsinger (1968), Meader and Muyskens (1950), Paget (1930), and Sweet (1877, 1890).

Comment about nasality as a feature of voice quality was already being made in writings on phonetics in the eighteenth century, when Bayly (1758:130) wrote that

The most remarkable ill tones arise from what is called speaking through the nose and in the throat

and Herries (1773:55), (writing about denasality), refered to

that dull, disagreeable sound, which we call sneveling or SPEAKING THROUGH THE NOSE. The latter term is entirely wrong, because it is the defect of NOT speaking thro' the nose, which occasions that impropriety of articulation.

Webster (1789:106–9) referred to nasality in these terms:

the drawling, nasal manner of speaking in New England ... The great error in their manner of speaking proceeds immediately from not opening the mouth sufficiently. Hence the words are drawled out in a careless lazy manner, or the sound finds passage through the nose. Nothing can be so disagreeable as that drawling, whining cant that distinguishes a certain class of people: and too much pains cannot be taken to reform the practice.

By the first part of the nineteenth century, the label 'nasal', was being used for a quality of the voice, by writers such as Rush (1827) and Willis (1829) without any need for explanation, and by the time Sweet (1877, 1890) and Bell (1908) were writing about voice quality, it was fairly firmly established. Luchsinger and Arnold draw attention to an interesting instance:

The old speech pathologists, notably H. Gutzmann, Sr. (1901), and Nadoleczny (1929), quoted the examples of habitually nasal speech among many Prussian Imperial Guard lieutenants, and the widespread nasality among priests and pastors in the eighteenth century, of whom it was said 'Humilitatis gratia nasalitatem affectant' (For the sake of humility, they affect nasality). (Luchsinger and Arnold 1965:666)

We can mention in passing that a variety of terms are used for 'nasal voice' and 'denasal voice' in the technical vocabulary of speech pathology, where there is no established single usage. They include not only 'nasality' and 'denasality' (Moore 1957), but also such labels as: 'rhinophonia' (Travis 1931); 'rhinolalia (clausa, aperta, mixta)' (Luchsinger and Arnold 1965); 'hyperrhinophonia', 'hyporhinophonia', 'hyperrhinolalia', 'hyporhinolalia' (Greene 1964); and 'hypernasality' and 'hyponasality' (Van Riper and Irwin 1958).

An alternative to the phrase 'velopharyngeal settings' used here could be 'velic settings', and 'velic setting' will often be used as an informal paraphrase throughout this section. 'Velopharyngeal' is preferred to 'velic' in the formal vocabulary of the descriptive system for a good reason, however. That is, there is a good deal more to consider in the physiology of nasality and denasality than just the position of the velum; and it is in keeping with the theme running through the whole of the descriptive model, of interdependence of muscle systems in different parts of the vocal apparatus, that 'velopharyngeal' is used as a reflection of the effect of velic activity on the activities of the pharynx (and hence of the tongue and the larynx). We shall see that some of the vagueness and misconceptions about nasality could well be attributed to the over-simplistic view of velopharyngeal action as involving only the positioning of the velum that is continually repeated in much of the phonetic literature.

The neutral velopharyngeal setting was said earlier to have velopharyngeal closure on all segments except those where audible nasality is criterial for their phonological identity in a given language, and on contextually-nasalized segments immediately preceding them. The question arises as to what constitutes the neutral amount of anticipatory nasalization of this latter, contextual sort. The position will be adopted here that a neutral amount of anticipatory nasality is that brought about by physiologically-inevitable, general human constraints applying to the temporal integration of the activity of different muscle systems of the vocal tract.

This approach to the definition of the neutral setting has the apparent disadvantage of bringing phonological considerations to bear on what is commonly supposed to be the independent field of general phonetic description; but this might not be the disadvantage that it seems at first sight, because a reasonable case can be argued for the position that any linguistically-motivated theory of general phonetics must have its foundation in phonological assumptions of one sort or another. For the moment, then, the neutral setting of the velum will be taken to be the one where the velum is closed except for fully nasal segments and the minimum possible stretch of preceding articulation. Not enough is known at the moment about unavoidable constraints on the operation of the various muscular systems of the vocal tract to be able to assert that French, for example, characteristically requires more than the minimum amount of anticipatory nasalization, or only the minimal amount, so the definition of the neutral position is here something of a convenient fiction.

It will be understood from the earlier comments about the 'phenomena of nasality', that the concept of 'nasality' is taken to include a number of auditorily distinguishable voice qualities, which can reasonably be grouped together as variations of the single major category of a *nasal voice*. The acoustic criteria by which this can be justified will be set out after an account of the physiology of the velopharyngeal system and a discussion of conventional phonetic treatments of the area of nasality.

The physiology of the velopharyngeal system has been the subject of research by many workers, though largely from other disciplines than general phonetics. The facts about the action of the groups of muscles that serve to open and close the velum are reasonably well established, with not many areas of controversy, and the account given here represents the consensus of opinion amongst the summary reports of Greene (1964), Hardcastle (1976), Kaplan (1960), Luchsinger and Arnold (1965), Van Riper and Irwin (1958) and Zemlin (1964).

The mechanism which lowers the velum consists basically of two inverted muscular slings, made up of the *palatoglossus* and the *palatopharyngeus*, both of them paired muscles. A schematic diagram of the location and action of the two muscles was given earlier in Figure 9, in

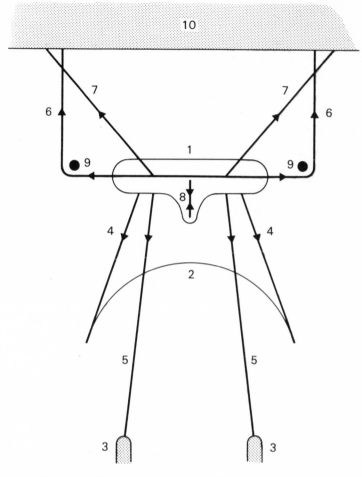

Figure 12. Schematic diagram of the action and location of the velopharyngeal
muscles, seen from behind (adapted from Van Riper and Irwin
1958)

1. Soft palate
2. Tongue
3. Thyroid cartilage
4. Palatoglossus muscle
5. Palatopharyngeus muscle

6. Palatal tensor muscle
7. Palatal levator muscle
8. Azygos uvulae muscle
9. Hamular process of the
   pterygoid bone
10. Skull

the section on faucal settings. This information is included for
convenience of reference in Figure 12, which is a combined schematic
diagram of the action of the muscle systems which raise and lower the
velum.

The palatoglossus is a relatively weak muscle, with sparse muscle fibres. It has its point of origin in the forward part of the body of the soft palate, and curves laterally forward and down to insert into the sides and upper part of the back of the tongue, where its fibres blend with the styloglossus, the transverse lingual muscle and the hyoglossus. The palatoglossus forms the forward arch of the faucal pillars, and was discussed briefly in the earlier section on faucal settings. In contraction, its effect is normally to approximate the sides of the forward faucal arch, and to pull the velum downwards, when the body of the tongue is braced against its tension. When the tongue is not braced, however, palatoglossal contraction tends to pull the body of the tongue slightly upwards and backwards.

The palatopharyngeus, which is a relatively powerful muscle, also has its points of insertion in the body of the soft palate, and curves laterally downward through the side walls of the pharynx, to insert in the back border of the thyroid cartilage of the larynx. The upper part of the muscle forms the back arch of the faucal pillars, and was discussed briefly in the earlier section on faucal settings. Contraction of the palatopharyngeus approximates the sides of the back faucal arch, and pulls the velum downwards, if the larynx is braced by the infrahyoid system. If it is not braced, then the larynx and the lower pharynx tend to be pulled slightly upwards.

The palatoglossus and the palatopharyngeus have been said to combine synergistically to lower the velum, acting as a pair of slings with their concavity directed downwards. A number of researchers have put forward the view that the act of lowering the velum is not merely a passive relaxation of the muscles which lift the velum, allowing the velum to open by gravity alone. Fritzell (1969), and Lubker, Lindqvist and Fritzell (1972), using electromyography and cineradiography, have shown that the palatoglossus in particular is active in pulling the velum downwards. It should be said, however, that not all experimental findings are in accord with this position. Bell-Berti (1973) showed that, on the basis of electromyographic evidence, nasality is not necessarily accompanied in all speakers by active contraction of the palatoglossus. We are thus obliged to accept that different speakers may achieve auditorily (and perhaps articulatorily) similar results by physiologically different means. This is very likely to be true not only of the velopharyngeal mechanism, but of the entire speech apparatus.

The action of the palatoglossus, when tensed, affects other settings of the supralaryngeal vocal tract. Diamond (1952) suggests that not only is the palatoglossus inserted into the sides of the back of the tongue, but that some fibres of the palatoglossus itself continue transversely through the body of the tongue to form a sphincter system rather than merely a sling system. Most writers support the sling interpretation of palatoglossal anatomy and physiology, but in either case, sling or sphincter, the articulatory action of the body of the tongue is likely to be slightly constrained when the palatoglossus contracts. In nasal voice, with the velum mostly held in a lowered position, there often seems to be an auditory component similar to the effect of slight velarization – that is to the effect of having a lingual setting in which the centre of mass of the tongue is moved slightly radially upwards and backwards. One explanation for this impression, if it is an accurate auditory judgement, is the muscular linkage between the lowered velum and the tongue. This is supported by a finding by Hixon (1949) that nasal speakers seem to retract and raise their tongues more than normal non-nasal speakers. An alternative or possibly complementary explanation is that the auditory effect labelled here as 'velarization' is the result, acoustically, of constricting the vocal tract at the velar region, and that this may be achieved not only by the movement of the body of the tongue, but also by the downward movement of the soft palate and the inward, coronal movement of the faucal pillars, particularly the palatoglossal arch.

Lowering of the velum in nasal voice will have an effect on a number of other types of settings. The palatopharyngeus, connecting the velum and the thyroid cartilage of the larynx, has an influence, when it contracts, on the fine detail of the mode of vibration of the vocal folds in laryngeal settings, both when the larynx is free to be pulled upwards and when the infrahyoid complex resists the upward pull. Nasal voice has been shown to have a special mode of phonation associated with it by Fletcher (1947), who is cited by Van Riper and Irwin (1958:244) for his high speed cinefilms of the action of the vocal folds in various voice qualities. They report that he found that 'in his subject, the vocal folds opened more abruptly and assumed a different shape in nasal phonation than they did in normal phonation'. Apart from this muscular linkage, the effect of nasality on the fine detail of phonation can also be partially ascribed to the changed acoustic coupling between the resonatory system of the tract and the larynx source.

There is another aspect of the interaction of the palatopharyngeus and the larynx. When the larynx is not braced by the infrahyoid musculature, and is pulled slightly upwards, the resulting change of the longitudinal axis of the vocal tract is reflected in changes of the resonatory characteristics, and this would contribute another factor to the change in the source – system acoustic coupling. Van Riper and Irwin (1958:244) give a personal finding that supports this: 'Clinically, we have found many cases of hypernasality who showed a marked elevation of the thyroid on their highly nasalized vowels which did not appear on those less nasalized.' Phonetically, it is easy to test this tendency for the thyroid cartilage to rise slightly during the production of nasality, by lightly resting a finger tip in the central notch in the top of the thyroid while changing an oral vowel to its nasalized counterpart.

The mechanism which acts to raise the soft palate to give velic closure is more complex, and to some degree more controversial. Van Riper and Irwin (1958:388–95) give a very clear account of differences of opinion that exist in this area, and the comments incorporated here of Bloomer, Buck, Calnan, Harrington and Podvinec are found in their outline.

The difficulty in giving a precise account of the velopharyngeal closing mechanism lies partly in the fact that not only is its action different in speech from its involvement in the biologically primary function of swallowing, according to Calnan (1954), Bloomer (1953) and Lubker, Fritzell and Lindqvist (1972), but also that the closing action differs between different individuals (Bloomer, 1953; Buck, 1954), and between different sounds in the speech of the same individual (Calnan 1953; Harrington 1944). Another aspect is that not only do the structure and condition of the nasal tract differ organically from person to person, just as the rest of the vocal apparatus does, but the resonatory condition of the nasal tract of any given speaker also changes from day to day, in respect of such details as the consistency of the mucal lining (House 1957). As Van Riper and Irwin point out (1958:388–9), when factors such as these are coupled with the complicated anatomy of the velopharyngeal system, and its relative inaccessibility to direct observation, broad generalizations about the functioning of the system are difficult to make, and it is not surprising that a certain amount of controversy should still prevail.

Some agreement does exist, however, about the anatomy and physiology of the velopharyngeal system and the mechanisms which serve to raise the velum to give velic closure.

There are certainly four muscles involved in raising the velum, and possibly six. The four chief muscles are the *palatal tensor*, the *palatal levator*, the *superior pharyngeal constrictor*, and some fibres of the upper part of the *palatopharyngeus*. The two other muscles possibly involved are the uvular muscle (the *azygos uvulae*), and the *salpingopharyngeus*.

The paired palatal tensor has a number of points of attachment on the skull above and to the sides of the soft palate. It is connected vertically downwards to a tendon, which then bends at right angles round the hamular process of the pterygoid like a rope around a capstan, and continues inwards to insert horizontally into the sides of the soft palate. Contraction of the tensor, as the name suggests, tautens the tendon, which serves to spread and tense the soft palate laterally. It also provides a fixed band within the body of the soft palate to which other palatal muscles are attached.

The paired levator also has its points of origin on the skull, above and behind the soft palate. It passes downwards, forwards and inwards to insert laterally in the back upper surface of the soft palate, forming most of the velic mass. Contraction of the levator lifts the body of the velum, which has been tensed by the tensor. The bending of the soft palate to form a palatal 'knee' may be helped by the contraction of the small uvular muscle, the azygos uvulae, which forms the body of the uvula and serves to shorten it. The levator and the azygos uvulae, together with the tensor, are shown schematically in Figure 12.

One view of the lifting sling action of the levator, together with the other components just mentioned, is that it should not be seen as a totally independent mechanism, but rather as the forward component of a velopharyngeal sphincter slightly tilted from the horizontal. Van Riper and Irwin (1958: 391) cite measurements made by Calnan (1953) of this sphincter, giving the transverse diameter (at rest) of about 3 cm and the sagittal diameter of 1 cm or less, so that the opening is oval, flattened from front to back. The back half of the sphincter, in the form of a sling with its concavity directed forwards, is composed of some fibres of the palatopharyngeus, which are said to have fused with the upper part of the superior pharyngeal constrictor. In contraction, these two muscles can pull the back wall of the nasopharynx slightly forward. (The physiological complexity of the velopharyngeal system can be seen in the double function of the palatopharyngeus muscle, which acts both as a palatal depressor (primarily), and as a palatal elevator (synergistically).)

Luchsinger and Arnold (1965: 449) emphasize the importance of the sphincteric view of the closure mechanism:

It is to be stressed that the velum does not move like a hinged trap door ... as is so often claimed in various books. In reality, the palate represents the anterior portion of the complex velopharyngeal valve, which functions mainly as a *circular sphincter*. The actual point of contact between the palate and the protruding pharynx occurs at the level of the palatal knee ... Besides palatal elevation, the entire closely interwoven and always synergistically active musculature of the pharynx is part of palatopharyngeal occlusion.

Not all writers agree, however, on the importance of the contribution of the palatopharyngeus–superior pharyngeal constrictor combination. Kaplan (1960: 207) suggests that 'In the normal person the closure of the nasopharyngeal valve is effected chiefly by the highly movable soft palate, so that the importance of Passavant's cushion is questionable.' Passavant discovered that, in a case of cleft palate, velopharyngeal closure was achieved by the formation of a muscular bar, or cushion, on the back wall of the nasopharynx at the point where it is touched by the lifted velum. This cushion is formed by the contraction of the superior pharyngeal constrictor and the upper fibres from the palatopharyngeus that are fused with it, and which were stated above as pulling the back wall of the nasopharynx slightly forward in closing the velopharyngeal sphincter. Kaplan's position is supported, against that of Luchsinger and Arnold (1965), by a number of writers on the subject of Passavant's cushion, who all deny the importance of the cushion in normal speakers (Bosma 1961; Calnan 1954; Greene 1964). Greene (1964:47) cites Russell's (1931) X-ray photographs which 'do not show the bulge of Passavant's muscle, or significant forward movement of the posterior pharyngeal wall'. It may be that vigorous contraction of the superior pharyngeal constrictor and palatopharyngeus is a compensatory action in speakers with a short soft palate or a cleft palate, providing a large cushion to make up for velic inadequacies, while normal speakers manage efficient velopharyngeal closure largely by the movement of the velum, as Kaplan suggests, and hence do not need to exploit the potential contribution of the posterior part of the sphincter mechanism. A small bulge of the back wall of the nasopharynx can be seen in Figure 1, which is based on an X-ray photograph of the author.

Van Riper and Irwin (1958: 389–91) argue for a compromise position in the sphincter–sling controversy, where they suggest that the sphincteric action is secondary to the primary sling-type action of the levator and tensor muscles. They point out that the amount of lateral contraction of the nasopharyngeal orifice is greater than can be accounted for by sphincteric action, and is probably due to the contraction of the salpingopharyngeus, a paired muscle independent of the sphincter system, which was described in the earlier section on pharyngeal settings. They also cite an observation by Podvinec (1952) that 'the closure of the nasopharyngeal passageway is too rapid in speech to be accomplished by sphincteric action of large muscles, particularly in view of the large size of the opening', and that 'anatomically, there is no recognizable dilator that would open the sphincteric passageway quickly or surely and with control'.

In thinking about the physiological correlates of nasality, it is probably sensible to adopt the compromise position of Van Riper and Irwin (1958: 391), that the action of the velopharyngeal system is 'a combination of valvular movement on the part of the soft palate and sphincter movement by the superior constrictor and its related fibres'.

It may be useful at this point to note some observations on the speed of velic movement, and characteristic areas of the velopharyngeal opening in different degrees of nasality, made by Björk (1961) using cineradiography and tomography, synchronized with sound spectrography. He found that the velum moves from closure to an open state in 130 msec, and from an open to a closed state in 160 msec. He also established that the rate of velic movement does not vary directly with speech rate, but lags behind: with a speech rate change of 100 to 200 to 300, the rate of velic movement in the same nominal terms was 100 to 130 to 160. The areas of the velopharyngeal opening that he found were 60 mm^2 for slight nasality, and 250 mm^2 for heavy nasality. So we are discussing a structure that moves fast, over rather small distances.

The outline of the anatomy and physiology of the velopharyngeal system given above is one which, within certain limits, most workers in the study of speech would accept, as a simplified account of a very complex area. Unfortunately, while an understanding of the working of the velopharyngeal system is necessary to an understanding of the phenomena of nasality, it is not enough.

This inadequacy arises from three aspects of the concept of nasality. Firstly, *nasality is above all else an auditory concept*, and not primarily an articulatory one able to be specified in terms of the position of the velum during speech. This means that the interim articulatory definition of the neutral velopharyngeal setting will have to be modified. Secondly, *'nasality' is a cover term for a number of auditorily similar but not identical phenomena*, as noted earlier, and the 'apparent homogeneousness of nasality is caused ... by empathic reactions of the listener in referring what he hears to the speaker's "nose"' (West, Ansberry and Carr

1957:156). West *et al.* also say, as an extension of this, that sometimes a quality heard as 'nasal' is made 'in such a manner as to exclude the possibility that resonance through or in the nasal chambers plays any part in the production of the "nasal" quality. Indeed, it is unfortunate that the term *nasal* has been applied to this quality of tone' (West, Ansberry and Carr 1957: 196–7). Thirdly, *nasality is a condition of resonance of a special kind.* West *et al.* suggest that 'The timbre, or overtone structure, usually given the name *nasality* is the result of resonance in a cul-de-sac resonator, a chamber opening off from the passageway through which a sound is resonated and delivered to the outer air' (West, Ansberry and Carr 1957:196–7). They refer to Russell (1931) for the original discussion of cul-de-sac resonance in nasality. Russell (1931), West (1936), and West, Ansberry and Carr (1957) suggest various possible locations for this cul-de-sac resonance, apart from the most usual location, the nasal cavity. We shall return to this cul-de-sac resonance theory in a moment.

As we shall see below, nasality is a complex topic, and one should be cautious about extending explanations of the mechanisms underlying segmental nasality to cover the production of nasality as a setting feature.

Segmental nasality is treated in most textbooks on general phonetics in a somewhat simplified fashion, and the simplifications are not always explicitly acknowledged. Of course, considerations of pedagogic expedience can quite reasonably inhibit writers of introductory texts from embarking on the often complicated explanations necessary to do justice to the detailed realities of nasality. So it may be helpful here to try to give a brief, explicit account of these simplifications, in order to see more clearly how the mechanisms normally put forward to explain the production of segmental nasality may relate to mechanisms responsible for nasality as a setting in voice quality.

The first simplification is the view that *when the velum is closed speech is free from nasality, and conversely, that when speech is free from nasality, the velum is closed.* For example, Sweet (1877: 7–8) wrote that 'In forming all the non-nasal sounds the uvula is pressed up so as to cover the passage into the nose. If the passage is open the sound becomes nasal.' This view, not unreasonable in Sweet, over a hundred years ago, is still not uncommon. Chomsky and Halle (1968: 316), for instance, write that 'Nasal sounds are produced with a lowered velum which allows the air to escape through the nose; nonnasal sounds are produced with a raised velum so that the air from the lungs can escape only through the mouth.'

It is not for the lack of available research data that this partial, simplistic account of the mechanism of nasality is perpetuated. Even in the late nineteenth century, Rousselot (1901) noticed that the velum is held slightly open throughout most of the course of normal speech without audible nasality. Van Riper and Irwin (1958 : 239–51), in one of the best reviews of the literature of the difficult area of nasality, say that experimental evidence has been offered 'for the belief that the velum does not completely close off the pharyngeal passage to the nose in normal speech', by Hixon (1949), Kaltenborn (1948), Nusbaum, Foley and Wells (1935), and Wolfe (1942). Later in their book (1958 : 392), Van Riper and Irwin also mention Kantner and West (1941), McDonald and Baker (1951) and Heffner (1949 [= 1950]) as resisting the simplification. Berry and Eisenson (1956) also support this view, and further point out that the degree of velic opening is variable. Warren (1964:161) has shown that velic opening up to a maximum of 10 mm^2 is 'adequate for the required oropharyngeal pressure of occlusive ... consonant production'. Kaltenborn (1948) quantified the characteristic sizes of the openings into the mouth and the nose from the pharynx in non-nasal and nasal speakers: the typical size of the opening to the nose (presumably on the front to back diameter) for non-nasal speakers was 1 mm, and for the opening to the mouth 11 mm; the measurements for speakers judged as nasal were 8.8 mm for the opening to the nasal cavity, and 3.1 mm for the opening to the mouth. He is quoted by Van Riper and Irwin (1958:241) as concluding that 'nasality is caused by having too wide an opening into the nasopharynx in comparison with the opening into the oral cavity'.

The second simplification, commented on by Heffner (1950: 31–2), is that *nasal airflow always gives rise to nasality*, and conversely that *nasality always requires nasal airflow*. It is certainly true that airflow can give rise to nasality, but only under certain conditions. If, as we have seen above, the velum may be held slightly open in normal non-nasal speech, then logically it follows that it should be possible to have airflow through the nasal cavity without giving rise to audible nasality. Benson (1951) found 'no relationship between the degree of judged nasality and the amount of nasal airflow in his subjects' (Van Riper and Irwin 1958 : 242). Nusbaum, Foley and Wells (1935) assert that 'It is quite possible to utter vowel sounds free from nasality even when air is flowing out of the nose' (Van Riper and Irwin 1958:243). Thus, clearly, airflow through the nasal cavity is not itself a necessary or a sufficient condition for the production of audible nasality. Nasality is essentially a condition of resonance, as asserted above, and the nasal cavity can resonate without the passage of air through it; one has only to think of the possibility of very marked nasality where the nostrils are held tightly closed, for example.

Considering for a moment exclusively the participation of the nasal cavity in the production of nasality, it is possible to suggest, following Kaltenborn (1948) and Van Riper and Irwin (1958), that a vital factor in inducing resonance in the nasal cavity is the ratio of the latitudinal cross-sections of two openings – the relatively horizontal opening from the pharynx into the nasal cavity, and the relatively vertical opening from the pharynx into the mouth. We have seen that Kaltenborn's cineradio-graphic study of velopharyngeal action showed that in non-nasal and nasal voices there is a major difference in the ratio in the two cases: in non-nasal voice, the ratio of the nasal port to the oral port was 1 : 11, and in the nasal voice was 8.8 : 3.1 (Kaltenborn 1948). We also noted that Björk (1961) found that the cross-sectional area of the nasal port increased from 60 mm^2 in slight nasalization to 250 mm^2 in heavy nasalization, presumably with a concomitant decrease in the oral port areas. That the oral port is rather smaller in nasal voices than in neutral voices is a conclusion reasonably drawn from the comment reported earlier by Hixon (1949), that nasal speakers retract and raise their tongues more than normal speakers. This was attributed above to the effect of the palatoglossus, which, in pulling the velum downwards also tended to pull the tongue body upwards and backwards. Van Riper and Irwin (1958 : 241), commenting on Hixon's finding, suggest that nasality sets in whenever the nasal port is relatively larger than the oral port.

One of the difficulties in achieving any precise quantification of the actual cross-sectional areas involved is that complete confidence in cineradiographic results is not usually possible (Trenschel 1969). This is especially the case with the small distances concerned in velopharyngeal activity, particularly given that one is looking at the outline of tissues lacking the sharper definition of a bony structure. It is also difficult to be sure of the representative nature of radiographic evidence acquired with the help of radio-opaque paint, which makes for an unusual speaking situation. Another technique has recently been introduced into the range of experimental phonetic methods of analysis, however, which can give fairly exact results, if a number of aerodynamic factors are known. This is the use of a hydrokinetic equation to predict the velopharyngeal orifice area from a knowledge of the pressure differential across the orifice, and the rate of airflow through the orifice. Warren (1964) and Warren and

Dubois (1964) were the first to apply this, in relation to work on cleft palate speech. They proposed a slight modification to the hydrokinetic equation for use in the investigation of speech: they introduced a correction factor K (= 0.65), for the unsteady, non-uniform and rotational characteristics of airflow in the vocal tract, in the equation:

$$A = \frac{V}{K \sqrt{2\left(\frac{P_1 - P_3}{D}\right)}}$$

where A is the cross-sectional area of the orifice in cm^2, V is the rate of airflow through the orifice in cc/sec, $P_1 - P_3$ is the pressure differential across the orifice in dynes/cm^2, and D is the density of air (0.001 gms/cm^3).

This approach was tested by Lubker (1969) in an experiment with an actual model, and he reported that 'the area of the orifice can be predicted with considerable accuracy, thus strongly supporting the use of the Hydrokinetic Equation for predicting velopharyngeal orifice areas'. Given that airflow and pressure sensing devices can be used which do not interfere seriously with the naturalness of articulation, a more precise and confident quantification is possible of the interaction of aerodynamic and articulatory factors in speech. One important additional factor in the aerodynamic-cum-articulatory study of nasality has to be added to this approach, however. Nasal airflow is 'dependent not only upon the amount of velopharyngeal opening, but also upon the amount of oral constriction' (Lubker and Moll 1965: 271). 'This implies that one measure, such as the velopharyngeal orifice distance, is not sufficient to describe the articulatory factors related to nasal airflow' (Lubker and Moll 1965: 270).

The most important single factor in the production of nasality, then, according to Van Riper and Irwin (1958) and Kaltenborn (1948), is the ratio of the sizes of the posterior oral and nasal openings. The actual dimensions of the openings will naturally vary from speaker to speaker, and the degree of possible nasal airflow without nasality will depend on the anatomical differences between the speakers. Berry and Eisenson (1956) say that in some bass resonant voices, the nasopharynx is open most of the time, without producing audible nasality. It seems statistically reasonable to assume that most men with bass voices are men of larger stature and hence tend to have larger vocal organs. The absolute size of the posterior nasal opening can thus be quite large, and nasal airflow consequently quite copious, before audible nasality begins to be produced.

The third and last simplification often found in introductory phonetic textbooks is that *resonance of the nasal cavity is the only resonance responsible for the production of nasality*, and conversely that *nasality always requires resonance of the nasal cavity*.

Some experimental work has been done on the measurement of acoustic energy in the nasal cavity, but the findings are contradictory. Weiss (1954) found a correlation of 0.74 between the judged hyper-nasality of voices in his sample and sound pressure level in the nasal tract. But Shelton, Arndt, Knox, Elbert, Chisum and Youngstrom (1969) claimed that 'measurements of oral and nasal sound pressure level do not correlate highly enough with nasality judgments to serve as indices to nasality'.

We can concede that the resonance of the nasal cavity itself is the most common, and the most important factor to be considered in discussions of the acoustic and articulatory correlates of nasality. There are alternative possibilities, however, and to elucidate these, we return now to the notion of 'cul-de-sac resonance' mentioned above, first put forward by Russell (1931:18). West, Ansberry and Carr (1957:196–7) give a concise summary and illustration of the notion:

The timbre, or overtone structure, usually given the name *nasality* is the result of resonance in a cul-de-sac resonator, a chamber opening off from the passageway through which a sound is resonated and delivered to the outer air ... Whenever, along the tube from the larynx to the outer air, there is a side chamber whose only opening is into the main tube, there is a chamber capable of acting as a cul-de-sac resonator and/or producing a quality of tone usually referred to as nasal; and wherever this side chamber has an accessory opening through it to the outer air, it may still function as a cul-de-sac resonator if the necessary opening is smaller than the aperture connecting the side chamber with the main tube.

Amalgamating these comments on resonance produced in a *side chamber* (to adopt Pike's term (1943:87) in preference to 'cul-de-sac') with the earlier discussion about areal ratios of the entries into the back of the mouth and the back of the nasal cavity, we begin to approach a reasonable summary specification for the configuration of the vocal tract in the production of nasality, as far as the nasal cavity is involved. Four cross-sectional areas are concerned: that of the entry to the oral cavity, and that of its exit (that is, the narrowest oral constriction); that of the entry to the nasal cavity, at the velopharyngeal orifice, and that of its exit, at the nostrils. In producing resonance auditorily acceptable as nasality, the following conditions will apply. Firstly, either the nasal cavity or the mouth cavity has to constitute a side chamber relative to the other. Whichever cavity has the smaller exit becomes the side chamber, provided that the exit is itself smaller than the entry to that cavity. Secondly, if Van Riper and Irwin (1958) and Kaltenborn (1948) are right in their comments reported above about the ratios of the areas of the entries to the two cavities, the side chamber will generate audible nasality only when the entry to the side chamber has an area approximately equal to or greater than that of the entry to the other cavity. The nasal cavity is the usual side chamber of the two, in nasal voice, and anatomy facilitates the provision of a large entry area and a small exit area for the cavity. It will be recalled that the value for a typical velopharyngeal opening in heavy nasalization was given by Björk (1961) as 250 mm^2. The entry to the oral cavity is made correspondingly smaller, in nasalization, other articulatory factors being equal, by the intrusion of the lowered velum into the back of the cavity, which constrains the oral airflow to pass mostly through the relatively narrow openings of the faucal arches on each side of the pendent uvula. The fixed area of the exit from the nasal cavity into the nostrils is relatively very small compared with the large areas involved in the contribution of the velopharyngeal orifice to the production of nasality.

We can now consider briefly the relation between the production of nasality for purposes of segment performance and its production in voice quality.

In the production of most nasal stop contoids (those with a place of articulation forward of velar), the effective side chamber is the oral cavity inwards of the oral closure. In velar nasal stops, there may be a small side chamber formed by the approximation of the back of the tongue behind the velar contact to the undersurface of the uvula (Hahn, Lomas, Hargis and Vandraegen 1952), but as in uvular nasals, there is normally a lateral space between the two sets of faucal pillars. Also, in velar and in uvular nasals, the surface of the tongue forward of the closure with the soft palate, if touched with a finger tip, can be felt vibrating with any but the very weakest degree of voicing. The surface of the tongue can therefore excite the resonances of the front of the mouth, and the oral cavity forms a resonant chamber in the formation of these two nasal stops. The oral cavity is made to resonate here in much the same way that the nasal cavity can be in the voice quality popularly labelled as 'cold in the head voice', when entry to the nasal cavity is blocked by catarrhal mucus in a heavy cold, with the acoustic excitation being transmitted through the tissue of the soft palate itself, or perhaps through the mucal plug.

That velar and uvular nasals have oral as well as pharyngeal and nasal cavity resonance can easily be demonstrated by producing either of them with a strong whisper, and changing the position of the lips from a spread posture to a rounded one and back again. The pitch of the resonances of the front of the mouth can be quite clearly heard, falling markedly with increasing lip-rounding and rising again with the progressive lip-spreading.

The auditory effect that we perceive as 'nasality', in the case of velar and uvular nasals, is likely also to have part of its acoustic basis in the tuning that the nasal system applies as a resonator neck to the resonant frequency of the pharynx (Fant 1960:142).

In the production of nasalized segments, as opposed to nasal segments, conventional phonetic description specifies the nasal cavity as the necessary side chamber. The nasal cavity is thus implicated as a normal part of the production of all nasal and nasalized segments. Given that nasality, as a segmental quality, has to be able to be switched on and off rather rapidly, in the spasmodic articulatory fluctuations of continuous speech, it seems certain that conventional phonetic theory is quite right in attributing the control of segmental nasality to the action of the velopharyngeal system (Condax, Acson, Miki and Sakoda 1976).

In nasality as a feature of voice quality, however, where the auditory effect has to be nearly permanently present, the involvement of side chambers other than the nasal cavity has to be considered a distinct possibility, in at least a minority of cases. This is all the more plausible in view of the variety of auditory qualities that we are willing to accept as 'nasal', in terms of voice quality.

The possible location of side chambers other than the nasal cavity has been discussed by a number of writers. Van den Berg (1962) says that

Nasality is immediately recognized by the human ear, but the acoustical correlate is difficult to describe exactly ... This might seem unimportant for the phonetician and not for the phoniatrist, but this would be a mistake ... Nasal qualities, at least qualities which are interpreted as being nasal, may arise *without participation of the nose*, by too large damping factors at other places of the vocal tract, primarily in the vicinity of the larynx ... the clinician needs to be aware of this. (quoted by Greene 1964:183)

As in this comment, discussion of side chamber resonator locations other than the nasal cavity is very often in work addressed chiefly to workers in speech therapy and pathology. This is to be expected, given that the use of other side chambers than the nasal cavity is more likely in speakers who suffer from some disability in speech such as velic inadequacies of various sorts, and that speech therapists are more likely to meet speakers whose speech is idiosyncratic enough, whatever the cause, to distinguish them from most of the rest of their community, than are workers in other disciplines such as phonetics.

West, Ansberry and Carr (1957), in their book on the rehabilitation of defective speech, mention various possibilities for the locations of the nasalizing side chamber:

Frequently there comes to the clinic a person whose voice is distinctly 'nasal' in quality but whose vowel sounds are made with the nasal port unmistakably shut tight. Where is the cul-de-sac responsible for his nasality? Many guesses have been made in answer to that question. (West, Ansberry and Carr 1957:199)

They mention various possible locations, and suggest that the nasal quality usually disappears when overall muscle tension is reduced. They conclude that

It may well be that the contraction of the muscles pulls apart surfaces of the larynx and pharynx, of the epiglottis and tongue, or of the cheek and (external) alveolar ridges, that would otherwise be in contact, thus creating cavities in which 'nasal' quality can be produced. (West, Ansberry and Carr 1957: 200)

The most frequently posited location for the side chamber, other than the nasal cavity, is the pharynx (Eijkman 1926; Paget 1930; Russell 1931; West 1936; Tarneaud 1941; Wise 1948); Tarneaud (1941), for example, talks about nasality caused by tension in the pharyngobuccal cavity, as 'timbre mi-guttural, mi-nasalisé' with complete velic closure.

Greene (1964) localizes the possible side chamber in the lower pharynx and upper larynx, saying that

it should not be forgotten that nasality may also be imparted to the voice by muscular constriction in the laryngeal cavity and the relative positions assumed by the ventricular folds, aryepiglottic folds and the epiglottis, also elevation of the larynx by the suprahyoid muscles. (Greene 1964:184)

The sources of nasality in voice quality suggested by the writers above are rather varied, including as they do hypothesized resonatory contributions from the nasal cavity, the pharynx and the larynx. However, it is not too unreasonable to assume that the comments of all the above writers contain elements of truth, if one takes the position emphasized in this book that the muscular systems of the vocal tract form a unified, complex, interlinked and interacting unit, mechanically, physiologically and acoustically. From the details of the physiology of the velopharyngeal system outlined earlier, it seems safe to assume that any adjustment of the system will inevitably affect, in varying degrees, many settings elsewhere in the vocal tract. We saw for example that adjustment of the velum entailed changes in laryngeal, pharyngeal, faucal and lingual settings.

Recognizing that 'nasality' is an auditory concept should allow us, ideally, to distinguish between velopharyngeal nasality, as it were, and other types such as pharyngeal 'nasality', faucal 'nasality', laryngeal 'nasality', and so forth. It may be, for instance that the term 'nasal twang' tends to be used for the quality produced by these other sources of 'nasality', rather than for velopharyngeal nasality. Nasality which is not produced by the action of the velopharyngeal system can be separately attributed to settings of the relevant mechanism, when enough becomes known to do this with confidence, and nasality due to velopharyngeal action can be considered independently.

The discussion of side chamber resonance other than that involved in resonance of the nasal cavity is speculative at present, and it gives rise to a problem of descriptive terminology concerning the term 'nasality' and related forms. Should 'nasality' be applied to the whole field of side chamber resonance, or only to resonance of the nasal cavity? West, Ansberry and Carr (1957: 200) opt for the second position, and conclude that 'it would be better to refer to this quality as cul-de-sac resonance rather than *nasal* resonance' and that 'we are then justified in employing the term *nasal* to describe the speech of a person who, because of imitation of those in his environment or because of indifference to standards of good speech, utters all his vowels and semivowels with the nasal type of cul-de-sac resonance'. Leaving aside their prescriptive attitude about 'standards of good speech', they are right about the desirability of having a separate cover term for the variety of phenomena currently included under the umbrella of 'nasality'; and 'cul-de-sac resonance', or 'side chamber resonance' might be suitable candidates. The only sub-category of side chamber resonance that we currently really know enough about to use with some degree of confidence is resonance of the nasal cavity – nasal resonance in the strict sense of 'nasal'. Not enough is yet known, in phonetics at least, about the sources of side chamber resonance in locations such as the pharynx, larynx, or faucal pillars to be able to differentiate accurately between the different types on an auditory basis, and until this is possible, it seems premature to develop an over-delicate descriptive terminology.

It is sufficient for the phonetic study of voice quality to note the generality of the concept of a side chamber in producing the effect commonly referred to as nasality, and to retain the well-established labels of conventional phonetics in their technical meanings: 'nasality', 'nasal', 'denasal' and 'nasalization' will now be taken to refer to control of resonance involving the nasal cavity by means of velopharyngeal action, unless there is indication to the contrary.

The neutral velopharyngeal setting was characterized earlier as involving 'velopharyngeal closure throughout, except for phonologically nasal or contextually-nasalized segments'. This interim description should now be modified. The articulatory notion of necessary velopharyngeal closure for non-nasal segments can be abandoned, since it is clear from the preceding discussion that the actual position of the velum will be highly variable during speech, in response jointly to the type of segment being produced, and to the need to maintain the ratio of the oral and nasal port areas below the critical level which would induce audible nasal resonance.

Condax, Acson, Miki and Sakoda (1976) showed that the velum has five distinct positions during speech, depending on the type of segment being articulated. Extending this finding, and drawing on published experimental work on nasality using endoscopic, fiberoptic, cineradio-graphic, electromyographic and aerodynamic techniques, Cagliari (1978:159–66) proposes a very useful 'neutral velic scale', on an articulatory basis. Velic height, he notes, varies from maximally high in blowing to maximally low in the respiratory position. Within these limits, different types of speech segments correlate with different velic heights on this scale, in the following progression from highest to lowest: voiceless stops; voiced stops; voiceless fricatives; voiced fricatives; oral close vowels; oral open vowels; nasalized close vowels; nasalized open vowels; nasal segments. For the velopharyngeal setting to change from neutral to nasal, Cagliari suggests that at least some segments in the speech of the speaker concerned must show a drop in velic height, compared with the notional values of the neutral scale. Conversely, a denasal quality involves a rise in velic height, compared with the neutral scale. Cagliari also accounts for degrees of nasality by means of his concept of a velic scale:

the severity of the nasal quality in the voice of certain individuals or the degrees of nasalization for linguistic segments will increase proportionally to the displacement of velic position for the phonetic segments downwards in the velic scale. The opposite is also true in relation to the process of denasalization. So, according to the explanation suggested, different types of nasal quality may be produced when different individuals with nasalized voice use different scales of velic activity in their speech. (Cagliari 1978:165)

This concept of a neutral velic scale for segmental performance will be adopted here, and will be taken to underlie the position that the nasal settings of the velopharyngeal system include any setting of the velum which produces more audible nasality than is appropriate for the neutral setting. Similarly, denasal settings of the velopharyngeal system will be taken to include any setting of the velum which produces less audible nasality than is appropriate for the neutral setting.

Different degrees of nasality and denasality can be described with scalar labels such as 'slight', 'moderate' and 'extreme'. The general principle of scalar labelling will be discussed in Chapter 5. It is necessary here merely to say that any judgement of scalar degrees has to be made on absolute grounds, not grounds relative to the accent of the speaker's speech community, nor any other relative measure which is not general to all anatomically and physiologically normal human beings.

The *denasal* setting of the velopharyngeal system is one which minimizes the occurrence of audible nasality. One problem here is that the term 'denasal' has been used sometimes to refer to the voice quality of a speaker who has a cold in the head. Luchsinger and Arnold (1965:684) list as a synonym of 'denasal speech, hyporhinolalia, hyponasality' the label 'head-cold speech'. A speaker who has a cold in the head may well have a blockage of the nasal port above the velum, and the consequence is that no nasal airflow is possible. We saw earlier, however, that the presence of nasal airflow is by no means an obligatory factor in the production of an auditory quality that listeners are ready to accept as nasality. A posterior nasal blockage of this sort does not necessarily prevent the resonance of the nasal cavity; the cavity may well be acoustically excited by sound waves travelling either through the nasal plug or the tissue of the velum itself, just as earlier it was suggested that the oral cavity could be made to resonate quite audibly by whispering while maintaining a uvular closure and velic opening. If the tongue can demonstrably allow the transmission of the low amplitude sound waves produced by the whisper phonation type, then it does not seem unreasonable to suggest that the velum may allow the higher amplitude voiced waves to be transmitted into the nasal cavity. The quality of some (not all) voices of speakers with a head cold gives an impression not of 'denasality' in the strict sense of an absence of nasality, but rather of a special, very highly damped kind of nasality.

The problem of describing the voice quality of speakers with head colds is not, however, the responsibility of this descriptive system, which is explicitly confined to the description of phonetic settings able to be controlled by any speaker of normal anatomy and in reasonable health. It *is* legitimate to speculate on how healthy speakers go about the business of reproducing a quality of a speaker with a cold in the head, or other obstructions of the nasal port, such as adenoidal swellings, by means of phonetic adjustments of the normal vocal apparatus. This is the situation Abercrombie describes in the Liverpool accent. He suggests that

people can be found with adenoidal voice quality who do not have adenoids – they have learnt the quality from the large number of people who do have them, so that they conform to what, for that community, has become the norm. (Continuing velic closure, together with velarization, are the principal components needed for counterfeiting adenoidal voice quality.) (Abercrombie 1967:94–5)

It was suggested earlier that slight velarization is a frequent concomitant of nasal voice. Abercrombie here indicates velarization as one component in simulated 'adenoidal' voice, in association with velic closure. Palatoglossal involvement explains both tendencies. Whenever the palatoglossus contracts, both the velum and the tongue will be pulled towards each other, unless antagonist muscle systems resist the movement. In producing simulated 'adenoidal' voice, one is conscious of a degree of tension in the faucal area. Support for the idea that the palatoglossus is actively contracting in producing the voice quality characteristic of Liverpool can be found in the quotation from Knowles (1978:89) given earlier, in the section on lingual settings. He writes that 'In Scouse, the centre of gravity of the tongue is brought backwards and upwards, the pillars of the fauces are tightened . . .' (though he does not mention velic closure explicitly, attributing the 'adenoidal' quality mostly to a combination of the above factors, raised larynx, constricted pharynx and a close jaw position). If it is valid to suggest that an 'adenoidal' effect is achieved partly by palatoglossal contraction with a raised velic position, then there will be a consequent effect on lingual articulations generally, with a constraining tendency being exercised on the body of the tongue for all susceptible segments.

The physiology of the velopharyngeal system which is relevant to the velum being sufficiently raised to minimize the degree of audible nasality that the neutral velic scale would produce has already been specified in the earlier discussion of the palatal elevator complex.

We come now to a brief discussion of the acoustic characteristics of nasality.

There has been a fair amount of research devoted to this area, mostly as it relates to segmental nasality in nasal contoids and nasalized vocoids. The conclusions of the research tend to be rather varied, although there is a measure of agreement about the principal features. The variability can be partly explained by the multiplicity of physiological components which has just been discussed. Another important source of the variability derives from the anatomical variations between different speakers (Bjuggren and Fant 1964), and to some extent to the variability within the speech of a given speaker on different occasions, noted earlier (House 1957), in details of the consistency of the mucal lining of the nasal cavity, and the underlying tissues. The effect of all these variabilities is that a fairly wide range of acoustic phenomena are perceptually acceptable as indicators of nasality, as will be seen in the summary below of the acoustic characteristics.

Most accounts of the acoustics of nasality assume a simplified anatomy of the nasal cavity, treating it as a single tube. Fujimura, however, writes that 'In reality, of course, the nasal system at a central point branches into two separate tubes, each of which opens at one of the nostrils. If the system is symmetric with respect to the point at which the sound is measured, this geometrical branching is acoustically immaterial' (Fujimura 1962:240). In the case of substantial asymmetry of the tubes, Fujimura (*loc.cit.*) and Bjuggren and Fant (1964:6) state that additional high frequency nasal formants and anti-formants are introduced.

Fant (1960) gives an account of the anatomy of the nasal cavity which is relevant to a discussion of its acoustic properties. He estimates that the 'overall length of the nasal pathways measured as the shortest distance from the uvula to the outlet at the nostrils' is about 12.5 cm. He continues:

The left and right nasal channels run approximately parallel for a distance of about 8 cm. from the nose opening and combine in the nasopharynx. Each of the frontal halves contains a bottom, middle, and upper branch in full communication at any cross-section. These appear to be too closely coupled to function as independent resonators. Provided the left and right parts show complete symmetry, they will function as a single cavity system. This is the ideal configuration ... but it can be expected that asymmetry will cause an additional diffusion of spectral energy owing to the occurrence of formants from the left and the right pathways, and to the particular mixing in the nasal radiation. A greater damping of resonance in the nasal part than in the oral part of the vocal tract can be expected owing to the greater surface outline in area ratio of any cross-section except in the nasopharynx ... Nostril hairs will also contribute to the damping. (Fant 1960:140–1)

The acoustic results of adding a nasal tract to an oral tract can be discussed under two headings: the resonatory characteristics of the nasal tract, and their effect on those of the rest of the vocal tract.

The most commonly reported nasal formant has a centre-frequency between 200 and 300 Hz (Curtis 1942; Delattre 1954; Fujimura 1962; Hattori, Yamamoto and Fujimura 1956; House and Stevens 1956; Potter, Kopp and Green 1947). Another nasal resonance is reported at about 1000 Hz by House and Stevens (1956), Joos (1948) and Smith (1951), and one at about 2000 Hz by Delattre (1954) and Smith (1951).

The bandwidths of nasal formants are said by House (1957) to be 300 Hz for the lowest formant increasing to 1000 Hz for those near 2500 Hz.

Anti-resonances, or anti-formants, which derive from any shunting side-branch present in the vocal tract (House 1957:199), are each paired with a nasal resonance (Fant 1960:60, 149). Values for anti-resonances have been specifically mentioned by Hattori, Yamamoto and Fujimura (1956) as 500 Hz, by Fujimura (1962) as 700 Hz for the lowest he found, and between 900 and 1800 Hz, varying with segmental articulation, by House and Stevens (1956).

The effects on the rest of the vocal tract of coupling the nasal tract to it are reasonably well agreed. The most general effect is an overall loss of power (Dickson 1962; House and Stevens 1956; Kelly 1932). This attenuation is directly due to the introduction of anti-resonances by the side chamber resonator, which absorb acoustic energy, especially in the higher frequencies (Curtis 1942; House and Stevens 1956; House 1957). A reflection of the general attenuation is a broadening of all formant bandwidths (Kelly 1932), which has another consequence, that of flattening spectral peaks in the region between 800 Hz and 2300 Hz, giving an intensity plateau (Fujimura 1962). It is almost certainly this general attenuation which is responsible for the drop in intelligibility of nasal voices reported by Diehl and McDonald (1956) and Moser, Dreher and Adler (1955), though Glasgow (1944) attributes the diminished intelligibility to the notion that nasality can call attention to itself, distracting the listener.

Considering more specific indicators of nasality, the most widely reported finding, according to Fant (1960:149), is a marked drop in intensity of the first formant (Björk 1961; Delattre 1954; Hose and Stevens 1956; Kelly 1932; Smith 1951). Always comparing the characteristics of nasality with the non-nasal equivalent, Björk (1961) found a drop in the intensity of the second formant, although Delattre (1954) disagrees. The third formant shows a drop in both intensity and frequency (Björk 1961; Delattre 1954; Kelly 1932; Smith 1951). There is a general drop in intensity on all formants above the third.

The characteristic drop in intensity of the first formant is brought about by a number of factors: the low frequency nasal formant boosts the intensity of the low harmonics, below the frequency of the first formant, and another nasal formant at about 1000 Hz reinforces the harmonics just above most values of the first formant. Anti-resonances and an increase in all formant bandwidths then combine to lower the intensity of the first formant (Fant 1960:149).

The exact detail of changes in the acoustic spectrum attributable to nasality will depend, as House and Stevens (1956) and Curtis (1970) point out, on the momentary configurational state of the vocal tract, because of the acoustic interdependence of the resonating cavities concerned.

The acoustic characteristics of denasality, to the extent that they derive from velopharyngeal adjustments, consist of the minimization on susceptible segments of the acoustic characteristics of nasality just discussed.

Nasality as a setting is exploited linguistically in many languages, as noted in the Introduction. Denasality, in the sense used here, seems to be used in a linguistic connection only as a feature characterizing particular accents, marking membership of sociolinguistic communities such as Liverpool, as mentioned above. Paralinguistically, nasality is used in English in 'whining'. Denasality, as a paralinguistic feature colouring the auditory quality of linguistic segments, is sometimes heard as a signal of incipient laughter.

3 Phonatory settings

The domain of phonatory settings is limited by the same criterion that was applied to supralaryngeal settings: only those settings which can potentially be controlled by any speaker with a normal vocal apparatus will be admitted into the descriptive phonetic scheme.

Only a small number of basic types of phonation will be distinguished; although we shall see that these basic types can combine with each other in various ways to make up a larger number of composite phonatory qualities.

The term 'register' has been used very frequently, particularly in the literature on singing, to refer to particular modes of vibration of the vocal folds. The term will not be adopted here, however, nor is it proposed in this outline of major types of phonatory settings to go into the details of the different minor 'registers' such as 'head register' and 'chest register' that are claimed to exist. A thoroughly comprehensive account would have to include them, but the difficulty of giving such an account is that almost as many 'registers' are suggested as there are writers on the subject. 'Register' is also used, very often, to refer to 'voice pitch level', instead of 'mode of vocal fold vibration', and it is not always clear which meaning is involved. Mörner, Fransson and Fant (1963:18), in discussing the general area of 'registers', say that it 'suffers from an abundance of terms and an ambiguity of their use', and they list 107 different labels.

A different ambiguity underlies many examples of the use of the term 'register' by linguists. Introduced as a technical term in phonetics by Henderson (1951), its reference was initially clearly to laryngeal activity. Henderson writes, for example, that 'An important feature of Cambodian phonology is the presence of two contrasting voice registers, each with its appropriate vowel alternance' (Henderson 1951). She is referring to 'chest register' and 'head register', and distinguishes such laryngeal considerations of 'register' from associated supralaryngeal factors such as vowel quality. 'Register' has since tended to become a phonological concept rather than primarily a phonetic one and as such to act as a cover term not only for laryngeal activity but also for the associated supralaryngeal factors. For example, Shorto writes about Mon, a language of South East Asia, that

the paratonal register distinction is broadly similar to that described for Cambodian by Henderson. Its exponents are distributed throughout the articulatory complex but exclude pitch features. Chest register ... is characterized by breathy voice quality in association with a general laxness of the speech organs and a relatively centralized articulation of vowels. The more frequent head register ... is characterized by a clear voice quality, relative tenseness, and peripheral vowel articulation. (Shorto 1966:399–400)

In other words, as a linguistic concept, 'register' often now refers not solely to laryngeal behaviour, but rather to a constellation of activities at various levels of the vocal tract.

Phoneticians on the whole have been much more interested in supralaryngeal activities than in phonatory ones, and consequently more is known about the former than the latter. This is not without justification, when one thinks of the central importance phoneticians properly place on the capacity of speech to embody the distinctive patterns of language. The number of linguistic distinctions manifested by supralaryngeal activities is always much greater than those signalled by different types of phonation, in every known language of the world. Ladefoged (1971:16–18) suggests nine different modes of vibration of the vocal folds (which he says does not exhaust the total number found in different languages); and he points out that, taking the feature that he calls 'glottal stricture', no single language makes use of more than three out of the nine modes of vibration for manifesting linguistic oppositions. In a later book, Ladefoged amends this last statement by listing five different values, 'all of which are used in Beja, a language spoken in the Sudan' (Ladefoged 1975:261).

In attempting to characterize the different phonatory settings, the first requirement is to define the neutral mode of phonation against which the other modes can be contrastively described. The neutral mode of phonation is one where the vibration of the true vocal folds is periodic, efficient, and without audible friction. This description is worded to facilitate the discussion of other types of phonatory settings where one (or more) of the specified characteristics does not apply. There are thus settings where the phonation is not achieved by the true vocal folds alone (as in *ventricular voice*), or where the mode of vibration is aperiodic (as in *harsh voice*), inefficient and with slight audible friction (as in *breathy voice*), or with strongly audible friction (as in *whispery voice* and *whisper*). This still leaves some types of phonation without contrastive identification against the neutral mode of vibration – for instance, *falsetto, creak,* and *creaky voice.* This is partially put right by noting that the term adopted here for the neutral mode of vibration, *modal voice,* is Hollien's (1971), and that he says he chose the term 'modal' because 'it includes the range of fundamental frequencies that are normally used in speaking and singing' (Hollien 1971 : 320). This comment can be incorporated into the description of the neutral type of phonation, but it is important to bear in mind that matters of pitch as such are not strictly relevant to quality. Falsetto is then characterized as having a range of fundamental frequency potentially higher than that of modal voice, and creak as having a range potentially lower. (The reason for the cautious use here of 'potentially' is an awareness that the pitch range of falsetto can substantially overlap the range of modal voice (Broad 1973 : 153), in terms of what is physically possible, even though male speakers using falsetto tend to utilize only the middle to high part of the possible range, in Western culture at least ; and the inverse applies to creak, which can be made on a high enough pitch to overlap the bottom end of the modal voice range.) The characterization of creaky voice is a problem which will be discussed later in this chapter.

None of these descriptions of phonation types is adequate however. The differences between modal voice and each of the other settings mentioned are of course more numerous and more complex than this brief sketch suggests. Even in the case of modal voice, it is only a description, and remains far from a definition : the issue is merely hedged by saying that modal voice is the type of vocal fold vibration which phonetic theory assumes takes place in ordinary voicing, when no specific feature is explicitly changed or added. It is very hard to construct a satisfactory, short definition of modal voice ; instead, its characteristics will be elaborated in a summary outline of the aerodynamic and physiological factors thought to be involved in producing this neutral mode of phonation. This base will then be used for the further discussion of the different phonation types.

The very widely accepted theory of vocal fold vibration is the *aerodynamic–myoelastic* theory. The myoelastic component was first stated by Müller (1837). He experimented with an excised human larynx set in a frame, exerting different tensions on the various muscles while air was blown through the glottis. He established that the vocal folds vibrate when they are *adducted* (i.e. brought together) to interrupt such an airstream, and that increasing longitudinal tension in the vocal folds is correlated with rising pitch.

The *aerodynamic* component is a relatively recent addition. Van den Berg (1958b) has shown that tension in the vocal folds is not the only factor to be considered in glottal vibration, in that the characteristic behaviour of airflow through narrow constrictions plays a very important part, particularly in closing the glottis. If we consider the train of events in one cycle of laryngeal vibration, the situation is basically as follows: with the glottis closed by muscular tensions acting on it in a number of dimensions (discussed later), sub-glottal air pressure builds up with pulmonic effort to expel the air from the lungs. It very rapidly reaches the pressure necessary to blow the vocal folds apart. They separate with a vertical phase difference, such that the lower parts of the vocal folds separate before the upper parts (Broad 1977; Farnsworth 1940; Flanagan and Landgraf 1968; Hirano 1977; Hollien, Coleman and Moore 1968; Ishizaka and Flanagan 1972; Matsushita 1969, 1975; Titze 1973, 1974; Titze and Strong 1975; Timcke, von Leden and Moore 1958). A jet of air shoots into the pharynx, momentarily relieving some of the sub-glottal over-pressure. The glottal margins of the vocal folds which a moment ago were in contact, now form a narrow constriction whose aerodynamic effect on the upward flow of air is to act as a venturi tube. This makes the jet of air from the lungs accelerate through the narrow gap, with the jet reaching a speed of between 2000 and 5000 cm/s (Catford 1977:98). The Bernoulli effect on the air molecules in this accelerating jet causes a very local drop in air pressure in the constricted passage between the vocal folds and the vocal folds are 'sucked' inwards towards each other by the drop in pressure. The sub-glottal air pressure, momentarily released into the pharynx, has now dropped sufficiently to be overcome by the two forces combining to close the glottis – the myoelastic tensions acting on and in the vocal folds, and the aerodynamic Bernoulli effect. The moment of glottal closure is usually the point in the phonational cycle at which the acoustic excitation of the supralaryngeal tract is most powerful. With the glottis closed, sub-glottal pressure builds up again, and the cycle of events repeats itself, between approximately 50 and 250 times a second in voiced segments uttered by average male speakers in ordinary conversation.

This picture of the combined aerodynamic and muscular forces at work in laryngeal vibration was built up by the work of a number of researchers in the 1950s, including Smith (1954a, 1954b, 1956a, 1956b, 1957), and Faaborg-Andersen (1957). The major contribution came from van den Berg himself (1954a, 1956, 1957a, 1957b, 1958a, 1958b) and with colleagues (van den Berg, Zantema and Doornenbal 1959). Van den Berg gives his own summary of the forces which interact to produce laryngeal vibration:

[The aerodynamic–myoelastic] theory postulates that the function of the larynx is based on the interplay of three factors: (1) the aerodynamic properties of the air which actuates the larynx, (2) the adjustment of the larynx, brought about by the proper nervous activation of the various muscles, and the myoelastic properties of the laryngeal components, (3) the aerodynamic coupling between (a) the subglottal system and the larynx, (b) the left and right vocal fold, and (c) the larynx and the supraglottal system. (van den Berg 1968: 291–2)

This comment on the different aerodynamic coupling factors is important in considering the fine details of the auditory quality of the voice. It implies that the detailed mode of vibration of the vocal folds will depend partly on the degree of effort exerted sub-glottally by the pulmonic system, so that fine details of phonatory quality will necessarily co-vary with laryngeal intensity. Also, coupling factors between the left and right vocal folds become auditorily important when organic asymmetries of the larynx are considered, in such cases as nodules and polyps on one or other vocal folds. In addition, the articulatory state of the supralaryngeal vocal tract will influence the fine detail of the vibratory pattern of the vocal folds to some small degree. It was noted earlier, for example, in the section on velopharyngeal settings, that nasal voice has been observed to be associated with a particular mode of vibration of the vocal folds.

Although the aerodynamic–myoelastic theory of laryngeal vibration is very well established now, it is not the only candidate in the area. There are two others, the *neurochronaxic* theory of Raoul Husson and his fellow-workers, and the *muco-undulatory* theory.

Husson's theory is diametrically opposed to the assumptions of the aerodynamic–myoelastic theory. Essentially, it dismisses muscle tension and the Bernoulli effect as the prime mechanisms of phonation, and maintains that each cycle of vibration is the direct muscular response of the *vocalis* muscles (forming the vocal folds) to an individual neural command (Husson 1950a, 1950b, 1951, 1952, 1957, 1962, 1964; Laget 1953; Moulonguet 1954; Piquet and Decroix 1956; Piquet, Decroix,

Libersa and Dujardin 1957; Portmann and Robin 1956). This theory has been widely rejected (Rubin 1960a, 1960b; Lafon and Cornut 1960; von Leden 1961; Weiss 1959). One aspect of the theory hinges on whether or not the fibres of the vocalis muscle, which makes up the glottal part of each vocal fold, run at an angle to the vocal ligament running along the edge of each fold. Goerttler (1950) suggested that vocalis fibres were arranged in two groups, both inserting on the vocal ligament at a sufficient angle to allow their contraction to open the glottis. Wustrow (1952) disputed Goerttler's views on the course of the vocalis fibres, and maintained that they run mainly parallel to the edge of the glottis, and hence cannot act independently to open the glottis. Most anatomists agree broadly with Wustrow, and conclude that the possibility of vocal fold vibration being attributable directly to periodic contraction of the vocalis muscle is remote.

The muco-undulatory theory put forward by many researchers (Baer 1973; Broad 1977; Farnsworth 1940; Hiroto 1966; Matsushita 1969, 1975; Perelló 1962a, 1962b; Smith 1956, 1961) is of smaller scale, and is complementary to the aerodynamic–myoelastic theory, not antagonistic. It concerns the effect on phonation of a wave motion in the wet mucosal layer that covers the surfaces of the vocal folds and which is attached to the underlying muscle fibres by connective tissue. Titze and Strong (1975: 740) suggest that this undulation

involves the relative motions between the mucosa and the ligament vocalis, and occurs whenever the vocal cord is unstretched. A surface wave is seen to propagate laterally from the glottis toward the vocal cord boundary ... Due to the high surface tension of the mucosa (which is, of course, the tension of the mucous membrane), the surface wave is readily dispersed, but occasionally gets reflected from the boundary and travels back toward the glottis.

Wave motion of this sort has been observed in many high-speed and stroboscopic cinefilms of the vocal folds in phonation (e.g. Farnsworth 1940; van den Berg, Vennard, Berger and Shervanian 1960). Broad (1977) writes that

It is this wave motion of the mucosa which prompted Hirano (1975) to suggest that the vocal fold should be considered in a mechanical sense to be subdivided into a loose layer (the epithelium and superficial layer of the lamina propria) and a stiff layer (the deeper layer of the lamina propria and the vocalis muscle). Earlier, Hiroto (1966) had incorporated the wave motions of the loose, superficial layer of the vocal fold as an essential component of his *muco-visco-elastic-aerodynamic* explication of the theory of vocal fold vibration. (Broad 1977: 255–6)

A picture is thus presented of the vocal fold as a layered structure, with each deeper layer being stiffer than its superficial covering (Hirano 1977:21). During phonation, the cross-sectional shape of each vocal fold is subject to continuously changing deformation. Part of the dynamic deformation is attributable to the mucosal wave motion travelling up the external surfaces of the vocal folds and into the ventricles, and part to the more gross displacements involved in the vertical phase difference mentioned earlier. It is apparent that the detail of vocal fold vibration is highly complex.

Smith (1961) considers that the contribution of these mucosal phenomena is to the fine detail of the quality of phonation, and not to the fundamental frequency. Perelló (1962a, 1962b) believes the reverse. He argues that changes of fundamental frequency in the absence of muscular adjustments can occur when the consistency of the mucosal layer changes, as in laryngitis, or in premenstrual mucosal changes in women. Changes in the mucosal lining in this way constitute organic conditions of the vocal apparatus, and lie outside the scope of phonetic control.

It will be assumed from this point onwards that the vibrations of the vocal folds in modal voice are brought about in the way described by the aerodynamic–myoelastic and muco-undulatory theories.

3.1 Modes of laryngeal vibration in phonatory settings

We come now to a summary outline of the physiology of laryngeal vibrations in modal voice, with which that of the other phonation types may then be compared.

Three laryngeal cartilages form the basic frame within which the muscular control of phonation is exercised. These are the *thyroid*, the *cricoid* and the paired *arytenoid* cartilages. Figure 13 is a schematic diagram of the relative position of these cartilages.

The thyroid is the big, shielding cartilage protecting the front and sides of the larynx from injury. It forms the 'Adam's apple' in male speakers, with its characteristic protruding, slightly pointed shape, and a V-shaped notch in the top edge at the centre. It is made up of two quadrilateral cartilaginous wings, or plates, vertically fused at the front under the central notch. The muscles which make up the *true vocal folds* and the *ventricular folds* are attached to the front, internal surface of the thyroid, at the point where the lateral plates fuse together.

The cricoid lies immediately below the thyroid, and is the uppermost

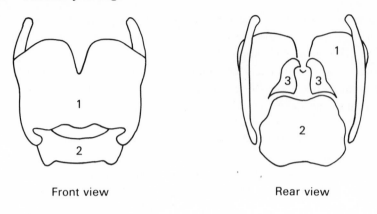

Front view   Rear view

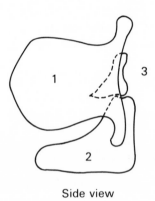

Side view

Figure 13. Schematic diagram of the principal laryngeal cartilages (adapted
         from Romanes 1978)
         1. Thyroid cartilage   3. Arytenoid cartilages
         2. Cricoid cartilage

of the tracheal cartilages. It is different from the other tracheal rings, in
that they are incomplete rings with a gap at the back, where the trachea
shares a common wall with the *esophagus*, whereas the cricoid is a
complete ring. It is often compared to a signet ring, as the etymology of
the name suggests, because the part at the back of the cricoid ring is
considerably larger than that at the front. The vertical dimension of the
'signet' at the back is usually about 25 mm in the adult male, and about
8 mm at the front. Together with the thyroid, it forms an effective
external protective structure for the rest of the larynx; it has also been

said to be 'the foundation of the structures which, as a functional group, are called the larynx' (Heffner 1950:15).

The arytenoid cartilages, much smaller than the thyroid and the cricoid, sit on the upper rim of the 'signet' of the cricoid at the back. They can rotate vertically and horizontally to a certain extent, as well as slide from side to side on the cricoid (Saunders 1964:72). They are shaped somewhat like small pyramids on a triangular base (Cates and Basmajian 1955). The posterior ends of the true vocal folds are attached to the lower, forward angles of the arytenoids, called the *vocal processes*. The posterior ends of the ventricular folds are attached to the apex of each arytenoid.

The thyroid is connected to the hyoid bone above it by the *thyrohyoid* muscle and ligament. When the larynx rises, pulled up by the action of the thyrohyoid muscle, or of the stylopharyngeus muscle (discussed earlier in this chapter, and which runs from the skull nearly vertically downwards at each side of the pharynx to insert in the back edge of the thyroid), the thyroid 'slips up under cover of the hyoid' (Kaplan 1960:115).

The thyroid is also connected not only to the arytenoid cartilages, as stated immediately above, but also to the cricoid, by the paired *cricothyroid* muscle. This runs upwards, backwards and laterally from the outer surfaces of the forward part of the cricoid to insert in the lower edge of the thyroid. The effect of its contraction is to pull the front of the cricoid ring upwards towards the thyroid, which has the mechanical consequence of rotating the back of the cricoid, with its attached arytenoids, downwards and backwards from its neutral position. This lengthens and tenses the vocal folds, thus contributing to pitch control in phonation (Sawashima 1974), and to the small changes in phonatory quality arising from changes in the fine detail of the cross-section of the folds. The retraction of the cricoid also tends to bring the vocal folds slightly closer to each other (Saunders 1964:73).

The laryngeal muscles of interest here fall into two groups: firstly, those which, like the cricothyroid, can change the positions of the cricoid relative to the thyroid; and secondly, those which affect chiefly the positions of the arytenoids relative to the cricoid.

Figure 14 is a schematic diagram of the location and actions of the muscles of the first category. A less schematic depiction of these muscles can be seen in Figure 14a. The muscles which can change the position of the cricoid relative to the thyroid are the cricothyroid muscles, and the paired *thyroarytenoid* muscles, which make up the true vocal folds and the ventricular folds. The thyroarytenoids, running from a fixed attachment

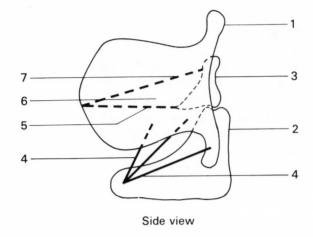

Side view

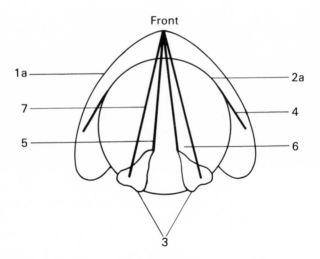

Front

View from above

Figure 14. Schematic diagram of the location of the laryngeal muscles
connecting the cricoid cartilage to the thyroid cartilage, and related
organs

1.   Thyroid cartilage
1a. External edge of thyroid
2.   Cricoid cartilage
2a. External edge of cricoid
3.   Arytenoid cartilages

4. Cricothyroid muscle
5. Glottal border of true vocal
    fold
6. Ventricle of Morgagni
7. Inner border of ventricular or
    false vocal fold

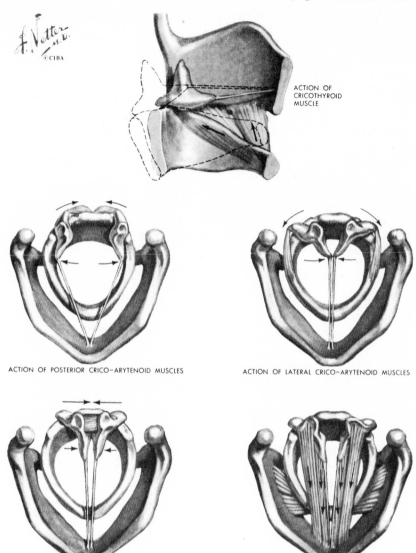

ACTION OF CRICOTHYROID MUSCLE

ACTION OF POSTERIOR CRICO–ARYTENOID MUSCLES

ACTION OF LATERAL CRICO–ARYTENOID MUSCLES

ACTION OF ARYTENOIDEUS MUSCLE

ACTION OF VOCALIS AND THYRO–ARYTENOID MUSCLES

Figure 14a. Action and location of the laryngeal muscles connecting the cricoid cartilage to the thyroid cartilage, and related organs, for comparison with the more schematic diagrams in figures 14 and 15.

at the fused angle of the thyroid to the mobile arytenoids, as noted above, are described by Heffner as follows:

Each [side] is divided into two parts – an upper and a lower – by a recess, or ventricle, which undercuts the upper portion throughout most of its length. The lower portion of each thyroarytenoid muscle is attached to the vocal process of the arytenoid cartilage. The upper portion is attached to the body and the upper tip of the arytenoid. Indeed, some of the upper fibers of the upper portion of the muscle run on upward into the folds which join the arytenoids with the edges of the epiglottis [i.e. the aryepiglottic folds]. When contracted, the thyroarytenoid muscles tend to draw the arytenoids forward, at the same time tilting them towards the thyroid cartilage. . . . The upper portions of this pair of muscles, with their covering mucous tissue, are known as the ventricular folds. . . . The lower portions . . . have a name of their own, the vocalis muscles [and they] constitute the vocal bands. . . . In cross-section the vocal bands are triangular, being shaped much like the cushions of a billiard table, and only their median edges are free. (Heffner 1950:17–18)

The ventricle mentioned is the *ventricle of Morgagni*, and it should be pointed out that the ventricular folds have a rather different composition of tissue than the true folds; Kaplan describes the ventricular folds as 'thick rounded folds of mucous membrane developed around the ventricular ligaments. They are soft and somewhat flaccid. Each contains . . . a few muscle fibers and numerous mucous glands' (Kaplan 1960:124–5). Saunders (1964:73) confirms that they contain only a few muscle fibres. Their vibration will therefore tend to be inefficient, with hypertension needed to adduct them sufficiently to phonate.

Longitudinal tension of the true and ventricular vocal folds can thus be achieved by two different actions. The first action is that of retraction and slight vertical rotation of the cricoid by means of the cricothyroid muscle, which puts longitudinal tension on the vocal folds by stretching them. The second action is contraction of the muscles which make up the vocal folds themselves, the thyroarytenoids.

The second category of muscles, those which control the positions of the arytenoid cartilage relative to the cricoid, have the function of opening and closing the glottis. Biologically vital in helping to control the airway to and from the lungs, they are small but powerful muscles, and are capable in combination of setting the glottis in a wide variety of adjustments. Figure 15 is a schematic diagram of these muscles and their action.

Only one muscle is normally used to open the glottis, the paired *posterior cricoarytenoids* (Kaplan 1960:150). These arise from the back,

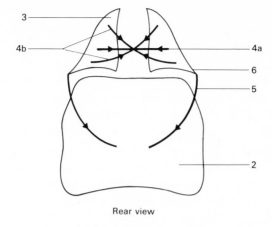

Rear view

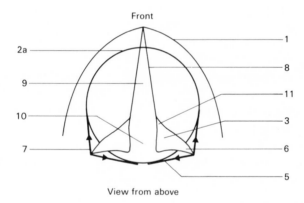

Front

View from above

Figure 15. Schematic diagram of the action and location of the laryngeal muscles connecting the arytenoid cartilages to each other and to the cricoid cartilage, and related organs

1. Thyroid cartilage
2. Cricoid cartilage
2a. External edge of cricoid
3. Arytenoid cartilage
4. Interarytenoid muscles
4a. Transverse arytenoid muscle
4b. Oblique arytenoid muscle

5. Posterior cricoarytenoid muscle
6. Muscular process of arytenoid
7. Lateral cricoarytenoid muscle
8. Vocal ligament
9. Ligamental glottis'
10. Cartilaginous glottis
11. Vocal process of arytenoid

outer surface of the cricoid and run upwards and to the side to join the arytenoids on their rearmost angles, called the *muscular processes*. Their contraction pulls the muscular processes in an arc towards the back, and the effect is to rotate the arytenoids, pivoting the other ends of the arytenoids, the vocal processes to which the vocal folds are attached, outwards. Heffner (1950: 20) says that this happens 'at every normal inhalation'. In speech, their action is the major contributor to opening the glottis for voicelessness (Hardcastle 1976: 76; Hirose and Gay 1972:158). Heffner continues: 'The action of these muscles is opposed to and can thus be controlled by the direct pull of the lateral cricoarytenoids and also by the direct pull of the thyroarytenoid muscles. The unopposed pull of the posterior cricoarytenoids widens the opening between the vocal bands to its maximum' (Heffner *ibid.*).

The muscular action which closes the glottis is more complex. The *lateral cricoarytenoids* run backwards from the outer and upper surface of the cricoid on both sides, and like the posterior cricoarytenoids, are attached to the muscular processes of the arytenoids. In contraction, as indicated above, the lateral cricoarytenoids directly oppose the action of their posterior counterparts, and swivel the arytenoid cartilages forward and inward (Hardcastle 1976: 78; Kaplan 1960:152), 'toe-ing' the vocal processes inwards. This action brings the vocal folds together, and closes the glottis along its length from the vocal processes of the arytenoids to the thyroid cartilage.

There are two other muscular actions which help to close the glottis along its full length. The first is that of the *arytenoid* muscle complex. The arytenoid muscle (sometimes referred to as the interarytenoid muscle) is made up of two sets of fibres: one of these sets is the *transverse arytenoid* muscle, which is an (unpaired)

thick, rectangular mass covering the entire deep posterior surface of both arytenoids. It may be considered to originate along the muscular process and lateral border of one arytenoid and to cross over to reach the lateral edge of the other arytenoid. It draws the arytenoids medially by a gliding action which adducts the vocal folds. (Kaplan 1960:151)

It opposes the action of the lateral cricoarytenoids. The other part of the arytenoid muscle complex is the *oblique arytenoid* muscle. It is a paired muscle in the form of the letter X, and it lies behind the transverse muscle, on its outer surface. Each branch of the oblique muscle starts low down on the backmost surface of the arytenoid and rises crossing to the highest angle of the other arytenoid. Its contraction tilts the tops of the arytenoids towards each other, and in conjunction with the transverse part of the arytenoid muscle, helps to *adduct* the vocal folds (Hardcastle 1976:79; Heffner 1950:21; Kaplan 1960:151; van den Berg 1968:294).

The second muscular action which can help to close the glottis is the contraction of the muscles forming the vocal folds themselves, the thyroarytenoids. The thyroarytenoids make a double contribution. The *vocalis* muscles (the part of the thyroarytenoids which make up the medial body of the folds nearest to the edges of the glottis) contract to exert *longitudinal tension* in the vocal folds, which reduces the length of the glottis (van den Berg 1968:294). Contraction of the outer, lateral parts of the thyroarytenoid muscles helps the lateral cricoarytenoids to bring the vocal processes of the arytenoids together.

To summarize the muscular actions which lead to glottal closure, then, van den Berg writes:

A contraction of the (powerful) interarytenoid muscles primarily adducts the apexes of the arytenoids and closes the back part of them so that no wild air can escape ... A contraction of the lateral cricoarytenoid muscles adducts the vocal processes of the arytenoids and therefore the body of the vocal folds. This adduction is augmented by a contraction of the lateral parts of the thyroarytenoid muscles (this contraction goes along with an adduction of the vocal folds). These adductional forces provide a medial compression of the vocal folds and reduce the length of the glottis which is effectively free to vibrate. (van den Berg 1968:294)

It is useful to set up a simple map for discussing the different locations in the glottis which are relevant to the characteristics of the different types of phonation. A useful point of reference for this is the *vocal ligament*, which runs along the glottal edge of each vocal fold at the point where it normally makes contact with the other. We can then follow Catford (1964:32) in using the term 'glottal', without any further qualification, to mean the whole length of the opening between the true vocal folds, from the front angle of the thyroid cartilage to the back of the arytenoids; and we can distinguish the *ligamental* glottis, which is the part of the full glottis formed by the vocalis muscles, with the length of the vocal ligaments along each edge, as opposed to the *cartilaginous* glottis, in the stretch where the arytenoid cartilages are located. The dimensions of these sections are of interest: Morris (1953) says that the 'intermembranous' (ligamental) part of the glottis is normally about 15.5 mm in the male, and 11.5 mm in the female. The length of the cartilaginous glottis is about 7.5 mm in the male and 5.5 mm in the female. This makes the full glottal length in males about 23 mm, and about 17 mm in females. Kaplan

(1960:128) adds that 'The widest part of the glottis is 6 to 8 mm in the male, and this can increase to about 12 mm, according to conditions.'

The nature of the glottis tempts one to regard it as a two-dimensional space; and for many phonetic purposes, that is sufficient. But in the case of contributions to the fine detail of phonatory quality, the need to take account of the changing three-dimensional configuration of the space between the vocal folds is very similar to the situation at the other end of the vocal tract, at the lips. The changing vertical thickness of the vocal folds from the outer wall inwards to the vocal ligaments at the edge of the glottal space reflects the interplay of the different tensions that are exerted in and on the folds by the laryngeal musculature, and this third, vertical dimension is one factor among others which differentiates the major settings of the phonatory mechanism.

We are now in a position to isolate some parameters of laryngeal control which are relevant to our discussion of different phonatory settings. From the account of laryngeal physiology offered above, three parameters of muscular tension emerge which have to interact with aerodynamic factors of pulmonic airflow and pressure. They are: *adductive tension, medial compression* and *longitudinal tension*. The second of these, medial compression, is the factor most in need of definition. As described by van den Berg and Tan (1959), van den Berg (1968), Broad (1973) and Hardcastle (1976), medial compression is a composite adductive product of the action of a number of muscles, including the interarytenoids, the lateral cricoarytenoids and the lateral parts of the thyroarytenoids. This conception of medial compression overlaps that of adductive tension, and it will be convenient to try to distinguish these two effects more sharply. One useful purpose in creating a distinction in this area is to facilitate a differentiation of phonatory settings, and to offer a tentative physiological explanation for some observed incompatibilities between settings which inhibit their co-occurrence. For this specific purpose, *adductive tension* will be defined here as the tension of the interarytenoid muscles, whose consequence will be to bring the arytenoid cartilages together, closing the cartilaginous glottis and hence also the ligamental glottis. *Medial compression* will be defined as the compressional pressure on the vocal processes of the arytenoid cartilages achieved by contraction of the lateral cricoarytenoid muscles and reinforced by tension in the lateral parts of the thyroarytenoid muscles. Medial compression will close the ligamental glottis, but whether the cartilaginous glottis also closes will depend on the analytically separate adductive tension achieved by the interarytenoid muscles. A possible acoustic correlate of medial compression is discussed in Chapter 4. *Longitudinal tension*, straightforwardly, is achieved by contraction of the vocalis and/or the cricothyroid muscles. The geometric relationship of these three parameters is illustrated schematically in Figure 16. Each different phonatory setting will be seen to have different specifications in terms of these three physiological parameters.

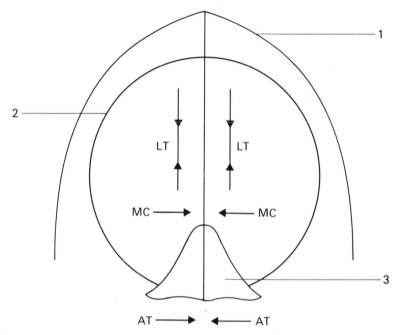

Figure 16. Geometric relationship between three laryngeal parameters

LT – longitudinal tension   1. Thyroid cartilage
MC – medial compression   2. Cricoid cartilage
AT – adductive tension   3. Arytenoid cartilage

3.1.1 *Modal voice*

Hollien (1974) makes the following comments about his choice of the term 'modal' for this phonation type:

The *modal* register is a term I have used for some years; originally, I favoured the term 'normal' to identify this register. However, as van den Berg pointed out (in a personal communication) the use of the label 'normal' would imply that the other registers were abnormal and, of course, his logic is correct. Accordingly, the modal register is so named because it includes the range of fundamental frequencies that are normally used in speaking and singing (i.e. the mode). It is a rather inclusive term and many individuals – especially workers in vocal music – would argue that this entity actually constitutes a set of registers or sub-registers including either two (chest and head) or three (low, mid and high) separate entities. I concede the tradition of such an approach, but ... I have yet to find reasonably convincing evidence that such sub-registers do indeed exist. (Hollien 1974:126)

It may well be that the type of phonation discussed in this book under 'modal voice' should be differentiated into at least two sub-types corresponding to what are called 'chest voice' and 'head voice'. But it will be assumed in what follows that the type of phonation involved in 'modal voice' essentially corresponds to the 'chest voice' register, to the extent that different workers seem to agree on aspects of its production.

The laryngeal characteristics of modal voice, as the neutral mode of phonation, are reasonably well agreed. Catford says that the full glottis is involved, 'both ligamental and cartilaginous, functioning as a single unit' (Catford 1964: 32). He specifies the following details:

Periodic vibration of the vocal folds under pressure from below ... For normal voice the liminal pressure-drop across the glottis is of the order of 3 cm of water. Rates of flow vary according to types of the voice ('registers'): for chest voice at about 100 cps the liminal rate of flow is about 5 cl/sec, maximal about 23 cl/sec. These are mean flow-rates: during the open phase of vocal fold vibration flow-rates much in excess of these must occur, and since the glottal area is small the general aerodynamic picture is of a series of high-velocity jets shot into the pharynx. (Catford 1964:31)

Citing Chiba and Kajiyama (1958), Fant suggests a 'normal air consumption of 140 cm^3/sec at a subglottal pressure of ... $16 \text{ cm H}_2\text{O}$ ... during phonation at medium intensity and Fo = 144 c/s ... the corresponding particle velocity is 5200 cm/sec and the mean glottis opening 0.027 cm^2' (Fant 1960:269).

Van den Berg specifies the physiological aspects of modal voice (i.e. chest voice register) as follows:

This register is characterized by large amplitudes of the vocal folds at low pitches. This requires small passive longitudinal tensions in the vocal ligaments. The minimal values of the interarytenoid contraction and medial compression are small. The vocal folds are short and thick. An increase of the active longitudinal tension in the vocalis muscle increases the pitch. Contraction of the cricothyroid muscles increases the pitch, but, when the passive longitudinal tension in the vocal ligaments increases beyond a rather small value, the vibrations either cease, at a small medial compression, or transit suddenly to the falsetto type, at a sufficiently large medial compression. (van den Berg 1968: 297)

By 'passive longitudinal tension' van den Berg means the tension exercised on the vocal ligament by the action of the strong cricothyroid muscle; such passive tension in the vocal ligament 'can be increased far beyond the maximal active tension in a contracting muscle, on account of the fact that the forces supplied by the comparatively thick cricothyroid muscles are exerted upon the comparatively thin vocal ligaments' (van den Berg, 1968: 295–6).

The production of modal voice is thus carried out with only moderate adductive tension and moderate medial compression, with moderate longitudinal tension when the fundamental frequency is in the lower part of the range used in ordinary conversation. The vibration of the larynx in this condition is regularly periodic, efficient in producing vibration, and without audible friction brought on by incomplete closure of the glottis. A laryngogram of modal voice is included in Figure 17, and a spectrogram in Figure 18.

During phonation, the opening of the adult male glottis has been described by Fant as having the following dimensions:

The glottis slit has an effective length of the order of 12 mm in the chest register and the maximal width is of the order of 2.5 mm at a moderate voice effort. The depth of the passage in the direction of the air stream that comes into contact during the closed phase is of the order of 2–5 mm. (Fant 1960: 266)

The acoustic characteristics of modal voice, as the neutral laryngeal setting, have already been given in Chapter 1.

Having outlined the characteristics of modal voice, we can now move on to the description of other phonatory settings, and their various possibilities of combination.

Each of the major phonatory settings will be discussed individually, but there are two criteria by which they can be grouped into categories, and the classification of the different settings into these categories reveals some useful generalities that might be lost sight of in a simple, sequential listing. The description of the different phonatory settings will be prefaced, therefore, by an outline of the classification.

The two criteria of classification can be expressed as questions. Firstly, 'Can the phonation type occur alone, as a *simple* type?', and secondly, 'Can the phonation type occur in combination with other phonation types, as a *compound* type, and if so, with which?'.

On this basis, there are three different categories involved.

The first category is made up of *modal voice* and *falsetto*. The

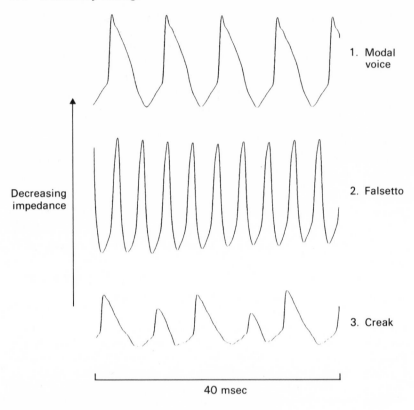

Figure 17a. Laryngograms of simple phonation types
1. Modal voice   2. Falsetto   3. Creak

qualification for membership of this category is that they can each occur alone, as simple types, and can individually combine with members of other groups, as compound types, but *not* with each other.

The second category consists of *whisper* and *creak*. These can occur alone, as simple types, and together as a compound type, to give *whispery creak*. They can also occur as compound types with either member of the first group, giving *whispery voice* and *whispery falsetto*, and *creaky voice* and *creaky falsetto*; and they can occur as compound types with members of the first group *and* with each other, giving *whispery creaky voice* and *whispery creaky falsetto*.

The third category is formed by modificatory settings which can *only* occur in compound types of phonation, and never by themselves as simple types. These are *harshness* and *breathiness*.

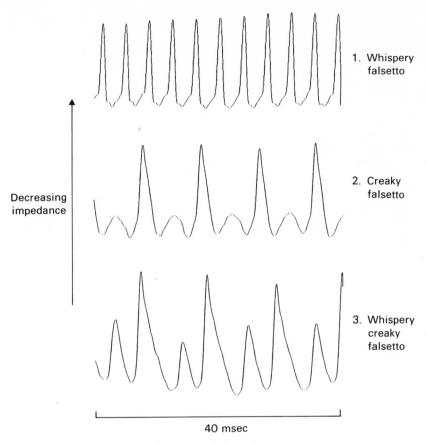

Figure 17b. Laryngograms of compound phonation types
    1. Whispery falsetto   3. Whispery creaky falsetto
    2. Creaky falsetto

    Harshness can combine with modal voice and with falsetto, to produce *harsh voice* and *harsh falsetto*. Breathiness can only combine with modal voice, to give *breathy voice*; the reasons for the incompatibility of falsetto and breathiness will be explored later. Harshness and breathiness cannot combine with the phonation types from the second category, whisper and creak and whispery creak, unless there is a member from the first category, either modal voice or falsetto, also present. Because the mutual incompatibility of breathiness and falsetto still applies, the only multiple compound products of this category of settings are thus *harsh whispery voice, harsh whispery falsetto, harsh creaky voice, harsh creaky falsetto, harsh whispery creaky voice,* and *harsh whispery creaky falsetto*.

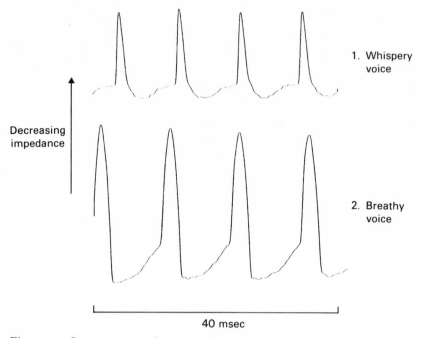

1. Whispery voice

Decreasing impedance

2. Breathy voice

40 msec

Figure 17c. Laryngograms of compound phonation types
1. Whispery voice   2. Breathy voice

The omissions of nominal possibilities from the above list, such as *breathy falsetto*, are to be explained by either redundant or conflicting acoustic requirements, or by conflicting physiological requirements. A tentative physiological explanation will be advanced in terms of mutually exclusive specifications of the phonatory settings involved on one or more of the three muscular parameters of longitudinal tension, adductive tension and medial compression, as indicated earlier. It is important to emphasize the tentative nature of this proposed explanation: it is offered here as a physiological hypothesis that emerges from the wide range of laryngeal research cited. The attractiveness of the hypothesis is clear: the auditorily-observed compatibility and incompatibility of the various different phonatory settings in compound phonations is given a physiological basis. But the hypothesis must be subjected to empirical test by physiological research before it can be elevated to the status of a reliable explanation.

There is one sub-category that should be mentioned, and it is a sub-category of the harshness setting. This is the setting where the ventricular

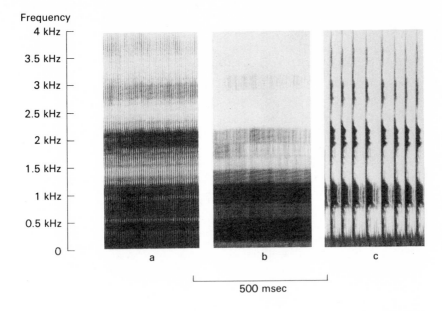

500 msec

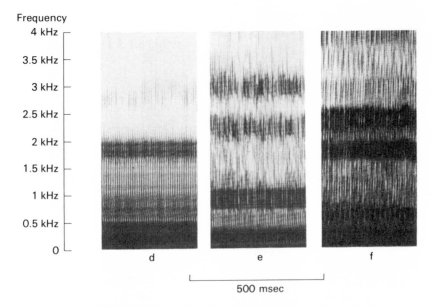

500 msec

Figure 18. Spectrograms of steady-state vowels with six phonatory settings
    a. modal voice   d. breathy voice
    b. falsetto   e. whispery voice
    c. creak   f. harsh voice

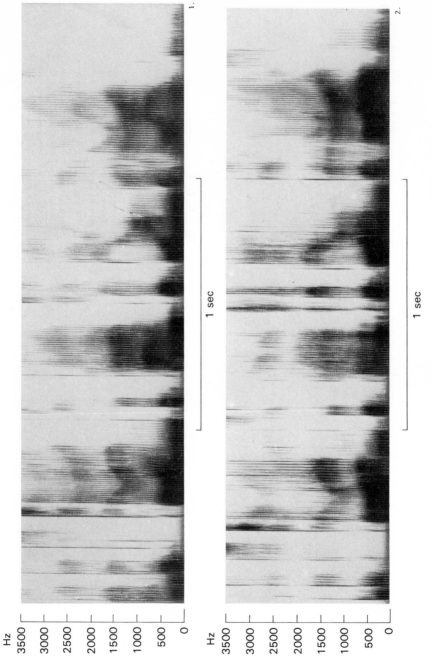

Figure 19a. Spectrograms of the phrase 'its two ends apparently beyond the
horizon', with different settings
1. Neutral setting   2. Lowered larynx setting

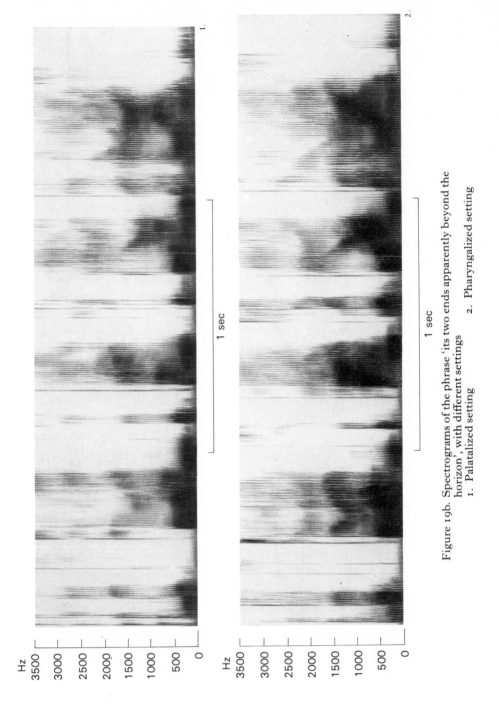

Figure 19b. Spectrograms of the phrase 'its two ends apparently beyond the
horizon', with different settings
1. Palatalized setting   2. Pharyngalized setting

folds become involved in the phonation of the true vocal folds by squeezing closed the ventricle of Morgagni and pressing down on the true vocal folds, with the effect that the true and the ventricular folds combine to vibrate as more massive, composite elements. In order to bring the ventricular folds to this position, a high degree of muscular tension is needed, and the effect is normally to make phonation auditorily very harsh. *Ventricular voice* will therefore be used in the descriptive system, but only as a synonym for 'extremely harsh voice'. The use of the label 'ventricular' is physiologically explicit, but not enough is yet known about phonation with the ventricular folds, in terms of combinatorial possibilities, to give ventricular phonation independent status as a separate phonation type.

3.1.2 *Falsetto*

Hollien (1971:329) suggests that modal voice and falsetto are 'completely different laryngeal operations'. Earlier, modal voice was described as having moderate adductive tension, moderate medial compression, and moderate longitudinal tension. Falsetto is different in all three respects. Van den Berg (1968:298) states that adductive tension of the interarytenoid muscles is high, medial compression of the glottis is large, and longitudinal passive tension of the vocal ligaments is also high (though there is little active longitudinal tension in the vocalis muscles).

There is a reasonably wide measure of agreement in recent accounts of the laryngeal mechanisms responsible for the production of falsetto. The summary account below of the physiology of falsetto is based on a number of sources: Chiba and Kajiyama 1958: Hollien 1971; Hollien and Colton 1969; Judson and Weaver 1942; Kaplan 1960; Luchsinger and Arnold 1965; Rubin and Hirt 1960; van den Berg 1968; Van Riper and Irwin 1958; Zemlin 1964.

The consensus of these sources describes the production of falsetto as follows. The arytenoid cartilages adduct the vocal folds, by contraction of the interarytenoid and the lateral cricoarytenoid muscles. The vocalis muscles along the glottal edge of each vocal fold remain relaxed, but the mass of each vocal fold is made stiff and immobile by contraction of the thyroarytenoid muscles, which make up the outer bulk of the folds. The vocal ligaments along the glottal edge of the vocal folds are put under strong tension by the contraction of the cricothyroid muscle. This results in the vertical cross-section of the edges of the vocal folds becoming thin. The glottis often remains slightly apart, and the characteristic sub-glottal air pressure is lower than for modal voice (Van Riper and Irwin 1958, 228; Kunze 1964). Van Riper and Irwin suggest here that with the vocalis muscles relaxed, and only the thin margins of the vocal folds participating in phonatory vibration, the expenditure of air is bound to be reduced. They cite Trojan (1952) as showing that oxygen consumption is decreased in falsetto voice, compared with modal voice.

The finding that the glottis often remains slightly open has prompted a number of writers to suggest that falsetto voice is usually accompanied by 'friction noises' (Judson and Weaver 1942: 74) or 'breathiness' (Zemlin 1964:155). Given that the width of opening is small, this fricative component is much more likely to be of the whispery rather than the breathy sort. This position is reinforced by van den Berg's statement that the forces giving medial compression of the folds (i.e. a compressive tendency at right angles to the front-to-back axis of the glottis) are strong (van den Berg 1968: 298). On the other hand, the whispery effect may be only slight, if transglottal airflow is small. Chiba and Kajiyama (1958: 28) report a finding that supports this:

It is found that the edges of the vocal chords remain covered here and there with small lumps of mucus, which means that the air is not exhaled abruptly. (In the chest register, especially in 'sharp voice', the small lumps of mucus on the edges of the vocal chords are blown away as soon as the voice starts.)

(Chiba and Kajiyama's 'sharp voice' is discussed in the next chapter, on overall tension settings.) Laryngograms of falsetto, whispery falsetto, creaky falsetto and whispery creaky falsetto are included in Figure 17. A spectrogram of falsetto is shown in Figure 18.

Falsetto is characterized acoustically by a number of factors: the first is that the fundamental frequency tends to be considerably higher than in modal voice. The pitch-control mechanism is different from that in modal voice; van den Berg (1968: 298) writes that

In chest voice the passive tension in the vocal ligaments needs to remain small when the active tension in the vocalis muscles is increased to attain the highest pitches. In falsetto voice, however, the active tension in the vocalis muscles needs to remain small when the passive tension in the vocal ligaments is increased [by the cricothyroid muscle – J.L.] to attain the highest pitches. The registers overlap in the region of medium pitches.

Hollien and Michel (1968: 602) found that the average pitch-range for male falsetto was 275–634 Hz, as against the average range for modal voice, which was 94–287 Hz.

The second acoustic characteristic derives from the interaction of high fundamental frequency and the mode of vibration of the vocal folds. Zemlin writes that

High speed motion pictures of the larynx during falsetto production reveal that the folds vibrate and come into contact only at the free borders, and that the remainder of the folds remain relatively fixed. Further, the folds appear long, stiff and very thin along the edges ... The quality of tone produced by falsetto is almost flute-like in nature. This is partly due to the rather simple form of vibration executed by the vocal folds, and partly due to the high rate of vibration ... when the fundamental frequency is very high, the harmonically-related overtones are widely separated in frequency, and consequently in any given frequency range there will be fewer components in the sound produced than there is in a voice with a lower fundamental frequency. This partly accounts for the rich quality of the bass voice when compared with the 'thin' quality of the tenor voice. (Zemlin 1964:155)

The third acoustic characteristic is that the slope of the spectrum of the laryngeal waveform is much steeper than for modal voice, falling at about −20dB per octave (Monsen and Engebretson 1977:988). Also, whereas the spectrum of modal voice falls off more steeply with increasing frequency, falsetto seems to have a more regular decrement (Monsen and Engebretson, *loc. cit.*) Finally, while modal voice has a closing portion of the laryngeal waveform as the more abrupt component, in falsetto it is the opening portion that is steeper (Monsen and Engebretson *loc. cit.*).

In the Hanson experiment mentioned in the Introduction, the general finding was that less efficient modes of phonation (such as falsetto, and compound creak phonations) all have a greater spectral slope than modal voice, and that as fundamental frequency rises within a given phonation type, the spectral slope becomes steeper (Hanson, personal communication).

Falsetto is a phonation type that does not seem to be exploited for linguistic purposes. But it frequently has a paralinguistic function, governed by conventional usage, in a variety of cultures. In Tzeltal, a Mayan language of Mexico, speakers 'use sustained falsetto as [an] honorific feature; it is enjoined in greeting formulae, and may spread over an entire formal interaction' (Brown and Levinson 1978:272).

3.1.3 *Whisper*

The physiology of the whisper setting of the phonatory mechanism is not controversial. Nearly all writers agree that the chief physiological characteristic of whisper is a triangular opening of the cartilaginous glottis, comprising about a third of the full length of the glottis (Pressman 1942). The shape of the glottis in whispering is often referred to as an inverted letter Y. (Luchsinger and Arnold 1965:119). In weak whisper, the triangular opening can be fairly long, including part of the ligamental as well as the cartilaginous glottis. With increasing intensity, the glottis is increasingly constricted until only the cartilaginous section remains just open. Taken together, these factors suggest low adductive tension, and moderate to high medial compression.

The triangular opening of the glottis is achieved by the following factors: the lateral cricoarytenoid muscles contract, 'toe-ing in' the vocal processes of the arytenoid cartilages (Zemlin 1964:169). The muscles which normally approximate the bodies of the arytenoid, the inter-arytenoid muscles, remain relaxed (Heffner 1950: 20). This facilitates the toe-ing in of the arytenoids as they pivot on the cricoid. As the air flows past the edges of the open cartilaginous glottis, the characteristic 'whisper' sound quality is produced by 'eddies generated by friction of the air in and above the larynx' (van den Berg 1968: 297).

The whisper setting is a very uneconomical use of airflow (Luchsinger and Arnold 1965:119; Zemlin 1964:169). Catford describes the aerodynamic and acoustic aspects of whisper in the following terms:

Glottis constricted (estimated area, from the smallest possible chink up to about 25% of maximal glottal area). Critical rate of flow about 2.5 cl/sec, estimated critical velocity about 1900 cm/sec. Maximum rate of flow about 500 cl/sec. Turbulent flow, with production of high-velocity jet into pharynx. Acoustic spectrum similar to breath but with considerably more concentration of acoustic energy into formant-like bands. Auditory effect: a relatively 'rich' hushing sound. (Catford 1964: 31)

When whisper combines with another laryngeal setting such as modal voice or falsetto, to give compound phonations of whispery voice or whispery falsetto, then there is necessarily a greater amount of interharmonic noise than in the simple phonations of modal voice or falsetto alone (Hanson, personal communication).

Laryngograms of whispery voice, whispery falsetto and whispery creaky falsetto can be seen in Figure 17. A spectrogram of whispery voice is shown in Figure 18.

Whisper does not seem to be used for contrastive linguistic purposes. However, it is phonetically characteristic of the utterance-final devoicing process in many languages, including English and French. Ladefoged cites Doke (1931) as reporting that the use of whisper as 'a ·prosody associated with the otherwise voiced sounds in final syllables … is common in the Bantu family' (Ladefoged 1971:16). Whisper is also found in a similar role in English, in juxtapositional assimilation. Partial regressive assimilation of voicelessness often results in an otherwise voiced consonant being whispered, as in the phrase 'his son' pronounced with the final consonant of 'his' with the vocal folds in a whisper position (Abercrombie 1967:137).

The use of whisper in a paralinguistic function is very widespread. In English, and perhaps in the vast majority of cultures, to whisper is to signal secrecy or confidentiality.

3.1.4 *Creak*

Creak is also called *vocal fry* or *glottal fry* in the phonetic literature, particularly by American researchers.

Catford gives the following details:

Low frequency (down to about 40 cps) periodic vibration of a small section of the vocal folds. Mean rates of flow very low – of the order of 1.25 to 2 cl/sec. The precise physiological mechanism of creak is unknown, but only a very small section of the ligamental glottis, near the thyroid end, is involved. The auditory effect is of a rapid series of taps, like a stick being run along a railing. (Catford 1964:32)

The low fundamental frequency of this creak type of phonation is one factor that distinguishes it from harsh voice, which is otherwise somewhat similar. While the mean fundamental frequency for creak has been found to be 34.6 Hz, in an average range for male speakers of 24–52 Hz, the mean fundamental frequency for harsh voice is said to be 122.1 Hz, with a range similar to that of modal voice, whose average range is 94–287 Hz, according to Michel and Hollien (1968), and Michel (1964). Michel (1968) also reports that harsh voices seem to have fundamental frequencies consistently above 100 Hz, and vocal fry (i.e. creak) consistently below 100 Hz. It is fundamental frequency characteristics of this sort that led Hollien, Moore, Wendahl and Michel (1966:246) to suggest that vocal fry 'is best described as a phonational register occurring at frequencies below those of the modal register'.

The specification of fundamental frequency characteristics is not, of course, enough. Comment on laryngeal factors contributing to auditory quality is also needed. These factors are described by Hollien, Moore, Wendahl and Michel (1966:247) as follows:

(1) the vocal folds when adducted are relatively thick and apparently compressed, (2) the ventricular folds are somewhat adducted also, and (3) the inferior surfaces of the false folds actually come in contact with the superior surfaces of the true vocal folds. Thus, an unusually thick, compact (but not necessarily tense) structure is created prior to the initiation of phonation. Under these conditions it might be expected that the false vocal folds would vibrate in synchrony with the true folds. However, since there is no evidence to support this conjecture, it is possible that their position is either the incidental result of basic laryngeal adjustments or serves to produce a damping of the vocal fold movement. It would be predicted also that vibration is initiated and maintained by relatively low subglottal pressures; that airflow, if measured, would be considerably less than for most other phonational events.

A number of experimental studies support their hypotheses. Moore (1971), on the basis of frontal stroboscopic laminagrams, suggests that

vocal fry may ... be produced when the mass of the vibrators is increased by the collaboration of the ventricular folds. These structures appear in x-ray photographs to combine the ventricular folds functionally with the vocal folds to form massive bilateral vibrators that move with relatively small amplitude. It is presumed that this mechanism is capable of both impeding the flow of air, even when there is considerable pressure, and of releasing a series of pulses in which the channel is open for relatively short portions of the cycle. (Moore 1971:72)

Fónagy (1962) investigated the influence of affective states on the mode of phonation, by means of laryngoscopy, tomography and asymmetrical radiography, and described what he called the 'creaky' voice of 'suppressed rage' as having ventricular folds pressed hard against each other, the ventricle of Morgagni wrinkled, the vocal folds held tightly together and the air column vertically through the larynx narrowed to a line – all matching the picture suggested by Hollien and his co-workers of phonation with strong adductive tension and medial compression, but little longitudinal tension, and with vigorous ventricular involvement.

More recent work by Hollien, Damsté and Murry (1969), has provided some support also, in their finding that the control of fundamental frequency in vocal fry is not achieved by the same mechanism as in modal voice; while vocal fold length in modal voice increases with fundamental frequency, and vocal fold thickness is inversely related to the frequency (Hollien and Michel 1968), in vocal fry neither the length nor the thickness of the vocal folds seem to vary with changes in pitch. This suggests that control of fundamental frequency is managed by the aerodynamic component of the aerodynamic–myoelastic phonatory action, rather than the myoelastic component, and the sub-glottal air pressure should reflect this. This has not yet been established experimentally, although Murry and Brown (1971) have shown that, consistent with the hypothesis of Hollien *et al.* mentioned above, the overall sub-glottal air pressure in vocal fry is 'always less than that for the modal phonation' (Murry and Brown 1971:446); McGlone (1967) and Murry (1969) have found lower airflow values for vocal fry than for modal voice.

Monsen and Engebretson (1977:989) give an account of 'creaky voice', which for them is synonymous with 'vocal fry', in broadly similar terms:

> The fundamental frequency of creaky voice ranges from 30 to 90 Hz. Because of the way it is produced (slack vocal folds and low subglottal air pressure), the period-to-period variations in fundamental frequency are quite high. In the extreme, one period may last 33 msec, followed by one of 11 msec and then one of 18 msec. The glottal waveform of creaky voice is thus highly irregular ... The glottal spectrum of creaky voice falls off less steeply than that of all other glottal samples, but because of the extremely low fundamental frequency, the overall distribution of energy associated with normal voice phonation is maintained.

A different aspect of creak, or vocal fry, is the 'auditory effect ... of a rapid series of taps, like a stick being run along a railing' that Catford (1964) mentions in the passage quoted at the beginning of this section on creak. The effect of continual, separate taps in rapid sequence is an essential part of the characteristic auditory quality of creak. Hollien and Wendahl (1968:506) have described the acoustic correlate of this effect as 'a train of discrete excitations or pulses produced by the larynx', using 'pulse' to mean 'any of a variety of glottal waveforms of brief duration separated by varying periods of no excitation'. In this connection, Wendahl, Moore and Hollien (1963:254) have suggested that 'the primary criterion which must be met in order for the signal to be perceived as vocal fry is that the vocal tract be highly damped between glottal excitations'. They also note that the fundamental frequency of vocal fry can vary between 20 and 90 Hz, and still be heard as vocal fry provided that the vocal tract is nearly completely damped in between the occurrence of successive wave-fronts. Coleman (1963) specifies that vocal fry is perceived whenever the vocal tract wave is allowed to decay by 42 to 44 dB of its maximum amplitude for a single pulse, and when the wave is allowed to decay by only 30 dB between the excitation pulses, vocal fry is not perceived. This criterion also allows for the possibility not only of trains of single, discrete pulses, but also for a sub-category of vocal fry where there is 'a vibratory pattern in which the vocal cords separate twice in quick succession and then approximate firmly in a relatively long closed phase'; this double-pulse train was discovered in an investigation using very high-speed cinefilm of the vibrating glottis, and was given the name 'dicrotic dysphonia' by the investigators (Moore and von Leden 1958:235). Monsen and Engebretson (1977:989) also refer to the possibility of 'double-pulse' phonation of this sort. Double-pulsing can be seen in the laryngogram of creak that is included in Figure 17. (Laryngograms of creaky falsetto and whispery creaky falsetto can also be seen in the same figure.) Hollien and Wendahl (1968:509) have also suggested the possibility of triple-pulse trains in vocal fry.

The perceptual necessity of damped laryngeal pulses gives quite strong plausibility to the suggestion by Hollien, Moore, Wendahl and Michel (1966:247) noted earlier, that the function of the ventricular folds coming into contact with the surfaces of the vocal folds may be to damp the movements of the vocal folds; damping of this sort would also have the effect, observed in creak, of elongating the closed phase of each vibratory cycle (Moore 1971:72).

This damped aspect of vocal fry also lends credibility to the comment reported in the previous chapter on velopharyngeal settings, made by Van Riper and Irwin (1958:244) to the effect that they 'suspect that some of what has been termed "nasal twang" is merely the presence of glottal fry'. The validity of their remark resides in the fact that nasality shares what is arguably one of its most important characteristics with vocal fry – that of a damped vocal system.

An example of the low-frequency, discrete pulses of creak can be seen in the spectrogram shown in Figure 18.

A term often used in the linguistic literature as a synonym for creak (and creaky voice, a compound phonation blending modal voice and creak, discussed in more detail below), is 'laryngealization'. Ladefoged writes that:

Another mode of vibration of the vocal cords occurs in laryngealized sounds. In this type of phonation the arytenoid cartilages are pressed inward so that the posterior portions of the vocal cords are held together and only the anterior (ligamental) portions are able to vibrate. The result is often a harsh sound with a comparatively low pitch. It is also known as vocal fry and creaky voice. (Ladefoged 1971:14–15)

Ladefoged makes it clear that in his view only a small length of the ligamental glottis is in vibration (1971:8), and also indicates that while a distinction may be drawn between creak and creaky voice, for his own linguistically-motivated purposes such a distinction is not necessary (1971:15). With allowance for these two points, Ladefoged's description of laryngealization is in accord with the description offered here of creak (rather than of creaky voice). Laryngealization plays a phonological role in many languages, including Arabic, Chadic and Nilotic languages (Ladefoged 1971:15, 42). In Danish, 'two such words as *hun* "she" and *hund* "dog" are pronounced alike except for a difference of register, the second having creaky voice' (Abercrombie 1967:101). In many tone languages, syllables with low or falling tones are phonetically charac- terized by creak or creaky voice. In English, in the paralinguistic regulation of interaction (Laver 1976:351), speakers of Received Pronunciation often use creak or creaky voice, simultaneously with a low falling intonation, as a signal of completion of their turn as speaker, yielding the floor to the listener. When used throughout an utterance, creaky voice signals bored resignation, in the paralinguistic conventions of English. In Tzeltal, the Mayan language mentioned earlier, creaky voice is used paralinguistically 'to express commiseration and complaint, and to invite commiseration' (Brown and Levinson 1978:272).

Another term in the linguistic literature which has a partial overlap with 'creak' and 'creaky voice' is 'glottalization'. However, this has been used as a cover term for such a wide variety of other phenomena as well, such as 'ejectives, implosives, laryngealized sounds, and pulmonic articulations accompanied by glottal stops' (Ladefoged 1971:28), that it is probably best to disregard it here, except to note one salient principle apparently held in common by the reference of both 'laryngealization' and 'glottalization'. That is, whatever else they may refer to, both terms suggest a tendency to constriction at the laryngeal level. This is strongly in keeping with the general laryngeal characterization of creak and creaky voice offered here, where the glottis is subjected to strong adductive tension and medial compression, with vigorous ventricular involvement.

3.1.5 Harshness

It will be recalled that 'harshness' is a quality taken on by a number of other phonation types. It will be discussed here as a modification of modal voice, for convenience of exposition. Applied to modal voice, harshness should be thought of not as contributing substantially new parameters to the mode of phonation, but rather as boosting the values of some of the parameters already operating. We shall return to this in a moment.

A number of writers have given auditory descriptions of the quality associated with *harsh voice*. Sherman and Linke (1952) call it 'an unpleasant, rough, rasping sound'; Holmes (1932) says it is 'a raucous voice quality'; Milisen (1957) writes that harsh voice is a 'rasping sound associated with excessive approximation of the vocal folds'; Van Riper (1954) calls it 'strident'. The widely used label for this quality, 'harshness', seems well-chosen.

The acoustic characteristics of harsh voice are concerned chiefly with irregularity of the glottal wave-form and spectral noise. Fairbanks (1960) said that 'Irregular, aperiodic noise in the vocal fold spectrum is the distinguishing feature of harshness.' Michel (1964) also says that 'harsh voices are characterized by aperiodicity or noise in the spectrum, a normal fundamental frequency level and larger than normal perturbations about the mean fundamental frequency'. The view that small cycle-to-cycle variations in fundamental frequency are associated with voices judged to be harsh is supported by Coleman (1960), Moore (1962), Thompson (1962) and Wendahl (1963). Wendahl (1964) carried out an acoustic analysis of the role of amplitude variations of the laryngeal waveform in voices judged to be harsh, and found that successive wave-fronts tended to be of unequal amplitude. Using LADIC, an electric laryngeal analogue for producing synthetic waveforms, he established that these characteristic amplitude irregularities made a significant contribution to the perception of harsh 'roughness' (Wendahl 1964).

The predominant characteristic is the aperiodicity of the fundamental frequency, which is heard as a component of auditory *quality* rather than of auditory pitch. This aperiodicity has been referred to as a pitch 'jitter' (Cooper, Peterson and Fahringer 1957:183). Listeners are very sensitive to even very small amounts of such jitter. Wendahl (1963) used LADIC in his investigations of laryngeal waveform irregularity to establish the contribution of pitch jitter to harshness. He presented listeners with synthetic stimuli which

varied in the magnitude of frequency differences between successive cycles. For each of two median fundamental frequencies, a 100 and a 200 cps condition, stimuli were generated to have frequency variations on successive cycles of $+/-$ 10 cps, 8 cps, 6 cps, 4 cps, 2 cps, and 1 cps. 535 listeners judged the stimuli on the basis of which sounded the most rough. The results show that even very slight frequency variations, as little as $+/-$ 1 cps around a median fundamental frequency of 100 cps, sounded rough. (Wendahl 1963: 248)

Wendahl also showed that greater auditory roughness was related to greater deviations from the fundamental frequency, and that the same absolute amount of deviation sounded less rough when superimposed on a fundamental of higher frequency; so if the 100 Hz median frequency were taken to represent a male voice and the 200 Hz median a female one, then the same deviation, say $+/-5$ Hz, would make the male voice sound rougher (*op. cit.* pp. 248–9). The same principle underlies Hess's finding that harshness in higher-pitched voices is judged as less severe than in lower-pitched ones (Hess 1959). This may help to explain the impression that harsh voice is heard much less commonly in women than in men.

Coleman and Wendahl (1967) also used LADIC to make synthetic stimuli in an experiment investigating the relationship between the proportion of pitch-jitter present in a stimulus and the degree of perceived roughness. They found that:

As the relative duration of jitter elements within a signal is increased, listeners will evaluate the signal as increasing in roughness. It makes little, if any, difference to listeners whether jitter segments occur at the beginning or end of stimuli. A large jitter signal of short duration may be judged to be less rough than a small jitter signal of less jitter excursion [i.e. less degree of frequency deviation from the median – J.L.] but having longer duration within a stimulus. (Coleman and Wendahl 1967:92)

The relevance of this last study, which will be commented on in more detail in a moment, lies in the relationship between segmental pronunciation and the everyday perception of voice quality. A number of researchers have found that the judged severity of harshness is correlated with some variables of segmental articulation. Rees (1958), for example, found that harshness on vowels was judged to increase with the openness of the vowel; to be greater when the vowel is in a voiced environment; and more marked on vowels in isolation when initiated with a glottal stop than with a 'soft', 'aspirated' beginning. In connection with this last comment, Craig and Sokolowsky (1945) said that excessive and continuous use of a 'glottal attack' on vowels gives a person's speech a characteristic harsh quality. Van Riper and Irwin (1958:232) agree with this, when discussing harshness as a functional disorder of the voice: 'Very characteristic of this disorder ... is the manner of vocal attack. Glottal catches and stops are common. Vocalization is sudden.' Sherman and Linke (1952) suggest that harshness is judged to be more severe with greater duration of the harsh utterance. Linke (1953) came to the same conclusion as Rees (1958) when she showed that high vowels are judged as less harsh than open vowels; she also showed that, as one would predict, lax vowels are less harsh than their tense counterparts. Although

Coleman and Wendahl used synthetic stimuli (very necessary for precise control of the stimulus variables), their results are nevertheless of direct relevance to the perception of voice quality in the normal situation of spoken interaction. Combining the results of the study by Coleman and Wendahl (1967) with those of Rees (1958), Sherman and Linke (1952) and Linke (1953), we can conclude that harshness in ordinary voices will be of intermittent occurrence, and of variable relative severity depending on the nature, context and duration of the segments involved. The example of the perception of harshness here can be extrapolated to the general perception of voice quality. This is to say that we perceive voice quality by attending to signals of differing duration and auditory prominence, distributed intermittently and irregularly through the stream of speech.

One physiological correlate of harshness is widely agreed. It is laryngeal tension, which underlies what Milisen (1957), quoted above, describes as 'excessive approximation of the vocal folds'. Gray and Wise (1959: 52), for example, say that harshness 'results from overtensions in the throat and neck; it is often if not usually accompanied by hypertensions of the whole body'. Van Riper and Irwin (1958: 232) write that in the case of speakers with harsh voices 'Most of these individuals show marked hypertension both of the (larynx) and of ... the pharynx. Both the suprahyoids and the infrahyoids tend to be strongly contracted, as palpation will demonstrate.' They quote Russell (1936), to the effect that 'as the voice begins to become strident and blatant, one sees the red-surfaced muscles which lie above the vocal cords begin to form a tense channel'. They add that

Most harsh voices are relatively low in pitch, with the average pitch level close to the bottom of the range. The intensity appears louder than in the normal voice, though some of the apparent loudness may come from resonation effects due to the tenseness of the oral and pharyngeal cavities. (Van Riper and Irwin 1958: 232)

Zemlin (1964) agrees with Van Riper and Irwin, when he writes that

the distinguishable feature which differentiates the normal from the harsh voice is aperiodic noise of aperiodic vocal fold vibration. Such vocal fold vibration may well be due to excessive tension in the folds. Support for this line of reasoning comes from the fact that persons with harsh voices tend to initiate phonation with glottal attacks. There is some evidence to suggest that persons with harsh voice quality are phonating at an inappropriate pitch level, usually slightly low for their vocal mechanism. (Zemlin 1964:165)

Kaplan (1960) is quite clear about the responsibility of laryngeal tension for harshness. He says that

Where the folds are drawn too tightly together during phonation rather than being lax, a shrill, harsh, creaking noise, which is called stridency, or stridor, enters the tone. An obstruction of some type is present. Some causes include general tension, spastic paralysis, or often a throat strain or 'pinched throat'. There is excessive constriction of muscles all through the vocal tract, and the tension is great in the external laryngeal muscles. The vibrations of the vocal chords are hindered, and supraglottal friction noises are introduced. (Kaplan 1960:167–8)

Accepting laryngeal tension as established, the question arises as to which type of tension, in the categories set up earlier of *adductive tension, medial compression* and *longitudinal tension*, is involved. Michel (1968) was reported, in the earlier section on creak, as stating that while vocal fry (creak) was characterized by fundamental frequencies consistently below 100 Hz, harshness showed fundamental frequencies consistently (but not markedly) above 100 Hz. This strongly suggests that the laryngeal tension in harshness is not chiefly longitudinal tension, the main mechanism in modal voice for controlling the frequency of vibration of the vocal folds. From the comments noted above, such as 'excessive approximation of the vocal folds', and 'the folds are drawn too tightly together', it seems reasonable to conclude that the exaggerated laryngeal tension in harsh voice is a combination of extreme adductive tension and extreme medial compression, brought about by over-contraction of the muscle systems responsible for these two parameters in modal voice. This is supported by Brackett (1940), cited by Van Riper and Irwin (1958:232), who describes the inflammation of the vocal folds which results from their traumatic abuse by the deliberate, experimental production of harsh voice.

Earlier in this chapter, it was suggested that when harshness became very severe, the ventricular folds become involved in phonation, pressing down on the upper surface of the true vocal folds. *Ventricular voice* was offered as a physiologically more explicit synonym for *severely harsh voice*. It may be helpful to end this section on harshness with some brief comments about this mode of phonation. We can note, initially, that ventricular voice involves considerably greater tension of the ventricular folds than occurs in the ventricular participation in creak mentioned earlier.

Van den Berg (1955) says that 'harsh, metallic voice is made ... when the ventricular folds withdraw into the adjacent tissue, leaving almost no space in the ventricles'. He then goes on to discuss the way that this setting of the larynx serves to boost the relative amplitude of the higher harmonics: spectral features of this sort are summarized in the next chapter, on overall tension settings of the vocal system, and will not be considered further at this point.

Frederickson and Ward (1962), in an article about the possibilities of damaging the larynx by strenuous muscular exertion, say that in pronounced physical effort, 'the true cords are no longer completely approximated, while the false cords remain competent'. Under these circumstances 'the full force of the intralaryngeal pressure is exerted at the ventricular level'. Ventricular voice can be visualized, then, as phonation at extreme effort, with a fine degree of control over the audible quality made impossible by the comparatively large muscular forces exerted. Plotkin (1964) says that ventricular voice, 'once heard is never forgotten', and that the 'characteristic deep, hoarse voice, alike in male and female, causes an almost sympathetic tightening of the listener's throat'. Freud (1962), quoted by Aronson, Peterson and Litin (1964), gives a rather similar picture, of 'ventricular dysphonia', where he 'depicts it as a total, tight, spastic apposition of the constrictors of the larynx and hypopharynx, giving the voice a groaning, animal quality and suggesting to the listener the exertion of extreme effort. The words sound as if they are being chopped off' (Aronson, Peterson and Litin 1964: 369).

These descriptions by Frederickson and Ward, and by Freud, are of course descriptions of voices which have been classed as 'dysphonic', and it does not follow that all voices phonetically classifiable as examples of ventricular voice would use ventricular phonatory effort of quite such extreme degrees. One can hear voices which make use of some contribution by the ventricular folds fairly commonly in everyday life. Sweet noted a quality he called 'the pig's whistle' effect, which he said gave 'a wheezy character to the voice' and which he suggested arose from a 'narrowing of the upper glottis' (Sweet 1877: 97–9): he said that 'it may be heard from Scotchmen [sic], and combined with high key gives the pronunciation of the Saxon Germans its peculiarly harsh character' (Sweet 1906: 73). In the terms offered here, this quality would be called ventricular voice, or possibly whispery ventricular voice. It is still frequently heard as a component in the voice quality characterizing some urban Scots accents. A spectrogram of harsh voice is shown in Figure 18.

Harsh voice and ventricular voice are both used in English as paralinguistic signals of anger. It seems not implausible to suggest a conventional scalar relationship between the degree of harshness and the degree of anger expressed. In this sense, ventricular voice is a signal of more extreme anger, being also correlated with more extreme muscular tension.

3.1.6 *Breathiness*

'Breathiness' is a quality which is quite often heard as a modification of modal voice, giving *breathy voice*. By comparison with modal voice, the mode of vibration of the vocal folds is inefficient, and is accompanied by slight audible friction. Muscular effort is low, with the result that the glottis is kept somewhat open along most of its length, and the folds never meet on the mid-line. Because each closing movement of the folds tends to be abortive, the lessened glottal resistance leads to a higher rate of air-flow than in modal voice.

Catford describes the characteristics of breathy voice as follows:

the sound of voice mixed in with breath. The effect is somewhat like that of sighing. This is *breathy voice*: the glottis is narrowed from its most open position, but not narrowed enough to generate whisper, that is, it is still at considerably more than 25 per cent of its maximal opening, probably, in fact, around 30 to 40 per cent. The vocal folds are vibrating, but without ever closing or, indeed, coming anywhere near closing. They simply 'flap in the breeze' of the high velocity air-flow. The liminal volume-velocity for the production of breathy voice is of the order of 90 to 100 mm^3/s: more commonly, however, it is much faster, around 900 to 1000 cm^3/s. (Catford 1977: 99)

It is clear that the notion of 'breathy voice' thus involves a type of phonation which can be produced on a very wide range of air-flow. Catford takes the position that most examples of what he would classify as breathy voice use a very high rate of air-flow. He suggests, for example, that one should

try filling the lungs to capacity and then generating breathy voice for as long as you can. Owing to the high volume–velocity of breathy voice, this probably will not be more than four or five seconds. Breathy voice often occurs when one tries to blurt out a message when extremely out of breath. It is also the phonation type of 'voiced h' [sic] (Catford 1977: 99).

While agreeing with Catford that breathy voice produced at the lower end of the range of airflow has enough auditorily in common with breathy voice produced at a very high rate of air-flow to justify the use of the same identifying label for such voices, the position is taken here that in normal speaking situations, most examples of breathy voice will use air-flow rates from the *lower* end of the range. Most speakers with breathy voices will thus be able to speak relatively continuously, without needing to pause every four to five seconds to draw breath, unlike the speakers Catford describes who use flow-rates of up to $1000 \ cm^3/s$.

The muscle tension adjustments necessary for breathy voice can be seen as involving minimal adductive tension and weak medial compression, just sufficient to allow aerodynamic forces in the comparatively large volume of transglottal airflow to superimpose on the outflowing air a very inefficient vibration of the vocal folds, with the folds not meeting at the centre line. The one laryngeal tension factor that is controlled more finely is longitudinal tension, in the production of appropriate variations of fundamental frequency for the purposes of intonation. We can assume that the degree of longitudinal tension is rather low, generally. High pitched breathy voices seem rare. Fairbanks (1960:179) comments that 'Breathy quality is almost invariably accompanied by limited vocal intensity [and] low pitch.' A laryngogram of breathy voice can be seen in Figure 17, and a spectrogram in Figure 18.

Breathiness can combine with only one other type of phonation, in the system of describing voice quality offered here: that is, modal voice. This is because, while modal voice requires only moderate medial compression, all the others, falsetto, whisper, creak, harshness and ventricular voice, need a greater amount than is compatible with breathiness.

Many writers have used the label 'breath' to describe components in given voice qualities that should rather have been called 'whispery'. In the descriptive scheme used here it would not be possible, for example, to accept a label which combined 'breathiness' and 'harshness', such as *harsh breathy voice*, for the voice quality often described as 'husky' or 'hoarse', because of the mutually exclusive prerequisites of *breathiness* as here defined and *harshness*. Such a quality would instead be labelled *harsh whispery voice*.

However, it is reasonable to acknowledge that there is a close auditory relationship between breathy voice and whispery voice, as these two compound types of phonation are understood in this descriptive scheme. Both involve the presence of audible friction; to the extent that such friction is concerned, the transition from breathiness to whisperiness is part of an auditory continuum, and the placing of the borderline between the two categories is merely an operational decision. The physiological relationship between the two is a good deal more distant, however, when their specification in terms of the muscular parameter of medial compression is considered, as indicated immediately above. Breathy voice has extremely weak medial compression, with little tendency on the part of the lateral cricoarytenoid muscles to swivel the vocal processes of the arytenoids in towards each other. The whisper component of whispery voice requires moderate to high medial compression, so that the whisper-producing channel is relatively confined to the cartilaginous glottis.

From an auditory point of view, it is practical to use the label 'breathy voice' for the range of qualities produced with a low degree of laryngeal effort, and where only a slight amount of glottal friction is audible. If one thinks of the friction component and the modal voice component as being audibly co-present but able to be heard individually, then the balance between the two components in breathy voice is one where the modal voice element is markedly dominant. 'Whispery voice' can then be used for phonations produced with a greater degree of laryngeal effort, and where a more substantial amount of glottal friction, from a more constricted glottis, is audible. The audible balance between the friction component and the periodic component is different from that in breathy voice; the friction component is more prominent than in breathy voice, and may on occasion even equal the periodic component, (and sometimes dominate it strongly, as in 'extremely whispery voice'). In the interpretation offered here, the friction component of whispery voice can thus be subdivided into a larger number of audible increments than can the friction component of breathy voice.

It is perhaps unfortunate that some writers simply collapse the two phenomena. Kaplan (1960:167), for example, describes 'breathiness' as a voice quality 'said to have an aspirate quality, and the effect is as though a whisper were added to the normal tone'. In this and in other cases, although 'whisper' is a term in the writers' descriptive repertoire for voice quality, it is not used for the description of a *compound* type of phonation with (modal) voice or any other type, and 'breathy voice' is the label used for any quality where there is a fricative escape of air during phonation. Zemlin writes, for example, that

The most common correlate of Breathiness is a persistent glottal chink in the posterior portion of the vocal folds. Critical examination of a large number of larynxes reveals that a good many persons with apparently healthy, normal sounding voices display a glottal chink in the area of the arytenoid cartilages. We can suppose that there is a point at which the magnitude of glottal chink will result in a breathy voice quality. The exact relationship between magnitude of glottal chink and vocal quality is not well understood. (Zemlin 1964:165)

In the situation that Zemlin describes, it would seem likely that as the 'glottal chink' grew in size, whispery voice would set in first, and that it would have to enlarge to a much greater proportion of the total possible glottal area before breathy voice either as described here or by Catford was heard.

With the considerable amount of air that is wasted in breathy voice, there is an inverse relationship between intensity of the voice and breathiness (Pronovost 1942). Some of the acoustic energy would also be lost by the damping effect of the general relaxation of the muscles of the whole vocal system in *lax voice*, of which breathy voice is almost always a component. This damping effect is discussed in the next chapter on tension settings of the vocal system. Breathy voice, however, contributes its own damping effect to the general energy loss. Fant (1972:50) points out that the broadening of the bandwidth of the first formant in lax voice can be partly attributed to the high damping effect of 'weak, breathy voice' on the rest of the vocal system.

Breathy voice does not seem to be used phonologically as often as whispery voice. Paralinguistically, however, breathy voice is exploited in English for the communication of intimacy.

3.2 Compound phonation types

A number of combinatorial constraints on the co-occurrence of individual phonation types to form a *compound* type have already been mentioned. In this section, we shall look briefly at some of the factors underlying the *compatibility*, or the lack of it, between different individual phonation types, with respect to their potential co-occurrence. There are two general conditions under which compatibility between phonation types is possible.

The first condition is where the individual settings apply to different parts of the laryngeal structure, so that competition for the same vocal apparatus is avoided.

The second condition is where the same part of the laryngeal apparatus *is* concerned in the production of two different phonation types, but where the vibratory patterns of the two settings modify each other without either changing substantially enough to lose its auditory identifiability.

Examples of the first condition for compatibility, where different laryngeal locations are involved, would be *whispery voice, whispery falsetto*, and *whispery creak*. The whisper component is assumed here to be produced in a triangular gap between the arytenoid cartilages, in all three compound phonations, and creak made separately at the thyroid end of the glottis, with both modal voice and falsetto being limited to the ligamental section of the glottis. The triple compound types *whispery creaky voice* and *whispery creaky falsetto* would be further instances.

Examples of the second condition for compatibility, where two (or more) vibratory patterns modify each other, would be all the instances of *harshness* in compound phonations. The modification that harshness imposes on all compounds in which it participates is a boost in the parametric values of adductive tension and medial compression to an extreme degree. In this way, the compound type *harsh voice* is characterized by greater adductive tension and medial compression than the moderate values normally found in modal voice alone. In order to achieve phonation, the sub-glottal pressure has to be given a compensatory boost also, in order to re-assert aerodynamic participation in an aerodynamic–myoelastic phonatory equation in which the myoelastic component has had the elastic resistance of the glottis to airflow substantially increased. This does not mean that phonation types with low values on these parameters cannot combine with harshness. Whisper is a case in point, where low adductive tension is normally one of its characteristics: it does mean though that the whisper component in *harsh whispery voice,* say, is maintained by a much greater effort on the part of the lateral cricoarytenoid muscles to keep the arytenoid triangle open against the vigorous attempt by the interarytenoid muscles to close it. The auditory nature of the whisper component is likely to be rather different in such compound phonation, compared with its occurrence as a simple type. There are two general conditions, as suggested in Chapter 1, under which compatibility is *not* possible between individual phonation types, preventing the occurrence of particular compound phonations.

The first of these conditions is where the pre-requisite actions of the larynx for each of the two types of phonation involved are mutually exclusive.

The second condition is where perceptual factors make it impossible to hear the differences introduced by the addition of one phonation type to the other.

There are a number of examples of the first, physiologically pre-emptive condition. Modal voice and falsetto are one instance. Their membership of the first grouping of phonation types is based partly on this impossibility of co-occurrence. These two types of phonation need quite different types of vibration of the vocal folds, as described earlier in this chapter, and they therefore cannot combine. Similarly, we have seen that harshness and breathiness are mutually incompatible, because of their parametric prerequisites. Where harshness has extremely high adductive tension and medial compression, breathiness must have very low values of these parameters. Breathiness is a very unusual aspect of phonation in this respect, and is incompatible with almost every other phonation type. With very low adductive tension, and most importantly, very low medial compression, breathiness is compatible with only one other phonation type – modal voice, giving *breathy voice*, as discussed above. Modal voice has a moderate degree of medial compression, while every other type, falsetto, whisper, creak and harshness, has a high or very high degree. Also, modal voice has only moderate adductive tension, where falsetto, creak and harshness have high or very high degrees. It is true that whisper is similar to breathiness in having low adductive tension, but whisperiness and breathiness have been defined here as complementary actions of the same scale, so that their potential combination is excluded by definition.

Another example, which is covered by both incompatibility conditions, physiological and auditory, is the combination of harshness and whisper, preventing the occurrence of *harsh whisper* as a descriptive category. The physiological incompatibility is on a different basis than that of modal voice and falsetto, or of harshness and breathiness. It is not a matter of directly opposite physiological requirements, but of redundancy. The effect of adding the actions which produce harshness to those producing whisper is merely to boost the tensions pressing the vocal folds and the arytenoid cartilages together. Regardless of whether the type of whisper is one where a gap is left between the arytenoids, or one where the ligamental glottis is also kept slightly open, the effect of adding harshness will be to narrow the glottal aperture. This will only result in the audible whisper rising in amplitude until the gap is completely closed. While the whisper lasts, it will be heard as being louder, without a major change in quality.

The second, auditory, incompatibility condition applies not only to harshness and whisper, but also to modal voice and falsetto, and possibly to harshness and creak.

Harshness and whisper are both characterized acoustically by a factor of aperiodicity. To add the aperiodicity of harshness to that of whisper would, in that particular respect, be auditorily redundant. This is not to say that harshness and whisper do not combine; *harsh whispery voice* is a common compound phonation. But their interaction is primarily with the voice component, as it were, rather than with each other in the particular respect of aperiodicity.

The auditory incompatibility of modal voice and falsetto is straightforward: using the same vocal apparatus, they constitute different qualities.

Harshness and creak present a less clear-cut case of auditory incompatibility. It will be recalled that creak is sometimes characterized by a certain amount of moment-to-moment variability of its (normally very low) fundamental frequency. To modulate this variability by superimposing the essential variability (aperiodicity) of harshness would not produce a large change in auditory quality. However, given that variability of fundamental frequency in creak is not a necessary ingredient, but only an occasional characteristic, then to superimpose a continuous aperiodic factor on creak would produce a compound phonation that should logically be called *harsh creak*.

It is worth emphasizing once again, at this point, that these suggestions about compatibility are based on hypothesized definitions. The empirical incompatibilities that are suggested rest on the validity of the physiological and acoustic hypotheses. While the suggested principles of compatibility and incompatibility are able to give structure to most of the combinations of phonation types that can and cannot occur, they can only be applied where the physiological mechanisms and the auditory effects are reasonably well understood. There are some compound types of phonation where the necessary degree of analytic clarity does not yet obtain. Comments about these can therefore only be rather speculative.

For example, the physiological mechanism for the production of creak remains unclear. It has been treated in this description as if it were the product of an independent vibratory system at the forward, thyroid end of the glottis, following suggestions by a number of writers. The auditory impression of the creak component in compound phonations is sufficiently different in the various compound types to suggest that the auditorily identified phenomena we are willing to call 'creak' may possibly be produced by different mechanism in different compounds. The creak component in high-pitched *creaky falsetto* sounds different from that in *whispery creak*, for example.

The creak component in *creaky voice*, which is a common compound phonation, may well differ from speaker to speaker. One suggestion for the creak mechanism in creaky voice is that it is made, not at the thyroid end of the glottis, but at the arytenoid end: Abercrombie (1967:101) describes the phonation in creaky voice as one 'in which the cartilage glottis is vibrating very slowly, while the rest of the glottis is in normal vibration'. A somewhat similar comment is made by Ladefoged in his monograph on West African languages, where he discusses 'laryngealized voice' (which he equates with 'creaky voice'). He writes that 'In this state of the glottis there is a great deal of tension in the intrinsic laryngeal musculature, and the vocal cords no longer vibrate as a whole. The ligamental and arytenoid parts of the vocal cords vibrate separately' (Ladefoged 1964:16). Presumably the creak component in this description would be attributable to the arytenoid location, rather than to the ligamental section.

In the case of the triple compound phonation type *whispery creaky voice* referred to above, it seems more likely that the creak component would be produced at the extreme thyroid end of the glottis, leaving the cartilaginous glottis free for the production of the whisper and the rest of the ligamental glottis for the voice component – but this remains a speculation for the present.

There are also physiologically possible phonation types quite outside the descriptive system presented here, omitted because they seem never to be used in normal speech, whose possibilities of occurrence in compound phonations are not yet well analysed. To give one example, it is possible to produce phonation which sounds like *ventricular falsetto* (sometimes referred to as 'seal voice'), by very severe compressive effort of the whole larynx, and extreme pulmonic effort. There are also a number of auditorily different kinds of whisper, touched on by Catford (1964:32–3). A further, very high-pitched phonation type is mentioned by Hollien (1974:127) 'usually referred to as the "flute", "whistle" or "pipe" register . . . exhibited by a few women and children'.

Two compound phonation types in particular seem to be exploited for linguistic purposes. They are creaky voice, discussed earlier, and whispery voice. Ladefoged's term for whispery voice is 'murmur', and he describes murmur as figuring in phonological opposition in many Indo-Aryan languages, such as Hindi, Sindhi, Marathi, Bengali, Assamese, Gujarati, Bihari, and Marwari; he also comments that murmured consonants are common in Southern Bantu languages, such as Shona,

Tsonga, Ndebele and Zulu (Ladefoged 1971:12–14).

Paralinguistically, whispery voice is used in English, and in very many other cultures, as an indicator of confidentiality. It is quite distinct in this function from the more intimate use of breathy voice.

4 *Tension settings*

Discussion so far has been concerned with settings, both of the supralaryngeal vocal tract and of the phonatory mechanisms of the larynx, which can suitably be described as specific to some local part of the vocal system. We come now to settings of a different order from such local considerations. These are settings of overall degrees of muscular tension which exercise their effect throughout the vocal system. Two categories of tension settings will be discussed, as distinct from the neutral tension specification. These are *tense voice* and *lax voice*, which stand for a high degree of tension generally through the system, and a low degree, respectively. It is very difficult to find any absolute measure that can be used to specify the degree of overall muscular tension in the neutral setting, and which could figure legitimately in a general phonetic theory. So a nominal, relative measure is adopted, where the degree of tension in the neutral setting is the one lying midway between the two extremes of maximally tense and maximally lax settings.

There has been a certain amount of discussion in the literature on voice quality about the factors correlated with overall tension settings. The usual contrast is one which is drawn by the use of descriptive impressionistic labels such as 'metallic voice' and 'muffled voice', relating them to high and low degrees of tension. Some other labels for 'metallic' are 'brassy, bright, clear, keen, piercing, ringing, sharp, strident'; labels used for 'muffled voice' include 'dull, guttural, mellow, obscure, soft, thick' (Laver 1974). Bloomfield (1933:94–5) uses the terms 'metallic sound' and 'muffled sound', to refer to 'quality of resonance', and says that they have 'not been physiologically analyzed'. In fact, although the impressionistic labels used have been somewhat varied, and most probably cover a range of different degrees of muscular tension, more recent writers seem to agree reasonably well on the physiological, auditory and acoustic factors posited as characterizing such voices.

For Milisen (1957) 'metallic voice' is a 'sharp piercing voice ordinarily associated with tension of the side walls of the oral and pharyngeal cavities', and 'muffled voice' is a 'diffused voice not projected from the mouth and frequently associated with excessive relaxation of the oral and pharyngeal cavities'.

Greene (1964: 53) says that 'The relaxed muscular walls of the vocal resonators tend to "damp", stop or absorb high frequencies and produce mellow tone, whereas hard or taut muscular walls act as reflectors and produce harsh tone.' Later, considering voice quality in singing, and the relation between singing and nasality, Greene writes that 'Clear, bright ringing tones (voix blanche) are dependent on lifting and tensing of the velum. Low mellow tones are achieved with the faucal arches well relaxed, and the soft palate almost pendant' (Greene 1964: 56).

Chiba and Kajiyama (1958) in their book on the nature and structure of the vowel (first published in 1941), write that 'soft voice'

is usually described as a dull, guttural or obscure sound. A voice which contains some noise and has a comparatively strong fundamental and weak higher harmonic partials. It can be most easily produced either when the head is bent upwards or when the larynx is drawn downwards with the head kept in a normal position. (Chiba and Kajiyama 1958:17)

'Sharp voice', they say,

is often described as being keen, ringing, energetic or powerfully penetrating. We can easily produce this voice with our head drawn back while keeping it bent forward'. (*ibid.*:18)

It may already be becoming clear that tense voice and lax voice are each manifested by a constellation of more local settings at various points in the vocal system. It is because there is a common factor of general muscle tension underlying the multiple local settings which contribute to each of these two types of voice that it is analytically helpful to consider the effects of different degrees of overall muscular tension in this separate chapter.

The outline that follows will consider the local effects of tension settings, firstly at the larynx, and then at a number of points along the supralaryngeal tract.

One acoustic finding needs to be mentioned before starting on the discussion of local manifestations of the tension settings. It is that tense and lax voices seem to be acoustically differentiated chiefly by the relative amounts of energy in the upper harmonics (Van Dusen 1941), with tense voice having stronger upper harmonics than lax voice, as noted in the quotations above from Greene (1964:53) and Chiba and Kajiyama (1958:17). A specific suggestion of a measure of the degree of tension in a speaker's voice has been made by Frøkjaer-Jensen and Prytz (1976:3). They set up 'a new parameter, α, which is a measure of the intensity relations in the higher and lower parts of the speech spectrum' where

$$\alpha = \frac{\text{intensity above 1000 Hz}}{\text{intensity below 1000 Hz}}$$

Frøkjaer-Jensen and Prytz suggest that α is 'a good acoustic correlate to the physiological term "medial compression"' (*ibid.*).

Kaplan (1960) relates the acoustic differences between tense and lax voices to characteristics of the pharynx. Referring to Anderson (1942), he says that:

the role of the pharynx in resonation is more difficult to evaluate than that of the mouth or nose, but ... it is especially important to provide resonance for the fundamental and the lower overtones. This is said to give the voice a mellow, rich and full quality.

The texture, as well as the size and shape, of the pharynx and its apertures affects speech quality. A hard-surfaced resonator emphasizes the higher partials, or overtones, so that a pharynx tightly constricted by its muscles, takes on a metallic, strident, and tense tone. On the contrary, a soft surface, provided by relaxed throat muscles, increases the responsive range while damping the resonator. This in effect gives relative prominence to the fundamental and lower partials. (Kaplan 1960:199)

One major acoustic variable dependent on the overall tension setting is thus the system's damping characteristics, or factors of absorption of sound energy, in different parts of the larynx and vocal tract. Formant amplitudes and bandwidths are hence involved, but we shall also see that dynamic configurational properties of the tract play a part, and that therefore formant frequencies are sometimes affected.

Considering now the involvement of the larynx in the production of tense and lax voice, a number of writers have suggested that some of the control of damping lies with the upper larynx, notably in the ventricles of Morgagni and the ventricular folds. Pepinsky (1942) claimed that the ventricles may act as a low-pass filter, in normal voices (that is, voices without a marked degree of tenseness or laxness). Van den Berg (1955) agrees that in normal voice the ventricles behave as a low-pass filter suppressing the higher-frequency components of the glottal waveform, and also says that, in what he calls 'harsh, metallic voice', the ventricular bands decline and lay themselves against the wall of the ventricle until they firmly press upon the vocal folds. The ventricle disappears and the higher harmonics are not filtered. This accords with observations on certain singers with a particularly strong voice, who exhibited small ventricles. (van den Berg 1955:63)

Greene (1964:55) supports this point of view:

The ventricle of the larynx is also modified by the action of the false folds which follow the movements of the true folds. When relaxed they act as soft surface filters but when constricted they press down upon the folds and obliterate the ventricle. The tension favours high partials and produces the 'compressed tone' described by Aikin [i.e. Aikin 1951].

Chiba and Kajiyama (1958) do not agree completely with Pepinsky, van den Berg and Greene about the acoustic function of ventricular action in tense and lax voices. They concede that in 'soft voice' [lax voice], the 'edges of the false vocal cords are curved upwards and the rimae ventriculorum are wide, while in "sharp voice" [tense voice] the latter are found to be narrower than in any other type of voice' (Chiba and Kajiyama 1958:35). But they believe that the relative adjustments of the false vocal cords are 'caused by the adjustment of the (true) vocal cords', and are 'not designed to change the resonance of the larynx tone in the ventricles of Morgagni; or if there be any such change, the effect is not great' (*ibid.*:36). They prefer to attribute the spectral prominence of the lower harmonics in lax voice ('soft voice') to the following fact:

In 'soft voice' the vocal processes of the arytenoid cartilages are separated and the cartilaginous glottis is kept slightly open. During pronunciation the ligamentous glottis opens and shuts periodically. It opens into the shape of a spindle and shuts completely. But in this case it opens for a considerable time and shuts for a short time. This makes it impossible for air to be emitted abruptly. The result is that the lower harmonic partials are somewhat stronger, and the higher harmonic partials are somewhat weaker, than in any other kind of voice. (Chiba and Kajiyama 1958:20–1)

Whichever explanation one accepts, the ventricular hypothesis of Pepinsky, van den Berg and Greene, or the 'opening quotient' hypothesis of Chiba and Kajiyama, the acoustic results are not in question.

Another involvement of ventricular action can often be found in the production of tense voice. Because of the hypertension of such voices, the phonation type is likely often to be either *ventricular voice* or *harsh voice*. Notice, for instance, that both van den Berg (1955:63) and Greene

(1964: 53) include auditory harshness in their comments on what is here called tense voice.

Monsen and Engebretson (1977: 987) distinguish between 'soft voice' and 'loud voice'. They report that soft voice is characterized by a more symmetrical laryngeal waveform and a more steeply declining laryngeal spectrum, relative to modal voice. Loud voice, on the other hand, which they suggest has a typically higher fundamental frequency than modal voice, they report as having a closing portion of the laryngeal wave which is brief and abrupt, with 'a consequent measure of energy particularly in the higher frequencies' (Monsen and Engebretson *loc. cit.*).

The two muscular parameters that are most exploited in the laryngeal contributions to tense voice and lax voice are adductive tension and medial compression. In tense voice, the values of both parameters are boosted: harsh voice and ventricular voice are the consequence of extreme degrees of such increases of tension, and are common accompaniments of tense voice. But more moderate increases of tension on these two parameters are not uncommon, and the presence of auditory harshness is not a necessary aspect of tense voice. A perceptible result of increased adductive tension and medial compression beyond the neutral values is the production of what Catford variously calls 'ligamental voice' (Catford 1964: 32–3) and 'anterior voice' (Catford 1977:102–3). Ligamental voice (i.e. a laryngeal component of tense voice which is nevertheless not tense enough to cause the aperiodicity of harshness) is characterized as follows:

The arytenoid cartilages are tightly occluded both by contraction of the interarytenoid muscles and by the forward pull of the lateral cricoarytenoids, which may press the vocal processes together (medial compression). Phonation is thus actively restricted to the ligamental glottis. Laryngoscopy indicates that, in the author's pronunciation, ligamental phonation may often (perhaps always?) be accompanied by upper larynx constriction – the epiglottis tends to be pulled back over the top of the larynx ... Ligamental voice appears to be one of the two phonologically distinct voice-qualities in Logbara, and possibly other Nilotic languages: it is commonly the 'normal' voice (contrasting with whispery voice) in Hindi and other North Indian languages etc. (Catford 1964: 32–3)

This account is elaborated in Catford's later book:

In anterior phonation the arytenoid cartilages are apparently clamped tightly together and only the front, ligamental part of the glottis actively participates in phonation. At the same time, the whole upper part of the larynx may be constricted to some extent: it appears as if the arytenoidal constriction essential for anterior phonation is part of a general sphincteric constriction of the (upper) larynx. Voice produced at the anterior location has a somewhat 'tight', 'hard' quality and appears to be what Chiba and Kajiyama (1958) call 'sharp' and Lindqvist (1969) calls 'tense' voice ... Anterior, hard, voice is characteristic of many North German speakers. In Britain some degree of 'anteriorness' is very common in the dialects of North East Scotland, especially Aberdeenshire and Banff, as opposed to the very lax, full-glottal, voice commonly heard in Central Scotland. (Catford 1977:102–3)

Concomitants of greater and less laryngeal tension here would be, respectively, heightened and lowered sub-glottal pressure.

In lax voice, the values of the laryngeal parameters of adductive tension and medial compression are lower than in the neutral state of modal voice. This laryngeal hypotension tends to inhibit the occurrence of all phonation types other than modal voice; and a breathy modification of modal voice, in various degrees of breathiness, is a very frequent component of lax voice. The main phonatory characteristic of breathy voice, incomplete closure of the vocal folds, is consistent with Chiba and Kajiyama's comment reported above that 'in "soft voice" the cartilaginous glottis is kept slightly open' (1958:20–1). Their comment is also consistent with the production of whispery voice, as defined here, but the higher medial compression necessary for whispery voice would involve greater laryngeal tension than breathy voice. It may be that voices which are slightly lax are whispery in quality, while breathiness characterizes voices which are either moderately or extremely lax. However, while lax voice may have a slightly whispery phonation, whispery voice is not necessarily part of a voice characterized by overall lax muscular tension. Whispery voice *may* accompany certain examples of tense voice: in such cases, the cartilaginous glottis is kept open against adductive tension only by vigorous antagonistic action. In tense whispery voices of this sort, the laryngeal tension is often very audible, and can be empathetically felt, just as can the tension in harsh or ventricular phonation.

A major difficulty in the discussion of tense and lax voices is that the adjectives 'tense' and 'lax' have been applied in such a variety of senses by different writers. It is extremely difficult to find alternative terms which would appropriately capture the underlying generality of differences in overall muscular tension between the two categories. 'Tense' and 'lax' will be retained here, but it is essential to indicate some differences of usage between this book and other users of the terms 'tense voice' and 'lax voice'. The two principal users are Ladefoged (1971:7–22) and Catford (1977:93–116), and they both reserve these labels for the description of laryngeal behaviour, rather than for qualities arising from both laryngeal and supralaryngeal activity. As far as laryngeal factors are concerned, however, the phenomena discussed by Ladefoged and Catford are clearly basically the same as, or auditorily closely related to, those being described here. The occasional differences of associated terminology sometimes tend to obscure this fact, and it may be helpful to offer a clarification at this point.

Ladefoged (1971) is concerned to propose a method of describing all the systematic phonetic differences which occur among languages. Accordingly, his discussion of phonatory states (1971 : 7–22) deals only with those that have been shown to act as the phonetic realizations of phonological oppositions. He distinguishes nine such states, under the feature 'Glottal Stricture', which he regards as a continuum. He points out, as noted earlier, that 'No language has contrasts involving more than three states and most languages use only two states within this continuum' (Ladefoged 1971 :18). His proposal, which he emphasizes is very tentative, conflates the effects isolated here of adductive tension and medial compression into a single continuum of glottal constriction

extending from the most closed position, a glottal stop, to the most open position observed in speech, which is that in voiceless sounds. Starting from a glottal stop (which itself may have several degrees of tightness), it is possible to pass through a form of laryngealization (here called creak) in which the arytenoid cartilages are pulled toward one another, and the whole glottis remains constricted except for a small opening in the anterior portion. Slight (but not complete) relaxation of the pulling together of the arytenoids produces the next phonation type, creaky voice, in which a larger proportion of the glottis is vibrating. Thus, by further releasing the degree of constriction, one passes through stages which we may call tense voice, voice and lax voice (though of course recognizing, as with all the stages on this continuum, that there is no predeterminable point at which, for instance, tense voice should be considered to become voice). Further relaxation leads to a widening of the glottis, particularly between the arytenoids, so that lax voice becomes murmur, in which only the anterior portion is vibrating. This state can arbitrarily be distinguished from one in which there is an even greater flow through the glottis, which we may now call breathy voice. Finally, when even the anterior portion of the glottis is so far apart that it cannot be set in vibration we have the voiceless position. (Ladefoged 1971 :18)

It may be helpful to indicate translational equivalents, as it were, between Ladefoged's labels and those used in this book. 'Creak', 'creaky voice' and 'breathy voice' are used identically in the two systems. Ladefoged's 'murmur' is 'whispery voice' in the terms used here, as indicated earlier, and his 'voice' is 'modal voice'. His 'tense voice' is the type of tense voice described earlier as involving a slight increase of tension, compared with the neutral setting, and giving rise to ligamental phonation. Ladefoged's 'lax voice' is the type of lax voice described earlier as involving a slight relaxation of tension, compared with the neutral setting. Progressive relaxation, giving rise to the whispery voice of 'murmur' should also be equated with slightly lax voice, and breathy voice with the moderate to extreme degree of laxness at the laryngeal level. So Ladefoged's 'lax voice', 'murmur' and 'breathy voice' are all to be interpreted as possible laryngeal realizations of lax voice as here conceived.

Catford (1977:105–6) also comments on Ladefoged's terms 'murmur' and 'lax voice'. He equates 'murmur' with a type of whispery voice, and suggests that 'lax voice' may also be somewhat whispery.

Using his newer term 'anterior' for his earlier 'ligamental', Catford comments that 'Ladefoged's "murmur" (the "whispery voice" of Indian languages) is anterior voice plus posterior (arytenoid) whisper, while "lax voice" is simply pure, full glottal, whispery voice' (Catford 1977:106).

'Tense voice', in Catford's own usage, means voice produced by vibration of the ligamental glottis, as noted earlier.

At the laryngeal level, therefore, the analysis offered here is broadly similar to that in Ladefoged (1971) and Catford (1977), as far as concepts of tense voice and lax voice are concerned. But it deserves emphasis that Ladefoged and Catford are discussing solely laryngeal activity, while tension settings are being considered here as a matter of overall muscular tension throughout the vocal system. Lax voice, for example, will be realized by a constellation of different local settings, and breathy phonation at the laryngeal level will be merely one contributory factor amongst several.

Laryngeal factors so far discussed concern the mode of vibration of the vocal folds. Other laryngeal factors include the pitch and loudness characteristics of tense and lax voice. These, although not directly aspects of quality as such, derive from the same underlying cause of greater or less muscular tension than in neutral voices, and their perception is to some extent influenced by the concomitant voice quality, as we shall see.

There is a strong probability that in tense voice the pitch-range will be higher than in lax voice, and the loudness-range louder. It is certainly possible, though, to compensate for these tendencies (just as we noted the possibility of pitch compensation in the earlier discussion of raised and lowered larynx voices). It is noticeable, for example, that a certain proportion of American adult male voices are tense, harsh, and loud, but low-pitched rather than high-pitched.

Leaving these possibilities of compensations of pitch-range aside, it is interesting that even when the pitch-range of tense voice is not in fact high, in physical terms, it may be perceived as being higher than the fundamental frequency by itself justifies, because of spectral characteristics of tense voices: Landes (1953) found that voices with relatively greater energy in the upper part of the spectrum (as is typical of tense voice), tend to be perceived as higher pitched than those with less high-frequency intensity. They may also be perceived as louder: Van Riper and Irwin (1958: 452–3) point out that

the human ear is much more sensitive to tones in the frequency range 1,000 to 4,000 than it is to tones below or above the range. Thus ... voice qualities that have more of their energy in the upper than in the lower frequencies ... may sound louder than the actual energy reaching the ear would normally justify.

West, Ansberry and Carr (1957: 72) put this point very appropriately:

Two voices that, physically measured, have equal intensities or energy values may vary greatly in loudness, particularly if one has its energy concentrated in the fundamental tone and the other in a harmonic tone near 1000 vibrations per second, for it is the octaves between C^1 and C^3 to which the human ear is most sensitive. 'Piercing' voices are those whose energy values are in this middle region.

Lax voice tends to be accompanied by a low pitch-range and a soft loudness-range. The comments and findings cited above in the discussion of tense voice, from Landes (1953), Van Riper and Irwin (1958) and West, Ansberry and Carr (1957), show equally that lax voices will tend to be perceived as lower-pitched and softer, just as tense voices are heard as higher-pitched and louder, than strictly acoustic measures of fundamental frequency and overall intensity would indicate.

We turn now to consider supralaryngeal factors in tension settings. In lax voice, because of the relative relaxation of the musculature of the vocal tract, the local velopharyngeal system tends also to be relaxed, and lax voice is therefore frequently accompanied by moderate nasality. In tense voice, the velopharyngeal musculature tends to be tensed in such a way that the velum closes the velopharyngeal port, with the result that tense voice is less often accompanied by nasality. The remark of Greene (1964: 56) that 'Clear, bright ringing tones (voix blanche) are dependent on lifting and tensing of the velum' supports this. This is not to say, however, that tense voice never has side chamber resonance associated with it. So-called 'nasal twang' may be the popular label for side chamber resonance generated by tense adjustments of the upper larynx, pharynx or faucal pillars, as discussed in the section on velopharyngeal settings in Chapter 2.

There is also the possibility that in tense voice the faucal pillars will be approximated, without any lowering of the braced velum, and with the pharynx constricted and the larynx subjected to a vertical pull both from below by the infrahyoid complex and from above by the laryngeal elevator complex. The comments by Bell (1908:19–21), in the section on faucal settings in Chapter 2 about faucalization in deaf speakers leading to a quality he described as 'a peculiar metallic ring, somewhat like the tone of a brass musical instrument', and by Pike (1943:123–4), associating faucalization with 'lower pharyngeal constriction, glottal tension, and usually a raising of the larynx', are relevant here. Whether faucalization is involved in the majority of tense voices or not, Pike is right to suggest that a raised larynx position often occurs. Equally, in lax voices, a noticeable lowering of the larynx is common: it will be recalled from Chapter 2 that lowered larynx voice is often associated with a breathy phonation, and the auditory contribution of these two features seems frequently very prominent in the constellation of settings here jointly labelled 'lax voice'.

Tense voice and lax voice are correlated with two aspects of lingual settings. The major aspect is to do with the amount of radial movement of the centre of mass of the tongue from its neutral position, in the midsagittal plane, that characterizes the articulatory gestures of segmental pronunciation. The other, more minor aspect concerns the shape of the tongue from side to side, in the coronal plane.

Sweet (1877) was one of the earliest writers to relate degrees of overall tension to activities of the tongue, in his use of the two terms 'narrow' and 'wide'. He said that

the distinction depends on the *shape* of the tongue. In forming narrow sounds there is a feeling of tenseness in that part of the tongue where the sound is formed, the surface of the tongue being made more convex than in its natural 'wide' shape, in which it is relaxed and flattened. This convexity of the tongue naturally narrows the passage – whence the name. This narrowing is produced by raising, not the whole body of the tongue, but only that part of it which forms, or helps to form, the sound. (Sweet 1877:9)

He made it more clear that he was thinking of the convexity of the surface of the tongue as related to the front-to-back sagittal plane, and not to the lateral, coronal plane as such, in an article in 1911, when he wrote:

In forming narrow sounds there is a feeling of tension in that part of the tongue where the sound is formed, the tongue being clenched or bunched up lengthwise, so as to be more convex than in its relaxed or 'wide' condition. The distinction between narrow and wide ... generally depends on quantity; length and narrowness, shortness and wideness going together. (Sweet 1911:463)

We will return to the relation between tension and segmental duration below, but we can note here that in bunching the tongue along its sagittal axis, there will normally also be an accompanying tendency for the coronal surface of the tongue to be made more sharply convex from side to side. So tense voice, to the extent that susceptible segments reflect increased tension, is likely to have the surface of the tongue more steeply convex in both planes, as well as involving a greater departure of the centre of mass from its neutral position, for the articulation of susceptible segments, than the corresponding 'wide', 'flattened' segments of lax voice.

Sweet gives Alexander Melville Bell the credit for being the first to notice the distinction between the two categories that Sweet was to call 'narrow' and 'wide' (Sweet 1911:463) Bell's own terms were 'primary' and 'wide'. He wrote that

Primary vowels are those which are most allied to consonants, the voice-channel being expanded only so far as to remove all 'fricative' quality. The same organic adjustments form 'wide' vowels when the resonance-cavity is enlarged behind the configurative aperture; – the physical cause of 'wide' quality being the retraction of the soft palate, and expansion of the pharynx. (Bell 1867:71)

But Sweet rejected this explanation of the articulatory actions contributing to the two qualities, and said that because he himself had showed that the distinction depended on the shape of the tongue, he 'accordingly substituted "narrow" for Bell's "primary"'' (Sweet 1911:463).

Heffner (1950:96–7) discusses some of Sweet's comments about this area, and writes that 'Later scholars have substituted the terms tense and lax for narrow and wide, and recognized that this tenseness applied not merely to the tongue muscles but to the entire articulating complex.' Heffner is here referring to Sievers (1876), though why he refers to him as one of the scholars 'later' than Sweet is difficult to understand. Heffner then goes on to adopt the position that tense and lax (vowels) are differentiated by relative constriction of the glottal opening (in vocal fold vibration) and greater sub-glottal pressure for tense vowels, and relative openness of the glottal opening and less sub-glottal pressure for lax vowels. He suggests that terms such as tense and lax can be retained if their reference is shifted 'from tongue elevations and tongue muscle tensions to laryngeal positions [*sc.* the maximum degrees of glottal opening in vocal fold vibration – J.L.] and air pressure' (Heffner 1950:97). There are thus various different physiological parameters posited by the different writers on the topic of segmental tension as a momentary action of the vocal apparatus. It is interesting that the different observations made in this area of segmental tension may *all* be right, from the point of view of the variety of local manifestations of an overall tension state. Comments by phoneticians about tenseness and laxness as segmental features are thus relevant to the study of longer-term settings, if we choose to see the various alternative segmental suggestions as possible co-occurring local phenomena which all individually arise from a general tendency towards an overall tension state throughout the vocal system.

A summary of hypotheses about the basis for segmental tension can be found in an article by Jakobson and Halle (1964), where their own comments are prefaced by a short history of the discussion about tenseness and laxness as segmental concepts. They explore comments on the topic by Sweet, Bell, Winteler, Sievers, Meyer, Stumpf, Jones and Fant. Among the variety of articulatory and acoustic correlates which have been suggested, one comment by Jakobson, Fant and Halle (1952) is particularly interesting. They maintain that tense vowels show a greater deformation of the vocal tract from its 'neutral, central position'. They define the 'neutral position' of the tract as the one assumed by the vocal organs in producing a very open [æ], which is different from the specification of the neutral configuration used here but in this regard not importantly so. Chomsky and Halle (1968:325) write that 'We note that the difference between tense and lax consonants ... (involves) a greater versus a lesser articulatory effort and duration. The greater effort is produced by greater muscular tension in the muscles controlling the shape of the vocal tract.'

The tendency for segmental articulation to depart further from the neutral vocal tract position in a tense voice, and less in a lax voice, may explain some of the auditory implications in the impressionistic labels given at the beginning of this chapter – particularly about a tense voice being a 'sharp', 'penetrating' voice, and a lax one being 'dull', 'guttural' or 'obscure', and a 'diffused voice not projected from the mouth'. In this connection also Fairbanks (1960:170) says that 'muffled voice [lax voice] is a general term for the slighted consonants and neutralized vowels that result from limited or inconclusive movement of the articulatory structures (oral inactivity)'. The quotation in the previous chapter from Shorto (1966:400) on the phonetic exponents of register differences in Mon, is also relevant, where 'head register' was characterized as having 'clear voice quality, relative tenseness, and peripheral vowel articulation'.

We return now to consider the comment quoted from Sweet (1911:463), to the effect that 'The distinction between narrow and wide ... generally depends on quantity: length and narrowness, shortness and wideness going together.' Jakobson and Halle (1964:97) summarize the findings of a number of investigators when they say that

The heightened subglottal air pressure in the production of tense vowels is indissolubly paired with a longer duration ... The tense vowels are necessarily lengthened in comparison with the corresponding lax phonemes [sic]. Tense vowels have the duration needed for the production of the most clear-cut, optimal vowels; in comparison with them the lax vowels appear as quantitatively and qualitatively *reduced*, obscured and deflected from their tense counterpart toward the neutral formant pattern.

This last comment neatly characterizes one aspect of the acoustic differences between tense and lax voice – formant ranges are narrower in lax voice than in tense, because of the tendency of the susceptible vocoid segments to be centralized in lax voice, with less extensive radial movements of the centre of mass of the tongue away from the neutral configuration, and hence less deviation of the formant frequencies from their neutral values.

Jakobson and Halle conclude their article with a brief summary of their survey:

In producing lax phonemes [sic] the vocal tract exhibits the same behaviour as in generating the cognate tense phonemes but with a significant attenuation. This attenuation manifests itself by a lower air pressure in the cavity ... by a smaller deformation of the vocal tract from its neutral, central position, and/or by a more rapid release of the constriction. The tense consonants show primarily a longer time interval spent in a position away from neutral, while the tense vowels not only persevere in such a position optimal for the effectuation of a steady, unfolded, unreduced sound, but also display a greater deformation of the vocal tract. (Jakobson and Halle 1964:100)

Sweet's observation about the correlations between longer duration and 'narrowness', and shorter duration and 'wideness' is thus supported by Jakobson and Halle, though it is important to emphasize that there is no necessary connection between duration as such and degree of tension. There is no reason to suppose that these two factors cannot be neurophysiologically programmed quite separately. French, for example, has short, tense vowels. But there may be some tendency for long duration and heightened muscular tension to co-occur as a favoured pattern in the segmental patterns of the majority of languages. Fant (1960) supports the 'traditional' position, and adds a comment on the contribution of muscle tension in the walls of the vocal tract to the acoustic output of the system:

The effect of the muscular strain traditionally claimed to be associated with the tense stops is to prolong the fricative interval of semi-closure. In the case of the tense vowels, the muscular strain cannot be expected to affect the damping of the cavity walls and thus influence the formant bandwidths to any significant extent. The tenseness and the longer duration condition an articulation further away from the neutral position, and those formant bandwidths variations that do occur, are due to the varying degrees of opening. (Fant 1960: 225).

The moment-to-moment variations in formant bandwidth that can be observed during continuous speech are therefore to be attributed not to the fluctuations of muscle tension in the walls of the tract, but to the effect of momentary configurational changes of segmental articulation. However, it is possible that the degree of difference of muscular tension between tense voice and lax voice may sometimes be greater than the differences of tension in the speech of a given speaker between tense and lax segments. Accordingly, in tense voice and lax voice in such cases, it may be possible to link some of the narrowing of formant bandwidths with the reflective effect of tense cavity walls, and some of the broadening with the attenuating effect of lax walls. It was also noted earlier that some of the broadening of formant bandwidths in lax voice is due to the damping effect of the inefficient phonation of 'weak', breathy voice (Fant 1972: 50).

The constellation of individual local settings that make up tense voice, and those that make up lax voice, can be summarized in the following way. A tense voice will tend to have these characteristics: ligamental, harsh or ventricular phonation which will sound comparatively louder and higher-pitched; higher subglottal air pressure; slightly raised larynx; constriction of the upper larynx and lower pharynx, and possibly of the faucal pillars; a tensed velum; vigorous and extensive radial movements of the convex-surfaced tongue in segmental articulation;

vigorous activity of the lips; and a more mobile jaw. A lax voice will tend to have the opposite characteristics: breathy or whispery phonation which will sound comparatively softer and lower-pitched; lower sub-glottal air pressure; a slightly lowered larynx; an unconstricted pharynx; moderate nasality; inhibited, minimized radial movements of the relaxed, relatively flat-surfaced tongue in segmental articulation; minimal activity of the lips; and a relatively immobile jaw. Although these are gross characterizations, it is striking that it seems possible to relate tendencies to use one type of tension setting rather than the other to typical behaviour of speakers of particular languages. French and German pronunciation tends to use slightly tense voice; Received Pronunciation of British English tends to use rather lax voice (Honikman 1964).

In a phonological role, tense and lax settings offer an interesting example of settings with partial, complementary distributions over the inventory of segments of a language. An instance of complementary distribution of this sort is found in Etsako (Laver 1967, 1969). This is an Edo language spoken by some 120,000 people near the Niger–Benue confluence in Nigeria. In Etsako, differences of overall muscular tension in the production of syllables are used as the basis for a phonological opposition. In a traditional phonemic analysis, consonant-harmony can be said to operate, and three sets of consonants can be suggested. These are: a tense set, a lax set and a neutral set. Harmonic rules apply, in that tense and lax consonants cannot co-occur within a monomorphemic stretch of speech, though members of the neutral set can occur with either. Words which show a mixture of tense and lax consonants are thereby signalled as morphologically complex. To illustrate this, we can briefly consider a number of Etsako words. Using 'h' after a consonant symbol to denote the lax phoneme of a tense–lax pair (as does the local orthography), then morphologically simple words which show the tense – lax opposition are: /ɔka/ 'maize', /ɔkha/ 'porcupine'; /agogo/ 'bell', /aghogho/ 'brain'; /aru/ 'hat', /arhu/ 'louse'. Tone is not marked, but is not a conditioning factor. Morphologically complex words mixing tense and lax consonants are: /ukokorhe/ 'to gather', from /ukoko/ 'to collect' and /-rhe/ 'away from original position'; /urɛkhaa/ 'to accompany', from /urɛ/ 'to use' and /-khaa/ 'together, jointly'; and /igwogho/ 'dried stems of elephant grass' (for thatching), from /igwa/ 'bones' and /ogho/ 'elephant grass'.

It is clear that the differences of muscular tension are a matter of settings, from the following details of phonetic realization: /k/ is realized by a tense voiceless velar stop, /kh/ by a lax voiceless velar stop in free variation with a lax voiceless velar fricative; /g/ is realized by a tense voiced velar stop, /gh/ by a lax voiced velar stop in free variation with a lax voiced velar fricative; /r/ is realized by a tense voiceless alveolar tap, in free variation with a tense voiced alveolar tap, with a tense voiceless alveolar fricative tap allophone before back vowels, and /rh/ by a lax voiced alveolar tap in free variation with a lax voiced post-alveolar approximant. Tense consonants are of longer duration than lax consonants. There are seven vowel phonemes /i e ɛ a ɔ o u/. The allophones of /i e o u/ are closer and more peripheral when they occur in tense morphemes, and more open and more central in lax morphemes. Inter-consonantal allophones of all vowels are longer in duration after tense than after lax consonants. Utterance-final allophones tend to be glottalized after tense consonants, and pronounced with breathy voice after lax consonants. Utterance-initial allophones before a tense consonant are shorter than before a lax consonant (Laver 1967: 54–5).

5 *Labels and notation for phonetic settings*

The purpose of this chapter is firstly to offer a brief discussion of possible conventions for organizing a phonetic labelling system for settings used in voice quality. Secondly, a notational system is described, providing a list of symbols and diacritics for the transcription of phonetic settings.

5.1 Descriptive phonetic labels for phonetic settings

The descriptive system outlined in the earlier chapters yields a large number of different phonetic labels. Since many of these are capable of combination, to describe voices characterized by composite settings it is clearly desirable to have some explicit structural conventions governing the shape of the necessary composite labels. These conventions specify the sequence and combination of the terms used in composite labels.

The first convention is that composite labels should basically have only two possible overall structures. If labels for tension settings are represented for the sake of this discussion by T, those for supralaryngeal settings by S and those for phonatory settings by P, then the first of the alternative structures for a composite label should be TSP. An example of this would be *tense velarized falsetto*.

The second possible structure is the order TPS, where supralaryngeal settings are represented by the phrase 'with ...', as in *tense falsetto with velarization*, or *lax breathy voice with retroflex articulation*. The only other structure which should be used, if one is to avoid terminological chaos, is an amalgam of the two suggested above, with the labels representing S divided into the two possible positions, in a TSPS structure. An example of this is *tense pharyngalized creaky voice with nasality*.

Most often, it will not be necessary to fill all three structural places in a composite label. Whenever a structural place is left unfilled, it can be assumed that the *neutral* setting relevant to that place in structure is operating, or that the nature of the setting applicable to the unfilled place is irrelevant. For example, in a composite label such as *nasal creak*, the assumption will hold that the overall tension setting in that voice is neutral or irrelevant. The one structural place that should always be explicitly filled is P, the specification of the phonation type. This will most often merely be *voice*, as in *nasal voice*, and the assumption can be made that the use of *voice* without further phonatory specification means *modal voice*.

Some conventional internal structure can also be given to the different individual settings within each of the three major places in a composite label. The discussion of these conventions also affords a useful opportunity to bring together in one place all the labels for the many different settings that have been discussed in the earlier chapters, and to set them out in summary form.

No internal sequence is involved in the labels for tension settings. The choice is merely of one from two non-neutral possibilities, *tense* and *lax*.

Conventions for the sequence of labels within the supralaryngeal group are helpful. Arbitrarily, the convention can be that the order of labels in the S element of the composite label should be as follows: firstly, *longitudinal* settings, then *latitudinal* settings, and lastly *velopharyngeal* settings. Within each category, the assumption still holds that neutral values apply in the absence of explicit mention of a particular setting.

The sequential order of labels for settings within these categories largely follows the anatomical progression from the lips to the larynx. The summary list, with its implied sequence, is as follows:

LABELS FOR SUPRALARYNGEAL SETTINGS

Settings of the longitudinal axis of the vocal tract

labial	labial protrusion
	labiodentalized
laryngeal	raised larynx
	lowered larynx

Settings of the latitudinal axis of the vocal tract

labial	horizontal expansion of the interlabial space
	vertical expansion
	horizontal constriction
	vertical constriction
	horizontal expansion and vertical expansion
	horizontal constriction and vertical constriction
	horizontal expansion and vertical constriction
	horizontal constriction and vertical expansion

lingual

tip/blade	tip articulation
	blade articulation
	retroflex articulation
tongue-body	dentalized
	alveolarized
	palato-alveolarized
	palatalized
	velarized
	uvularized
	pharyngalized
	laryngo-pharyngalized
tongue-root	advanced tongue-root
	retracted tongue-root
faucal	faucalized
pharyngeal	pharyngalized
mandibular	close jaw position
	open jaw position
	protruded jaw

Settings of the velopharyngeal system

  nasal

  denasal

The terms describing labial activity are suitable for a precise discussion of the detailed articulatory aspects of the settings, but very often such specificity is not necessary. When brief labelling is adequate, then the more familiar labels of traditional phonetic description can be used, as briefly discussed in the section of labial settings. The phrase *with spread lips* or *with lip-spreading* can be used for every label in which *horizontal expansion* occurs. Similarly, *with rounded lips*, or *with lip-rounding* can be used for every label in which *horizontal constriction* occurs. When a slightly greater specificity is needed, *with open lip-rounding* can be used for *horizontal constriction with vertical expansion*, and *with close lip-rounding* translates both *horizontal constriction* and *horizontal constriction with vertical constriction*. It can normally be assumed that open rounding and close rounding will both have labial protrusion as a co-occurring setting, and *labial protrusion* in those contexts can be omitted.

Examples of the conventional sequence of supralaryngeal labels are: *tense, harsh voice with open rounding, pharyngalization and open jaw* (TPS structure); *whispery creaky voice with labiodentalization, tip articulation and nasality* (PS structure); *nasal voice with close lip-rounding and velarization* (SPS structure); and *velarized harsh whispery voice with raised larynx, open lip-rounding and nasality* (SPS structure). A certain flexibility is retained by not constraining the sequence of labels in the divided S-representatives in an SPS structure to follow the anatomical ordering that obtains within one S element.

It is useful to adopt similar general conventions for the phonatory labels. The first constraint, on permissible combinations of phonatory settings, has already been discussed in the section on compound phonation types. A related convention deals with the sequential order of the phonatory items in composite labels.

It will be recalled that the different phonation types were classified into three groups, depending on criteria of combinatory potentials. The first group was made up of *modal voice* and *falsetto*, the second of *whisper* and *creak*, and the third of *harshness* and *breathiness*. The sequential constraints on these labels take account of this classification. The convention is that if either member of the first group, *modal voice* or *falsetto*, is present, then it will take the final position in the P element of the composite label. If a member of the second group, *whisper* or *creak*, is present, then it will take the penultimate position in the P element, unless the first group is not represented, in which case *whisper* or *creak* will take the final position. If both *whisper* and *creak* are present, then arbitrarily *whisper* will precede *creak* to give *whispery creak*. Whenever a member of the third group, *harshness* or *breathiness*, is present, it will always take the initial position in the P element of the composite label. In this way, composite labels are produced such as *breathy voice*, for the combination of breathiness and modal voice, *creaky voice*, *whispery falsetto*, *whispery creaky falsetto*, *harsh whispery voice*, and so forth.

If all incompatible combinations of compound phonation types are omitted, the complete list of phonation types, in the descriptive framework offered here, is as follows:

LABELS FOR LARYNGEAL SETTINGS

Simple phonation types	modal voice
	falsetto
	whisper
	creak

Compound phonation types	whispery creak
	whispery voice
	whispery falsetto
	creaky voice
	creaky falsetto
	whispery creaky voice
	whispery creaky falsetto
	breathy voice
	harsh voice
	harsh falsetto
	harsh creak
	harsh whispery voice
	harsh whispery falsetto
	harsh creaky voice
	harsh creaky falsetto
	harsh whispery creaky voice
	harsh whispery creaky falsetto

The twenty-one items are not, of course, of equally frequent occurrence. The phonation types involving *falsetto* are much rarer than the others, for instance. *Breathy voice* is much more common than the single appearance in the list of the label *breathy* might suggest.

5.2 Scalar conventions for voice quality labels

It is sometimes necessary to go beyond the decision that a particular voice is characterized by the presence of some given setting, to an analysis of the scalar degree of that setting. At least three degrees of perceptual prominence of most settings can be fairly easily distinguished – *slight*, *moderate* and *extreme* degrees. We can thus refer, for example, to a *slightly velarized voice*, a *moderately breathy voice* or an *extremely tense voice*. When composite labels of some complexity are involved, then the application of each scalar label can be made clear by punctuation, as in a *slightly tense, moderately velarized, extremely whispery voice with slight nasality*.

Some economy can be made in the use of scalar labels by the convention that when no scalar label is explicitly given, then either the moderate value can be taken to apply, or the scalar degree is irrelevant.

The one component of a composite label that cannot be given a scalar specification is the last item in the phonatory element of the label. There are four phonation types that can appear in this position, *modal voice, falsetto, whisper* and *creak*. The first two never appear in any other position than the final one in the P element, so never have scalar labels attached to them in any circumstances. The last two, however, can appear not only in the final position, but also in the penultimate position, as in *whispery voice* and *creaky falsetto*. When penultimate, *whisper* and *creak* can properly have scalar labels attached to them, as in *slightly whispery falsetto*.

5.3 Notation for settings

It is convenient to have a set of symbols and diacritics for the phonetic transcription of settings, to be used in phonological, paralinguistic and voice quality applications. The notation suggested here covers nearly all the settings described in this book. It is designed to obey, wherever possible, the conventions of the International Phonetics Association for segmental transcription, and to be easy to read, write and print. There is a limit to the phonetic specificity of the notational symbols, just as there is in segmental transcription. When greater specificity is required, prose expansions of the notation are necessary.

It was suggested in Chapter 1 that settings can be abstracted from a chain of segments as the shared properties of those segments. This is reflected in the suggested notation system, in that the symbols for the transcription of settings are prefaced to the segmental transcription. The effect of abstracting some of the shared properties of the different segments in an utterance, and representing them in a separate setting symbol, is to make the segmental transcription less narrow. An example illustrating this would be two alternative transcriptions of an utterance pronounced with velarized voice. A traditional, narrow transcription of the phrase 'Sweet deserved an Oxford chair' in Received Pronunciation with velarization, where all the textual information (Abercrombie 1964) was carried by the segmental symbols, would be:

[ɐwiʈ dɪ̴zɜ̴vd ə̴ɴ ɒksfɘ̴d ʈʃɛ̴ə]

A phonetic transcription which abstracted the velarization component from susceptible segments for separate representation in the prefacing setting symbol would be:

Ɐ [swit dɪzɜvd ən ɒksfəd tʃɛə]

The two transcriptions of course reflect exactly the same utterance. They differ only in the location of information about aspects of the pronunciation. The gain in legibility is clear.

The symbols for settings are organized on a mnemonic basis, using T, L, J, V, F, W, and C for tension, larynx position, jaw position, voice, falsetto, whisper and creak respectively. The symbols and diacritics will be discussed according to the group of settings concerned, and then will be summarized in a single comprehensive list.

As a general convention, when no setting symbol is specified, then the neutral value will be taken to apply.

Settings of overall muscular tension can be symbolized by T for *tense voice* and T̟ for *lax voice*.

Settings of the longitudinal axis of the vocal tract are symbolized by L̂ for *raised larynx* and L̬ for *lowered larynx*. No separate symbol is suggested for labial protrusion alone, given that it is assumed to be a normal component of open and close lip-rounding, for which individual symbols are provided, and normally to be absent on other lip-settings. *Labiodentalized voice* is transcribed with a subscript diacritic on the general symbol V, as V̪.

V is used as the basis for the remaining latitudinal settings, with the exception of mandibular settings. The diacritics for the latitudinal settings are as follows:

open rounding	V̮
close rounding	V̮̮
spread lips	V̧
tip articulation	V̂
blade articulation (neutral)	V̬
retroflex articulation	V̢
dentalized voice	V̤
alveolarized voice	V̟̟
palato-alveolarized voice	V̟
palatalized voice	V̧
velarized voice	V̶
uvularized voice	V̶̠
pharyngalized voice	V̶̈
laryngo-pharyngalized voice	V̶̈

Mandibular settings are symbolized as Ĵ for *close jaw*, J̬ for *open jaw*, and J̟ for *protruded jaw*.

Velopharyngeal settings use the general symbol V, with $\tilde{\text{V}}$ for *nasal voice* and $\tilde{\text{V}}$ for *denasal voice*. Faucalization and tongue-root adjustments are left without suggested symbols in this list.

Symbols for phonatory settings are as follows: *modal voice* is indicated by the general symbol V, *falsetto* by F, *whisper* by W and *creak* by C. Compound phonation types are signalled by the use of diacritics on the symbol for the simple phonation type concerned. *Creaky voice* is symbolized by V̰, *creaky falsetto* by F̰, *whispery voice* by V̞, *whispery falsetto* by F̞, *whispery creak* by C̞, *breathy voice* by V̤, *harsh voice* by V!, *harsh falsetto* by F!, *harsh whispery voice* by V̞!, *harsh whispery creaky voice* by V̰!, and so forth.

A problem of legibility arises from the possibility of multiple diacritics being attached to single letters in this notation system. A composite voice such as *velarized nasal whispery creaky voice* could by symbolized by $\tilde{\text{V}}$. Such illegibility is clearly undesirable, however, and an alternative method is to use as many separate symbols as necessary. *Velarized nasal whispery creaky voice* could then be transcribed as V̴ Ṽ V̞ V̰, or as any convenient combination of these.

The use of multiple symbols makes the indication of scalar degrees of settings a more amenable problem. If slight, moderate and extreme degrees are indicated by the digits 1, 2 and 3 respectively, then *extremely tense, slightly velarized, moderately whispery voice* can be transcribed as 3T̟ 1V̴ 2V̞. If no scalar degree is explicitly indicated, then the degree can be assumed to be moderate or irrelevant.

Scalar degrees are useful in the indication of composite settings such as *ventricular voice*, as being synonymous with *extremely harsh voice* (3V!). Similarly, *whispery voice* with the modal voice component auditorily dominant can be transcribed as 1V̞, while *whispery voice* with the whisper component dominant can be indicated by 3V̞.

The symbols and diacritics for the notation of settings are summarized in Table 2.

Table 2. *Summary list of symbols and diacritics for the notation of settings*

Setting	Symbol	Setting	Symbol
tense voice	T̟	palatalized voice	V̵
lax voice	T̠	velarized voice	V̶
raised larynx	L̝	uvularized voice	V̴
lowered larynx	L̞	pharyngalized voice	V̴
labiodentalized voice	V̪	laryngo-pharyngalized voice	V̴
open rounding	V̜	close jaw position	J̝
close rounding	V̹	open jaw position	J̞
spread lips	V̺	protruded jaw position	J̟
tip articulation	V̝	modal voice	V
blade articulation	V̦	falsetto	F
retroflex articulation	V̨	whisper	W
nasal voice	Ṽ	creak	C
denasal voice	Ṽ	whispery voice	V̤
dentalized voice	V̪	creaky voice	V̰
alveolarized voice	V̟₊₊	breathy voice	V̤
palatoalveolarized voice	V̟₊	harsh voice	V!

Scalar degrees of settings can be indicated on a three-point basis; e.g. 'slightly harsh voice' = $1V!$, 'moderately harsh voice' = $2V!$, and 'extremely harsh voice' (synonymous with 'ventricular voice') = $3V!$ Composite settings can be indicated by either composite symbols or by multiple symbols; 'nasal whispery creaky voice', for example can be symbolized either as Ṽ̰, or as ṼV̤V̰.

References

Abercrombie, D. (1964) *English phonetic texts*, Faber, London

Abercrombie, D. (1967) *Elements of general phonetics*, Edinburgh University Press

Abercrombie, D., Fry, D. B., MacCarthy, P. A. D., Scott, N. C. and Trim, J. L. M. (Eds.) (1964) *In honour of Daniel Jones*, Longmans, London

Aikin, W. A. (1910) *The voice : an introduction to practical phonology*, Longmans, London (New edn edited by Rumsey, H. St. J.,) (1951)

Anderson, V. A. (1942) *Training the speaking voice*, Oxford University Press, London

Appaix, A., Sprecher, R., Hénin, J. and Favot, C. (1963) A propos de la rhinolalie dans l'amygdalectomie et de l'adenoidectomie, *Journal Français de l'Otorhinolaryngologie* 12 : 211–14

Ardener, E. (Ed.) (1970) *Social Anthropology and Language*, Association of Social Anthropologists Monograph No. 10, Tavistock Press, London

Arnold, D. G. F., Denes, P., Gimson, A. C., O'Connor, J. D. and Trim, J. L. M. (1958) The synthesis of English vowels, *Language and Speech* 1 : 114–25

Aronson, A. E., Peterson, H. W. and Litin, E. M. (1964) Voice symptomatology in functional dysphonia and aphonia, *Journal of Speech and Hearing Disorders* 29 : 367–80

Aubin, A. (Ed.) (1957) *Larynx et phonation – anatomie, physiologie, clinique, pathologie*, Presses Universitaires de France, Paris

Baer, T. (1973) Measurement of vibration patterns of excised larynxes, *Journal of the Acoustical Society of America* 54 : 318(A)

Bayly, A. (1758) *An introduction to languages, literary and philosophical, especially to the English, Latin, Greek and Hebrew*, J. & J. Rivington, J. Fletcher, P. Vaillant and R. & J. Dodsley, London

Bazell, C. E., Catford, J. C., Halliday, M. A. K. and Robins, R. H. (Eds.) (1966) *In memory of J. R. Firth*, Longmans, London

Bell, A. and Hooper, J. B. (Eds.) (1978) *Syllables and segments*, North-Holland, Amsterdam

Bell, A. G. (1908) *The mechanism of speech*, Funk & Wagnalls, New York

Bell, A. M. (1867) *Visible speech : the science of universal alphabetics*, Simpkin, Marshall, London

Bell-Berti, F. (1973) The velopharyngeal mechanism: an electromyographic study, Ph.D. dissertation, City University of New York

Benson, J. (1951) An experimental study of the relationship between amount of

166

nasal emission of air and judged nasality, M.A. thesis, University of West Virginia

Berg, J. van den (1954a) Sur les théories myoélastiques et neurochronaxiques de la phonation, *Revue de Laryngologie* 74: 494–512

Berg, J. van den (1954b) Uber die Koppelung bei der Stimmbildung, *Zeitschrift für Phonetik* 8: 281–92

Berg, J. van den (1955) On the role of the laryngeal ventricle in voice production, *Folia Phoniatrica* 7: 57–69

Berg, J. van den (1956) Physiology and physics of voice production, *Acta Physiologica et Pharmacologica Néerlandais* 5: 481–96

Berg, J. van den (1957a) Subglottic pressures and vibrations of the vocal folds, *Folia Phoniatrica* 9: 65–71

Berg, J. van den (1957b) Physiologie et physique de la vibration des cordes vocales, in Aubin, A. (1957) pp. 51–69

Berg, J. van den (1958a) On the myoelastic theory of voice production, *Bulletin of the National Association of Teachers of Speech* 14: 6–12

Berg, J. van den (1958b) Myoelastic–aerodynamic theory of voice production, *Journal of Speech and Hearing Research* 1: 227–44

Berg, J. van den (1962) Modern research in experimental phoniatrics, *Folia Phoniatrica* 14: 81–149

Berg, J. van den (1968) Mechanism of the larynx and the laryngeal vibrations, in Malmberg, B. (1968) pp. 278–308

Berg, J. van den and Tan, T. S. (1959) Results of experiments with human larynxes, *Practica Oto-Rhino-Laryngologica* 21: 425–50

Berg, J. van den, Vennard, W., Berger, D. and Shervanian, C. C. (1960) Voice production. The vibrating larynx, Film, SFW-UNFI, Utrecht

Berg, J. van den, Zantema, J. F. and Doornenbal, J. P. (1959) On the air resistance and the Bernoulli effect of the human larynx, *Journal of the Acoustical Society of America* 29: 626–31

Berry, M. F. and Eisenson, J. (1942) *The defective in speech*, Appleton-Century-Crofts, New York

Berry, M. F. and Eisenson, J. (1956) *Speech disorders*, Appleton-Century-Crofts, New York

Björk, L. (1961) Velopharyngeal function in connected speech. Studies using tomography and cineradiography synchronized with speech spectrography, *Acta Radiologica* (Stockholm), Supplement No. 202

Bjuggren, G. and Fant, G. (1964) The nasal cavity structures, *Quarterly Progress and Status Report* 4: 5–7, Speech Transmission Laboratory, Royal Institute of Technology, Stockholm

Bloomer, H. (1953) Observations on palatopharyngeal movements in speech and deglutition, *Journal of Speech and Hearing Disorders* 18: 230–46

Bloomfield, L. (1933) *Language*, Henry Holt, New York

Bosma, J. F. (1953) Studies of disability of the pharynx resultant from poliomyelitis, *Annals of Otology, Rhinology and Laryngology* 62: 529–47

Bosma, J. F. (1957a) Deglutition: pharyngeal stage, *Physiological Review* 37: 275–300

Bosma, J. F. (1957b) Poliomyelitic disabilities of the upper pharynx, *Pediatrics* 19:5ff.

Bosma, J. F. (1961) Comparative physiology of the pharynx, in *Congenital anomalies of the face and associated structures*, Thomas, Springfield

Bosma, J. F. and Fletcher, S. G. (1961) The upper pharynx: a review. Part I. Embryology, anatomy, *Annals of Otology, Rhinology and Laryngology* 70:953–73

Bosma, J. F. and Fletcher, S. G. (1962) The upper pharynx: a review. Part II. Physiology, *Annals of Otology, Rhinology and Laryngology* 71:134–57

Brackett, I. P. (1940) The growth of inflammation of the vocal folds accompanying easy and harsh production of the voice, M.A. thesis, Northwestern University

Broad, D. J. (1973) Phonation, in Minifie, F. D., Hixon, T. J. and Williams, F. (1973) pp. 127–67

Broad, D. J. (1977) *Short course in speech science*, Speech Communications Research Laboratory, Santa Barbara

Brown, P. and Levinson, S. (1978) Universals in language usage: politeness phenomena, in Goody, E. N. (1978) pp. 56–289

Buck, M. W. (1954) Post-operative velo-pharyngeal movements in cleft palate cases, *Journal of Speech and Hearing Disorders* 19:288–94

Bullen, A. (1942) Nasality: cause and remedy of our American blight, *Quarterly Journal of Speech* 28:83–4

Cagliari, L. C. (1978) An experimental study of nasality with particular reference to Brazilian Portuguese, Ph.D. dissertation, University of Edinburgh

Calnan, J. (1953) Movements of the soft palate, *British Journal of Plastic Surgery* 5:280–96

Calnan, J. (1954) The error of Gustav Passavant, *Plastic and Reconstructive Surgery* 13:275–89

Carterette, E. C. and Friedman, M. P. (Eds.) (1976) *Handbook of perception*, Vol. 7, *Language and speech*, Academic Press, New York

Cates, H. A. and Basmajian, J. V. (1955) *Primary anatomy* (3rd edn), Williams and Wilkins, Baltimore

Catford, J. C. (1964) Phonation types: the classification of some laryngeal components of speech production, in Abercrombie, D. *et al.* (1964) pp. 26–37

Catford, J. C. (1977) *Fundamental problems in phonetics*, Edinburgh University Press

Chiba, T. and Kajiyama, M. (1958) *The vowel: its nature and structure*, Phonetic Society of Japan, Tokyo (first published 1941)

Chomsky, N. and Halle, M. (1968) *The sound pattern of English*, Harper & Row, New York

Coleman, R. F. (1960) Some acoustic correlates of hoarseness, M.A. thesis, Vanderbilt University

Coleman, R. F. (1963) Decay characteristics of vocal fry, *Folia Phoniatrica* 15:256–63

Coleman, R. F. and Wendahl, R. W. (1967) Vocal roughness and stimulus duration, *Speech Monographs* 34:85–92

Condax, I. D., Acson, V., Miki, C. C. and Sakoda, K. K. (1976) A technique for monitoring velic action by means of a photo-electric nasal probe: application to French, *Journal of Phonetics* 4:173–81

Cooper, C. (1685) *Grammatica linguae anglicanae*, B. Tooke, London

Cooper, F. S., Peterson, E. and Fahringer, G. S. (1957) Some sources of characteristic vocoder quality, *Journal of the Acoustical Society of America* 29:183(A)

Craig, W. C. and Sokolowsky, R. R. (1945) *The preacher's voice*, The Warthburg Press, Columbus

Crystal, D. (1970) Prosodic and paralinguistic correlates of social categories, in Ardener, E. (1970) pp. 185–206

Curtis, J. F. (1942) An experimental study of the wave-composition of nasal voice-quality, Ph.D. dissertation, State University of Iowa

Curtis, J. F. (1970) The acoustics of nasalized speech, *Cleft Palate Journal* 7:380–96

David, E. E. and Denes, P. B. (Eds.) (1972) *Human communication: a unified view*, McGraw-Hill, New York

Davis, E. B. (1941) Nasal twang, *Le Maître Phonétique* 56:4–5

Delattre, P. (1954) Les attributs acoustiques de la nasalité vocalique et consonantique, *Studia Linguistica* 8:103–9

Diamond, M. (1952) Dental anatomy (3rd edn), Macmillan, New York

Dickson, D. R. (1962) An acoustic study of nasality, *Journal of Speech and Hearing Research* 5:103–11

Dickson, D. R. and Dickson, W. M. (1972) Velopharyngeal anatomy, *Journal of Speech and Hearing Research* 15:372–81

Diehl, C. F. and McDonald, E. T. (1956) Effect of voice quality on communication, *Journal of Speech and Hearing Disorders* 21:233–7

Doke, C. M. (1931) *A comparative study in Shona phonetics*, University of the Witwatersrand, Johannesburg

Dunstan, E. (Ed.) (1969) *Twelve Nigerian languages*, Longmans, Green, London

Eijkman, L. P. H. (1926) The soft palate and nasality, *Neophilologus* 11:207–18 and 277–8

Esling, J. H. (1978) Voice quality in Edinburgh: a sociolinguistic and phonetic study, Ph.D. dissertation, University of Edinburgh

Faaborg-Andersen, K. (1957) Electromyographic investigation of intrinsic laryngeal muscles in humans, *Acta Physiologica Scandinavica*, Supplement No. 140:1–149

Fairbanks, G. (1960) *Voice and articulation drill-book* (2nd edn), Harper & Row, New York

Fant, G. (1956) On the predictability of formant levels and spectrum envelopes from formant frequencies, in Halle, M., Lunt, H. and MacLean, H. (1956) pp. 109–20

Fant, G. (1957) Modern instruments and methods for acoustic studies of speech, *Proceedings of the 8th International Congress of Linguists*, Oslo, pp. 282–388. Also in *Acta Polytechnica Scandinavica* 1:1–81 (1958)

Fant, G. (1960) *Acoustic theory of speech production*, Mouton, The Hague

Fant, G. (1962) Descriptive analysis of the acoustic aspects of speech, *Logos* 5:3–17

Fant, G. (1964) Formants and cavities, *Proceedings of the 5th International Congress of Phonetic Sciences*, Münster

Fant, G. (1966) A note on vocal tract size factors and non-uniform f-pattern scalings, *Quarterly Progress and Status Report* 4:22–30, Speech Transmission Laboratory, Royal Institute of Technology, Stockholm

Fant, G. (1968) Analysis and synthesis of speech processes, in Malmberg, B. (1968) pp. 173–277

Fant, G. (1972) Vocal tract wall effects, losses, and resonance bandwidths, *Quarterly Progress and Status Report* 2–3: 28–52, Speech Transmission Laboratory, Royal Institute of Technology, Stockholm

Fant, G. (1975) Vocal-tract area and length perturbations, *Quarterly Progress and Status Report* 4:1–14, Speech Transmission Laboratory, Royal Institute of Technology, Stockholm

Farnsworth, D. W. (1940) High speed motion pictures of the human vocal cords (and film), *Bell Laboratories Record* 18:203–8

Firth, J. R. (1951) Modes of meaning, *Essays and Studies of the English Association* 4:118–49

Flanagan, J. L. (1958) Some properties of the glottal sound source, *Journal of Speech and Hearing Research* 1:99–116

Flanagan, J. L. (1965) *Speech analysis, synthesis and perception*, Springer, Berlin

Flanagan, J. L. and Landgraf, L. L. (1968) Self-oscillating source for vocal-tract synthesizers, *IEEE Transactions on Audio and Electroacoustics*, Vol. AU-16, 1:57–64, March

Fletcher, W. W. (1947) A high-speed motion picture study of vocal fold action in certain voice qualities, M. A. thesis, University of Washington

Fónagy, I. (1962) Mimik auf glottaler Ebene, *Phonetica* 8:209–19

Franke, F. (1889) Die Umgangssprache der Niederlausitz in ihren Lauten, *Phonetische Studien* 2:21–60

Frederickson, J. M. and Ward, P. H. (1962) Laryngocele ventricularis, *Archives of Otolaryngology* 76:568–73

Freud, E. D. (1962) Functions and dysfunctions of the ventricular folds, *Journal of Speech and Hearing Disorders* 27:334–40

Fritzell, B. (1969) The velopharyngeal muscles in speech: an electromyographic and cineradiographic study, *Acta Otolaryngologica*, Supplement No. 250:1–81

Frøkjaer-Jensen, B. and Prytz, S. (1976) Registration of voice quality, *Bruel and Kjaer Technical Review* 3:3–17

Fromkin, V. (1965) Some phonetic specifications of linguistic units: an electromyographic investigation, *Working Papers in Phonetics* No. 3, Department of Linguistics, University of California at Los Angeles

Fujimura, O. (1962) Analysis of nasal consonants, *Journal of the Acoustical Society of America* 34:1865–75

Fujimura, O. (1980) Elementary gestures and temporal organization – what does an articulatory constraint mean? in Myers, T. F., Laver, J. and Anderson, J. (1980)

Fujimura, O. and Lovins, J. B. (1978) Syllables as concatenative phonetic units, in Bell, A. and Hooper, J. B. (1978) pp. 107–20

Glasgow, G. M. (1944) The effects of nasality on oral communication, *Quarterly Journal of Speech* 30: 337–40

Goerttler, K. (1950) Die Anordnung, Histologie und Histogenese der quergestreiften Muskulatur in menschlichen Stimmband, *Zeitschrift für Anatomie und Entwickelungsgeschichte* 115: 352–401

Goody, E. N. (Ed.) (1978) *Questions and politeness: strategies in social interaction*, Cambridge University Press

Gray, G. W. and Wise, C. M. (1959) *The bases of speech* (3rd edn), Harper, New York

Greene, M. C. L. (1964) *The voice and its disorders* (2nd edn), Pitman Medical, London; (3rd edn), Lippincott, Philadelphia (1972)

Gregerson, K. J. (1973) Tongue-root and register in Mon-Khmer, *Proceedings of the 1st International Conference on Austroasiatic Linguistics*

Gutzmann, H. (Sr) (1901) *Von den verschiedenen Formen des Naselns*, Marhold, Halle/Saale

Hahn, E. F., Lomas, C. W., Hargis, D. E. and Vandraegen, D. (1952) *Basic voice training for speech*, McGraw-Hill, New York

Halle, M., Lunt, H. and MacLean, H. (Eds.) (1956) *For Roman Jakobson*, Mouton, The Hague

Hardcastle, W. J. (1976) *The physiology of speech production*, Academic Press, New York

Harrington, R. (1944) Study of the mechanism of velopharyngeal closure, *Journal of Speech Disorders* 9: 325–45

Harris, Z. (1944) Simultaneous components in phonology, *Language* 20:181–205

Hattori, S., Yamamoto, K. and Fujimura, O. (1956) Nasalization of vowels and nasals, *Bulletin of the Kobayasi Institute of Physical Research* 6: 226–35

Heffner, R.-M. S. (1950) *General phonetics*, University of Wisconsin Press, Madison

Henderson, E. J. A. (1951) The phonology of loanwords in some South-East Asian languages, *Transactions of the Philological Society*, pp. 131–58

Henke, W. L. (1966) Dynamic articulatory model of speech production using computer simulation, Ph.D. dissertation, Massachusetts Institute of Technology

Herries, J. (1773) *The elements of speech*, E. & C. Dilly, London

Hess, D. A. (1959) Pitch, intensity, and cleft palate voice quality, *Journal of Speech and Hearing Research* 2:113–25

Hirano, M. (1975) Phonosurgery. Basic and clinical investigations, *Otologia Fukuoka* 21: 239–440 [in Japanese]

Hirano, M. (1977) Structure and vibratory behavior of the vocal folds, in Sawashima, M. and Cooper, F. S. (1977) pp. 13–27

Hirose, H. and Gay, T. (1972) The activity of the intrinsic laryngeal muscles in voicing control – an electromyographic study, *Phonetica* 25:140–64

Hiroto, I. (1966) Patho-physiology of the larynx from the standpoint of vocal mechanism, *Practica Otologica Kyoto* 59: 229–92

Hixon, E. H. (1949) An X-ray study comparing oral and pharyngeal structures of individuals with nasal voices and individuals with superior voices, M.A. thesis, State University of Iowa

Holder, W. (1669) *Elements of speech*, F. Martyn, London

Hollien, H. (1971) Three major vocal registers: a proposal, *Proceedings of the 7th International Congress of Phonetic Sciences*, Montreal, pp. 320–31

Hollien, H. (1974) On vocal registers, *Journal of Phonetics* 2:125–43

Hollien, H., Coleman, R. and Moore, P. (1968) Stroboscopic laminagraphy of the larynx during phonation, *Acta Otolaryngologica* 65:209–15

Hollien, H. and Colton, R. H. (1969) Four laminagraphic studies of vocal fold thickness, *Folia Phoniatrica* 21:179–98

Hollien, H., Damsté, H. and Murry, T. (1969) Vocal fold length during vocal fry phonation, *Folia Phoniatrica* 21:257–65

Hollien, H. and Michel, J. F. (1968) Vocal fry as a phonational register, *Journal of Speech and Hearing Research* 11:600–4

Hollien, H., Moore, P., Wendahl, R. W. and Michel, J. F. (1966) On the nature of vocal fry, *Journal of Speech and Hearing Research* 9:245–7

Hollien, H. and Wendahl, R. W. (1968) Perceptual study of vocal fry, *Journal of the Acoustical Society of America* 43:506–9

Holmes, F. L. D. (1932) The qualities of the voice, *Quarterly Journal of Speech* 17:249–55

Honikman, B. (1964) Articulatory settings, in Abercrombie, D. *et al.* (1964) pp. 73–84

House, A. S. (1957) Analog studies of nasal consonants, *Journal of Speech and Hearing Disorders* 22:190–204

House, A. S. (1959) A note on optimal vocal frequency, *Journal of Speech and Hearing Research* 2:55–60

House, A. S. and Stevens, K. N. (1956) Analog studies of the nasalization of vowels, *Journal of Speech and Hearing Disorders* 21:218–31

Husson, R. (1950a) Etudes des phénomènes physiologiques et acoustiques de la voix chantée pendant la phonation, D.Sc. thesis, University of Paris

Husson, R. (1950b) Etudes des phénomènes physiologiques et acoustiques fondamentaux de la voix chantée, *La Revue Scientifique* 88:67–112; 131–46; 217–35

Husson, R. (1951) Etude stroboscopique des modifications reflexes de la vibration des cordes vocales déclenchées par des stimulations expérimentales du nerf auditif et du nerf trijumeau, *Comptes Rendus de l'Académie des Sciences* 232:1247–9

Husson, R. (1952) Sur la physiologie vocale, *Annales d'Oto-laryngologie* 69:124–37

Husson, R. (1957) Analyse des forces qui s'exercent sur les cordes vocales de l'homme pendant leur vibration avec ou sans pression sous-glottique, *Revue de Laryngologie*, Supplement No. 78:515–32

Husson, R. (1962) *Physiologie de la phonation*, Masson, Paris

Husson, R. (1964) Sur le fonctionnement phonatoire du larynx, *Proceedings of the 5th International Congress of Phonetic Sciences*, Münster

Ishizaka, K. and Flanagan, J. L. (1972) Synthesis of voiced sounds from a two-mass model of the vocal cords, *Bell System Technical Journal* 51:1233–68

Jakobson, R., Fant, C. G. M. and Halle, M. (1952) Preliminaries to speech analysis. The distinctive features and their correlates, *Technical Report* No. 13, Acoustics Laboratory, Massachusetts Institute of Technology

Jakobson, R. and Halle, M. (1964) Tenseness and laxness, in Abercrombie, D. *et al.* (1964) pp. 96–101

Jones, D. (1962) *An outline of English phonetics* (9th edn), Heffer, Cambridge

Jones, D. and Plaatje, S. T. (1916) *A Sechuana phonetic reader*, University of London Press

Joos, M. (1948) *Acoustic phonetics*, Supplement, *Language* 24

Judson, L. S. V. and Weaver, A. T. (1942) *Voice science*, Appleton-Century-Crofts, New York; (1966) 2nd edn

Kaltenborn, A. (1948) An X-ray study of the velo-pharyngeal closure in nasal and non-nasal speakers, M.A. thesis, North-Western University

Kantner, C. E. and West, R. (1941) *Phonetics*, Harper, New York

Kaplan, H. M. (1960) *Anatomy and physiology of speech*, McGraw-Hill, New York

Kelly, J. P. (1932) A phonophotographic study of nasality in certain speech sounds, Ph.D. dissertation, University of Iowa

Kelz, H. P. (1971) Articulatory basis and second language teaching, *Phonetica* 24:193–211

Kemp, J. A. (Ed., Trans.) (1972) *John Wallis : grammar of the English language, with an introductory treatise on speech*, Longmans, London

Kent, R. D. and Minifie, D. (1977) Coarticulation in recent speech production models, *Journal of Phonetics* 5:115–33

Key, M. (1967) *Morphology of Cayuvava*, Mouton, The Hague

Knowles, G. O. (1978) The nature of phonological variables in Scouse, in Trudgill, P. (1978) pp. 80–90

Kunze, L. H. (1964) Evaluation of methods of estimating sub-glottal air pressure, *Journal of Speech and Hearing Research* 7:151–64

Ladefoged, P. (1964) *A phonetic study of West African languages*, Cambridge University Press

Ladefoged, P. (1971) *Preliminaries to linguistic phonetics*, University of Chicago Press

Ladefoged, P. (1975) *A course in phonetics*, Harcourt Brace Jovanovich, New York

Lafon, J.-C. and Cornut, G. (1960) Vibration neuromusculaire des cordes vocales et théorie de la phonation, *Journal Français d'Oto-Rhino-Laryngologie* 9:317–24

Laget, P. (1953) Reproduction expérimentale de la vibration des cordes vocales en l'absence de tout courant d'air, *Revue de Laryngologie* 74:132–42

Landes, B. A. (1953) An investigation of the relationships between vocal harmonics and listeners' discrimination of fundamental pitch, M.A. thesis, Purdue University

Laver, J. (1967) A preliminary phonology of the Aywele dialect of Etsako, *Journal of West African Languages* 4 : 53–6

Laver, J. (1968) Voice quality and indexical information, *British Journal of Disorders of Communication* 3 : 43–54

Laver, J. (1969) Etsako (Aywele dialect), in Dunstan, E. (1969) pp. 47–55

Laver, J. (1974) Labels for voices, *Journal of the International Phonetic Association* 4 : 62–75

Laver, J. (1975) Individual features in voice quality, Ph.D. dissertation, University of Edinburgh

Laver, J. (1976) Language and nonverbal communication, in Carterette, E. C. and Friedman, M. P. (1976) pp. 345–62

Laver, J. (1977) Early writings on voice quality and tone of voice: from Cicero to Sweet, *Edinburgh University Department of Linguistics Work in Progress* 10 : 92–111

Laver, J. (1978) The concept of articulatory settings: an historical survey, *Historiographia Linguistica* 5 : 1–14

Laver, J. (1979) *Voice quality: a classified bibliography*, John Benjamins, Amsterdam

Laver, J. and Trudgill, P. (1979) Phonetic and linguistic markers in speech, in Scherer, K. R. and Giles, H. (1979) pp. 1–32

Leden, H. von (1961) The mechanism of phonation, *Archives of Otolaryngology* 74 : 660–76

Lindau, M. (1979) The feature 'expanded', *Journal of Phonetics* 7 : 163–76

Lindblom, B. and Sundberg, J. (1969) A quantitative model of vowel production and the distinctive features of Swedish vowels, *Quarterly Progress and Status Report* 1 : 14–32, Speech Transmission Laboratory, Royal Institute of Technology, Stockholm

Lindblom, B. and Sundberg, J. (1971) Acoustical consequences of lip, tongue, jaw, and larynx movement, *Journal of the Acoustical Society of America* 50 : 1166–79

Lindblom, B. and Sundberg, J. (1972) Observations on tongue contour length in spoken and sung vowels, *Quarterly Progress and Status Report* 4 : 1–5, Speech Transmission Laboratory, Royal Institute of Technology, Stockholm

Lindqvist, J. (1969) Laryngeal mechanisms in speech, *Quarterly Progress and Status Report* 2–3 : 26–32, Speech Transmission Laboratory, Royal Institute of Technology, Stockholm

Linke, C. E. (1953) A study of the influence of certain vowel types on human voice quality, *Speech Monographs* 20 : 163(A)

Lubker, J. F. (1969) Velopharyngeal orifice area: a replication of analog experimentation, *Journal of Speech and Hearing Research* 12 : 218–22

Lubker, J. F., Fritzell, B. and Lindqvist, J. (1972) Velopharyngeal function: an electromyographic study, *Proceedings of the 7th International Congress of Phonetic Sciences*, Montreal

Lubker, J. F., Lindqvist, J. and Fritzell, B. (1972) Some temporal characteristics of velopharyngeal muscle function, *Occasional Papers* 13 : 226–69, Language Centre, University of Essex

Lubker, J. F. and Moll, K. L. (1965) Simultaneous oral–nasal air flow measurements and cinefluorographic observations during speech production, *Cleft Palate Journal* 2 : 257–72

Luchsinger, R. (1968) Phonetics and pathology, in Malmberg, B. (1968) pp. 502–32

Luchsinger, R. and Arnold, G. E. (1965) *Voice – speech – language. Clinical communicology : its physiology and pathology*, Constable, London

Lyons, J. (1962) Phonemic and non-phonemic phonology: some typological reflections, *International Journal of American Linguistics* 28 :127–33

McDonald, E. T. and Baker, H. K. (1951) Cleft palate speech: an integration of research and clinical observation, *Journal of Speech and Hearing Disorders* 16 : 9–20

McGlone, R. E. (1967) Air flow during vocal fry phonation, *Journal of Speech and Hearing Research* 10 : 299–304

Malmberg, B. (Ed.) (1968) *Manual of phonetics*, North-Holland, London

Matsushita, H. (1969) Vocal cord vibration of excised larynges – a study with ultra-high-speed cinematography, *Otologia Fukuoka* 15, No. 2 : 127–42 [in Japanese]

Matsushita, H. (1975) The vibratory mode of the vocal folds in the excised larynx, *Folia Phoniatrica* 27 : 7–18

Meader, C. L. and Muyskens, J. H. (1950) *Handbook of biolinguistics*, Weller, Toledo Speech Clinic, Ohio

Meilanova, U. A. (1964) *Očerki Lezginskoj dialektologii*, Nauka, Moscow

Merritt, W. H., Nielsen, M., Bosma, J. F., Goates, W. A., Haskins, R., Ramsell, C. and Lamb, R. H. (1957) Studies of the pharynx: II, *Pediatrics* 19 :1080–7

Michel, J. F. (1964) Vocal fry and harshness, Ph.D. dissertation, University of Florida

Michel, J. F. (1968) Fundamental frequency investigation of vocal fry and harshness, *Journal of Speech and Hearing Research* 11 : 590–4

Michel, J. F. and Hollien, H. (1968) Perceptual differentiation in vocal fry and harshness, *Journal of Speech and Hearing Research* 11 : 439–43

Milisen, R. (1957) Methods of evaluation and diagnosis of speech disorders, in Travis, L. E. (1957) pp. 267–309

Miller, R. L. (1959) Nature of the vocal cord wave, *Journal of the Acoustical Society of America* 31 : 667–77

Minifie, F. D., Hixon, T. J. and Williams, F. (Eds.) (1973) *Normal aspects of speech, hearing and language*, Prentice-Hall, Englewood Cliffs

Monsen, R. B. and Engebretson, A. M. (1977) Study of variations in the male and female glottal wave, *Journal of the Acoustical Society of America* 62 : 981–93

Moore, G. P. (1971) *Organic voice disorders*, Prentice-Hall, Englewood Cliffs

Moore, P. (1957) Voice disorders associated with organic abnormalities, in Travis, L. E. (1957) pp. 653–703

Moore, P. (1962) Observations on the physiology of hoarseness, *Proceedings of the 4th International Congress of Phonetic Sciences*, Helsinki, pp. 92–5

Moore, P. and Leden, H. von (1958) Dynamic variations of the vibratory pattern in the normal larynx, *Folia Phoniatrica* 10 : 205–38

Mörner, M., Fransson, F. and Fant, G. (1963) Voice register terminology and standard pitch, *Quarterly Progress and Status Report* 4:17–23, Speech Transmission Laboratory, Royal Institute of Technology, Stockholm

Morris: (1953) *Human Anatomy* (11th edn), Ed. by J. P. Schaeffer, McGraw-Hill, New York

Moser, H. M., Dreher, J. J. and Adler, S. (1955) Comparison of hyponasality, hypernasality, and abnormal voice quality on the intelligibility of two-digit numbers, *Journal of the Acoustical Society of America* 27:872

Moulonguet, A. (1954) Enregistrement simultané sur l'homme et in situ, des potentiels d'action récurrentiels et de la voix, au cours d'une opération de laryngectomie totale, *Revue de Laryngologie*, Supplement No. 75:110–31

Müller, J. (1837) *Handbuch der Physiologie des Menschen*, Vol. 2, Holscher, Coblenz

Murry, T. (1969) Subglottal pressure measures during vocal fry phonation, Ph.D. dissertation, University of Florida

Murry, T. and Brown, W. S. (Jnr) (1971) Subglottal air pressure during two types of vocal activity: vocal fry and modal phonation, *Folia Phoniatrica* 23:440–9

Myers, T. F., Laver, J. and Anderson, J. (Eds.) (1980) (forthcoming) *The cognitive representation of speech*, North-Holland, Amsterdam

Nadoleczny, M. (1929) *Untersuchungen über den Kunstgesang*, Springer, Berlin

Nusbaum, E. A., Foley, L. and Wells, C. (1935) Experimental studies of the firmness of velar-pharyngeal occlusion during the production of English vowels, *Speech Monographs* 2:71–80

Öhman, S. (1966) Coarticulation in VCV utterances: Spectrographic measurements, *Journal of the Acoustical Society of America* 39:151–68

Öhman, S. (1967) Numerical model of coarticulation, *Journal of the Acoustical Society of America* 41:310–20

Paget, R. (1930) *Human speech*, Kegan Paul, London

Passy, P. (1914) *The sounds of the French language* (2nd edn, trans. by D. L. Savory and D. Jones), Clarendon Press, Oxford

Pepinsky, A. (1942) The laryngeal ventricle considered as an acoustic filter, *Journal of the Acoustical Society of America* 14:32–5

Perelló, J. (1962a) Le disfonia premenstruel, *Acta Oto-Rino-Laringologica Ibero-Americana* 23:561–3

Perelló, J. (1962b) The muco-undulatory theory of phonation, *Annals of Otolaryngology* 79:722–5

Peterson, G. E. and Barney, H. L. (1952) Control methods used in a study of the vowels, *Journal of the Acoustical Society of America* 24:175–84

Pike, K. L. (1943) *Phonetics*, University of Michigan Press, Ann Arbor

Pike, K. L. (1947) *Phonemics*, University of Michigan Press, Ann Arbor

Pike, K. L. (1967) Tongue-root position in practical phonetics, *Phonetica* 17:129–40

Piquet, J. and Decroix, G. (1956) Etude expérimentale peropératoire du rôle de la pression sous-glottique sur la vibration des cordes vocales, *Comptes Rendus de l'Académie des Sciences* 242:1223–5

Piquet, J., Decroix, G., Libersa, C. and Dujardin, J. (1957) Etude expérimentale peropératoire chez l'homme des vibrations des cordes vocales sans courant d'air sous-glottique, enregistrées à la caméra ultra-rapide, *Revue de Laryngologie*, Supplement No. 78:510–4

Plotkin, W. H. (1964) Ventricular phonation: a clinical discussion of etiology, symptoms and therapy, *American Speech and Hearing Association Convention Abstracts* 6:409

Podvinec, S. (1952) The physiology and pathology of the soft palate, *Journal of Laryngology and Otology* 66:452ff.

Portmann, G. and Robin, J. L. (1956) Myographies des cordes vocales chez l'homme, *Revue de Laryngologie* 77:1–10

Potter, R. K., Kopp, G. A. and Green, H. C. (1947) *Visible speech*, Van Nostrand, New York

Pressman, J. J. (1942) Physiology of the vocal cords in phonation and respiration, *Archives of Otolaryngology* 35:355–98

Pronovost, W. (1942) Research contributions to voice improvement, *Journal of Speech Disorders* 7:313–8

Quintilian *Institutiones Oratoriae* (Watson, J. S. (Trans.), *Quintilian's Institutes of oratory, or, education of an orator*, George Bell, London, 1899)

Rees, M. B. (1958) Some variables affecting perceived harshness, *Journal of Speech and Hearing Research* 1:115–68

Robins, R. H. (1953) The phonology of the nasalized verbal forms in Sundanese, *Bulletin of the School of Oriental and African Studies* 15:138–45

Robins, R. H. (1957) Vowel nasality in Sundanese, in *Studies in Linguistic Analysis*, Special Volume of the Philological Society of Great Britain, pp. 87–103

Romanes, G. (Ed.) (1978) *Cunningham's Manual of Practical Anatomy*, Vol. 3, *Head and Neck and Brain* (14th edn), Oxford University Press

Rousselot, P. J. (1901) *Principes de phonétique expérimentale*, Didier, Paris

Rubin, H. J. (1960a) The neurochronaxic theory of voice production – a refutation, *Archives of Otolaryngology* 71:913–20

Rubin, H. J. (1960b) Further observations on the neurochronaxic theory of voice production, *Archives of Otolaryngology* 72:207–11

Rubin, H. J. and Hirt, C. C. (1960) The falsetto: a high speed cinematographic study, *Laryngoscope* 70:1305–24

Rush, J. (1827) *The physiology of the human voice*, Griggs & Elliot, Philadelphia; 5th edn (Lippincott, Philadelphia, 1859)

Russell, G. O. (1931) *Speech and voice, with X-rays of English, French, German, Italian, Spanish, soprano, tenor, and baritone subjects.* Macmillan, New York

Russell, G. O. (1936) Etiology of follicular pharygitis, catarrhal laryngitis, so-called clergyman's throat; and singer's nodes, *Journal of Speech Disorders* 1:113–22

Sapir, E. (1921) *Language*, Harcourt, Brace and World, New York

Saunders, W. H. (1964) *The larynx*, Ciba Corporation, New Jersey

Sawashima, M. (1974) Laryngeal research in experimental phonetics, in Sebeok, T. (1974) pp. 2303–48

Sawashima, M. and Cooper, F. S. (Eds.) (1977) *Dynamic aspects of speech production*, University of Tokyo Press

Scherer, K. R. and Giles, H. (Eds.) (1979) *Social markers in speech*, Cambridge University Press

Sebeok, T. (Ed.) (1974) *Current Trends in Linguistics*, Vol. 12, Mouton, The Hague

Shelton, R. L. (Jnr), Arndt, W. B. (Jnr), Knox, A. W., Elbert, M., Chisum, L. and Youngstrom, K. A. (1969) The relationship between nasal sound pressure level and palatopharyngeal closure, *Journal of Speech and Hearing Research* 12:193–8

Sherman, D. and Linke, E. (1952) The influence of certain vowel types on the degree of harsh voice quality, *Journal of Speech and Hearing Disorders* 17:401–8

Shorto, H. L. (1966) Mon vowel systems: a problem in phonological statement, in Bazell, C. E., Catford, J. C., Halliday, M. A. K. and Robins, R. H. (1966) pp. 398–409

Sievers, E. (1876) *Grundzüge der Lautphysiologie*, Breitkopf & Haertel, Leipzig

Smith, S. (1951) Vocalization and added nasal resonance, *Folia Phoniatrica* 3:165–9

Smith, S. (1954a) Remarks on the physiology of the vibrations of the vocal cords, *Folia Phoniatrica* 6:166–78

Smith, S. (1954b) Vibration of the vocal cords (Film Part I and Part II), Government Film Office, Copenhagen

Smith, S. (1956a) Mouvements des cordes vocales (Film No. 4), Government Film Office, Copenhagen

Smith, S. (1956b) To what extent is the neurochronaxic theory necessary for explanation of pitch variation? Paper read at International Voice Conference, Chicago, May 1956

Smith, S. (1957) Théorie aérodynamique de la vibration des cordes vocales, in Aubin, A. (1957)

Smith, S. (1961) On artificial voice production, *Proceedings of the 4th International Congress of Phonetic Sciences*, Helsinki, pp. 96–110

Sondhi, M. M. (1975) Measurement of the glottal waveform, *Journal of the Acoustical Society of America* 57:228–32

Stevens, K. N. (1972) The quantal nature of speech: evidence from articulatory–acoustic data, in David, E. E. and Denes, P. B. (1972) pp. 51–66

Stevens, K. N. and House, A. S. (1955) Development of a quantitative description of vowel articulation, *Journal of the Acoustical Society of America* 27:484–93

Stevens, K. N. and House A. S. (1961) An acoustical theory of vowel production and some of its implications, *Journal of Speech and Hearing Research* 4:303–20

Stevens, K. N. and House, A. S. (1963) Perturbations of vowel articulations by consonantal context: an acoustical study, *Journal of Speech and Hearing Research* 6:111–28

Stewart, J. M. (1967) Tongue-root position in Akan vowel harmony, *Phonetica* 16:185–204

Sundberg, J. and Nordström, P.-E. (1976) Raised and lowered larynx – the effect on vowel formant frequencies, *Quarterly Progress and Status Report* 2–3: 35–9,

Speech Transmission Laboratory, Royal Institute of Technology, Stockholm

Sweet, H. (1877) *Handbook of phonetics*, Clarendon Press, Oxford

Sweet, H. (1890) *A primer of phonetics* Clarendon Press, Oxford (3rd edn, revised, 1906)

Sweet, H. (1911) Phonetics, *Encyclopaedia Britannica* (11th edn) pp. 458–67, Cambridge University Press

Tarneaud, J. (1941) *Traité pratique de phonologie et de phoniatrie, la voix – la parole – le chant*, Librairie Maloine, Paris

Thompson, C. L. (1962) Wavelength perturbations in phonation of pathological larynges, *Progress Report*, National Institutes of Health Grant No. NB-04398

Timcke, R., Leden, H. von and Moore, P. (1958) Laryngeal vibrations: measurements of the glottic wave. Part I. The normal vibratory cycle, *Archives of Otolaryngology* 68:1–19

Titze, I. R. (1973) The human vocal cords: a mathematical model, Part I, *Phonetica* 28:129–70

Titze, I. R. (1974) The human vocal cords: a mathematical model, Part II, *Phonetica* 29:1–21

Titze, I. R. and Strong, W. J. (1975) Normal modes in vocal cord tissues, *Journal of the Acoustical Society of America* 57:736–44

Travis, L. E. (1931) *Speech pathology*, Appleton-Century-Crofts, New York

Travis, L. E. (Ed.) (1957) *Handbook of speech pathology*, Appleton-Century-Crofts, New York

Trenschel, W. (1969) Zu Klärung des Problems der Nasalität, *Sonderschule* 14:311–17

Trojan, F. (1952) Experimentelle Untersuchunger über den Zusammenhang zwischen dem Ausdruck der Sprechstimme und dem vegetativen Nervensystem, *Folia Phoniatrica* 4:65–92

Trudgill, P. (1974) *The social differentiation of English in Norwich*, Cambridge University Press

Trudgill, P. (Ed.) (1978) *Sociolinguistic patterns in British English*, Arnold, London

Van Dusen, C. R. (1941) A laboratory study of the metallic voice, *Journal of Speech Disorders* 6:137–40

Van Riper, C. (1954) *Speech correction: principles and methods* (3rd edn), Prentice-Hall, Englewood Cliffs

Van Riper, C. and Irwin, J. V. (1958) *Voice and articulation*, Prentice-Hall, Englewood Cliffs

Wallis, J. (1653) *Grammatica linguae anglicanae, cui praefigitur, de loquela sive sonorum formatione, tractatus grammatico-physicus*, Lichfield, Oxford

Warren, D. W. (1964) Velopharyngeal orifice size and upper pharyngeal pressure-flow patterns in normal speech, *Plastic and reconstructive surgery* 33:148–62

Warren, D. W. and Dubois, A. B. (1964) A pressure flow technique for measuring velopharyngeal orifice area during continuous speech, *Cleft Palate Journal* 1:52–71

Webster, N. (1789) *Dissertations on the English language*, Isaiah Thomas, Boston

Weiss, A. I. (1954) Oral and nasal sound pressure level as related to judged severity of nasality, Ph.D. dissertation, Purdue University

Weiss, D. A. (1959) Discussion of the neurochronaxic theory (Husson), *Archives of Otolaryngology* 70: 607–18

Wendahl, R. W. (1963) Laryngeal analog synthesis of harsh voice quality, *Folia Phoniatrica* 15: 241–50

Wendahl, R. W. (1964) The role of amplitude breaks in the perception of vocal roughness, *American Speech and Hearing Association Convention Abstracts* 6: 406

Wendahl, R. W., Moore, P. and Hollien, H. (1963) Comments on vocal fry, *Folia Phoniatrica* 15: 251–5

West, R. (1936) Recent studies in speech pathology, *Proceedings of the American Speech Correction Association* 6: 44–9

West, R., Ansberry, M. and Carr, A. (1957) *The rehabilitation of speech* (3rd edn), Harper, New York

Wilkins, J. (1668) *An essay towards a real character and a philosophical language*, John Martyn, London

Willis, R. (1829) Vowel sounds, *Transactions of the Cambridge Philosophical Society*

Wise, C. M. (1948) Is nasal resonance actually nasopharyngeal resonance? *Le Maître Phonétique*, pp. 4–5

Wolfe, W. G. (1942) X-ray study of certain structures and movements involved in naso-pharyngeal closure, M.A. thesis, State University of Iowa

Wustrow, F. (1952) Bau und Funktion des menschlichen Musculus vocalis, *Zeitschrift für Anatomie und Entwickelungsgeschichte* 116: 506–22

Zemlin, W. R. (1964) *Speech and hearing science*, Stipes, Champaign, Illinois

Index